DBT & CBT SKILLS WORKBOOK FOR TEENS

A TEEN'S GUIDE TO EMOTIONAL REGULATION AND COPING WITH SEVERE ANXIETY

R.J. MILLER

TABLE OF CONTENTS

WHAT THE HECK IS DBT?

Introduction   9

1. THE FUNDAMENTALS OF DIALECTICAL
   BEHAVIOR THERAPY   17
   How DBT Differs From Other Therapies   22
   What Can DBT Help Treat   24
   The Core Principles of DBT   25

2. MINDFULNESS AND ITS SIGNIFICANCE
   IN DBT   29
   How Mindfulness Got Its Latest Revival   32
   The Role of Mindfulness in DBT   35
   The 7 Principles of Mindfulness   39

3. MINDFULNESS TECHNIQUES TO HELP YOU
   LIVE IN THE PRESENT   43
   How To Practice Mindfulness For Specific
   Reasons   46
   Mindful Breathing   53
   Mindful Walking   54
   Mindful Eating   55
   Body Scans   57

4. WHAT IS DISTRESS TOLERANCE?   61
   What is Distress Tolerance?   63
   What Does The Vagus Nerve Have to Do With
   This?   67
   Distress Tolerance and Vagus Nerve Stimulation
   (VNS)   68

5. PUTTING DISTRESS TOLERANCE INTO
   PRACTICE   75
   TIPP   77
   ACCEPTS   80
   IMPROVE   84

STOP 86
Radical Acceptance 87
Self-Soothe 89
Distractions 91

6. INTERPERSONAL EFFECTIVENESS AND
YOUR RELATIONSHIPS 93
Understanding Interpersonal Effectiveness 94
The Goals of Interpersonal Effectiveness 97
Factors that Block Interpersonal Effectiveness 99
Applying Interpersonal Effectiveness 104
Your Social Skills Assessment 108

7. STRATEGIES TO INCLUDE INTERPERSONAL
EFFECTIVENESS IN YOUR LIFE 113
DEAR MAN 114
GIVE 119
FAST 124
THINK 127
The Importance of Assertive Communication 129
Healthy Boundary-Setting 130

8. THE POWER OF EMOTIONAL REGULATION 133
Emotional Regulation vs. Emotional
Dysregulation 137
Know Your Emotional Triggers 143
Manage Your Emotional Triggers 146
Developing Emotional Self-Awareness 148

9. EXERCISES TO REGULATE AND MANAGE
YOUR POWERFUL EMOTIONS 153
Long-Term Stimulation of the Vagus Nerve 154
Label Your Emotion 156
The Emotional Mind, Rational Mind, and
Wise Mind 161
Opposite Action 163
ABC PLEASE 165
Positive Self-Talk 168
Problem-Solving 170
Journaling 172

Conclusion   181
References   185

WHAT THE HECK IS CBT?

Introduction   191

1. THE PHILOSOPHY BEHIND COGNITIVE
   BEHAVIORAL THERAPY   197
   What is CBT?   198
   What is CBT Used For?   211
   Is CBT For Everyone?   213

2. THE THOUGHT PROCESS AND
   CONSEQUENCES   219
   Where Do Our Thoughts Stem From?   220
   How Thoughts, Emotions, and Behaviors Are
   Linked   224
   Examining your Cognitive Distortions   231

3. HOW TO EFFECTIVELY REWIRE THE BRAIN   241
   What are Automatic Negative Thoughts (ANTs)?   242
   The Relationship Between ANTs and Rumination   247
   Stop Falling for Negativity Bias   250
   How to Reframe Negative Thoughts in Nine
   Steps   254

4. GETTING A GRIP ON STRESS   261
   Why Stress Should Not Be Dismissed   263
   Check Your Stress Symptoms   268
   Diaphragmatic Breathing   270
   Progressive Muscle Relaxation (PMR)   274
   Guided Meditation for Stress   277
   Taking a More Mindful Approach   280

5. TAKING CONTROL OF ANXIETY AND
   DEPRESSION   285
   Stress vs. Anxiety   286
   Understanding Anxiety Triggers   290
   CBT Strategies For Anxiety   295

The Depths of Depression — 302
How to Start Lifting Your Depression — 303

6. HOW TO COPE WITH PANIC ATTACKS — 313
Getting Acquainted With The Fight, Flight, or Freeze Response — 316
The Importance of Learning How to Control Panic Attacks — 322
Calming The Body Back to a Rest and Digest State — 326

7. OVERCOMING OBSESSIVE AND ADDICTIVE BEHAVIORS — 333
CBT and Obsessive-Compulsive Disorder — 335
Overcoming Addiction With CBT — 340
Self-Harm and Eating Disorders: How to Change Thoughts and Behavior — 346
Why Self-Care is Crucial — 352

8. MANAGING CHRONIC PAIN WITH CBT — 355
Common Causes of Chronic Pain — 357
Brain Mechanisms and Pain — 360
How Can CBT Help the Symptoms of Chronic Pain — 363
Pacing Yourself — 367
Questioning Thoughts Regarding Pain — 371
Body Scanning: Guided Meditation for Pain Relief — 374

Conclusion — 377
References — 381

WHAT THE HECK IS DBT?

THE SECRET TO UNDERSTANDING YOUR EMOTIONS AND COPING WITH YOUR ANXIETY THROUGH DIALECTICAL BEHAVIOR THERAPY SKILLS.

FREE INSIDER GIFT

As a BONUS for purchasing this book,
we would like to give you some
DBT skills worksheets to fastrack your success.

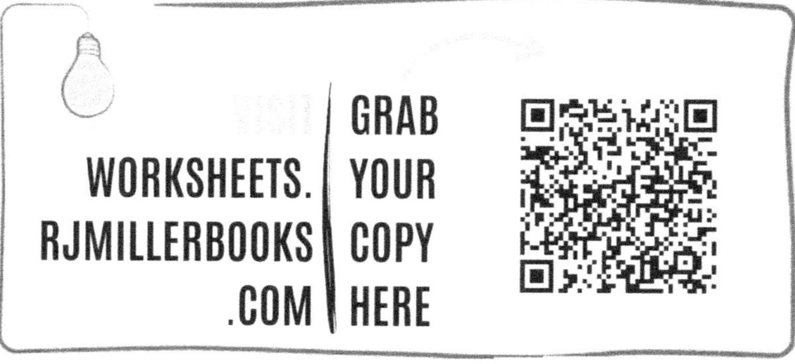

INTRODUCTION

"You can't calm the storm, so stop trying. What you can do is calm yourself. The storm will pass."

— TIMBER HAWKEYE

"Who would have thought life could be so interesting and fun! After so many years of suffering in silence and living in pain, I can now feel and enjoy life like everyone else!"

For many years, I couldn't appreciate simple things like the smell of coffee, birds chirping, watching the sun rise and set, and all the other amazing things nature has to offer. Instead, I was more engrossed in dealing with intense emotions. Every day felt like I was dealing with the worst heartbreak as I was in a *"pain loop"* with no escape route.

On the outside, it may look like I had it all together; I worked in a fantastic organization, had great friends and incredible parents. However, no one knew the demons I battled inside. I felt pressured to be perfect. Whenever I didn't do well, I felt hopeless and overwhelmed with emotions. When my girlfriends broke up with me, I saw them as the problem. "Why can't they accept me for who I am?" "Why are they pretending to love me when they don't?" "Why can't this, why can't that…." I always asked myself so many "whys."

Even though I failed to admit it, I've had many up-and-down moments. I knew there was a problem with how I reacted to things, but I could not pinpoint what was wrong with me or how to improve myself and the situation.

I never spoke about how I truly felt and never thought I would. I was worried that it would make people avoid me. Since how I felt did not make sense to me, how would it make sense to others? Besides, I have never been a talker; I was used to bottling my feelings and getting angry at myself. I was a more "traditional man" who grew up in a family where men hardly talked about their feelings and weren't encouraged to speak up. Speaking up as a man may portray you as weak, and that's the last thing I wanted people to see me as. So, I joined the bandwagon and had to pay the price.

I continued hiding my feelings and thoughts until they started keeping me awake at night. I would lay sleepless in my bed and cry for hours. I would be so tired the next day at work and highly unproductive. I would feel cranky, and everything my boss said became annoying. Whenever friends complained about my actions, I would turn it against them and feel like they didn't know how to have a good time.

This continued until I started having issues at the one place I excelled; my job! I loved what I did but didn't know what to do because it seemed like a never-ending cycle. I was in a bad place and eventually left the job I loved. I was now ALONE!

Luckily for me, my parents intervened. However, it took weeks of convincing from them before I finally agreed to see a doctor. The doctor assessed and diagnosed me with Borderline Personality Disorder (BPD). I remember feeling scared and upset when I heard about BPD. The diagnosis was upsetting because I had difficulty accepting my "disordered personality." However, despite the harsh words and stigma attached to it, the diagnosis still brought me some relief. I finally understood what was happening to me and realized that there was a way out of the ditch I was rotting in.

Let me guess; you're experiencing something similar? You see yourself swinging from one extreme emotion to another within seconds, acting impulsive and recklessly, and suddenly bored with life. You find it difficult to cope with your fluctuating emotions, your brain is overworking, and you're full of guilt and fear. You've never felt like you're good enough, leading to panic and anxiety because you're afraid your emotional distress will push others away and you will be alone.

Perhaps, you see yourself drowning in these intense emotions with no help. You are tired of not knowing the cause of your emotional problems and feel you've lost control of your life. If you feel like you're on a conveyor belt, and the inevitable end is a giant grinder with no idea of how to stop the belt or get off it, then you aren't alone.

Many have similar experiences as you; it was happening to me, and I realized there was a way out of the ditch I was rotting in.

Many expectations come with understanding and managing your emotions, but this isn't an inborn skill; you get to learn it. The situations I've described above should be easily fixed without much hassle. However, it becomes even more frustrating and self-loathing when you don't know where to start or how to go about it.

I understand that you're tired of where your life is right now, you've been seeking help, and you desperately want to see changes. You want to live like everyone else, do things and enjoy life like them.

So, what do you do? How do you escape this tunnel of deep pain and break free from this horror?

First, you need to understand that you're the only one responsible for your life, and only you can change it. This is the turning point. All the emotional turmoil you've experienced can change if you commit to helping yourself.

Although I can't promise that there's a magic wand that I can wave and take away your pain instantly, I can guarantee that this book will introduce you to Dialectical Behavior Therapy (DBT) in a simplified way.

DBT is a research-based psychotherapy that has been proven effective in helping people suffering from anxiety, depression, Borderline Personality Disorder (BPD), eating disorders, and substance abuse find relief. This evidence-based therapy strengthens your ability to handle distress without acting destructively or losing control. You will first accept your feelings as a valid part of your experience, build a tolerance to distress, and effectively regulate your emotions.

With DBT, you can understand and manage your fluctuating emotions, overcome impulsive behaviors, improve your self-awareness, and effectively deal with relationship issues you may have. DBT aims to help you control your emotions and be the best version of yourself!

The most rewarding thing about DBT is knowing that having intense feelings doesn't mean you should act on them; you have a choice on how to act in difficult situations. You need to acknowledge the emotions and be non-judgmental about them.

For many years, I was scared of letting people know how I felt or giving an explanation for my constant withdrawal from people. However, looking back now and considering the many years of living in pain, I am glad I am writing this book. This book will serve as a medium to share my experience and help other people with similar experiences as I find relief.

Before I got introduced to DBT, I tried traditional therapy without much luck. I knew I had to try something more hands-on that I could practice daily with quicker results rather than talking to someone weekly. No doubt, talk therapy also has its benefits. But, I wanted something I could do independently and get life-changing results.

I went online, researched DBT, and printed a heap of information on it. I highlighted essential lines on each page, which suddenly all made sense to me! Everything I bottled up that didn't make sense, that I couldn't put my fingers on, and that I couldn't explain to others were on those pages.

I used what I learned and started journaling the results of various DBT practices. My life completely changed within six months of applying DBT skills and tools! I was able to manage my stress and thoughts more effectively.

Even though it took me six months to see a significant difference, DBT is a lifetime practice that shouldn't be a headache or a chore. It's about continuously learning more about yourself and improving daily. The DBT skills I've learned have positively impacted every area of my life, career, family and friends, and meaningful relationships. Thanks to DBT, I can now manage my emotions successfully, something that not everyone can do, and it's something I am very proud of.

This book has been written to help you better understand the fundamentals of DBT and teach you how to use DBT skills to live in the present, tolerate distress, effectively manage your relationships, regulate your emotions, and improve your life. In addition, it offers easy and fun exercises to engage in and control your emotions.

I've written this book because I've been there. I've experienced chronic pain and felt broken and depressed. I've been aggressive over nothing, totally lost it when I shouldn't of, felt various discomforting emotions, and even had suicidal tendencies. I got tired of living that way and finally accepted that I needed help.

Acceptance was my first step to recovery, and from there, other measures followed. Trust me, it wasn't easy at first because I made many mistakes. But, I tested all I learned and sieved through to know strategies that work and those that don't.

For some time, I've had an enormous passion for this subject, and I want to help as many people struggling with their emotions as possible. What you will learn in the following chapters is a well-crafted and careful collection of my personal experience and information from experts in the field.

Even though it will be challenging initially, I know you will get through it. With this book, the ride ahead will be smoother. Your efforts will be worth it, and you will be confident knowing that you now have access to tools that will make a significant difference in your life. Always remember that you deserve to be happy and live a peaceful life.

Are you ready to break free from the shackles of your emotions, challenge your assumptions, react more rationally to situations, and learn to live in the present moment peacefully?

Let's get started as we uncover everything you need to know about the fundamentals of DBT in the first chapter.

THE FUNDAMENTALS OF DIALECTICAL BEHAVIOR THERAPY

"What exactly is this therapy?"

This was me asking my therapist about DBT when he suggested it. He hasn't practiced it himself, but he had opinions about it. Some of his perspectives suggested that DBT is a helpful therapy that provides skills for patients to practice. These skills allow you to connect with your spiritual side since it's practical and not difficult to understand and engage in. Also, the group component of DBT lets you see how others are using it and gives you hope that you can do it too. His explanation calmed me a bit, even if I still felt reluctant.

For many people unfamiliar with DBT, this concept may initially sound strange. Some may assume it is a complicated therapy and, like me, feel reluctant to try it. This chapter aims to set the record straight by clearly explaining what DBT entails, starting with its effectiveness in helping people suffering from a wide range of issues such as low self-image, impulsivity, and anger. Below, I will also introduce the four areas of DBT and why every human deserves a life worth living.

With so many therapies, it becomes hard to know one from another and know the best option for you. So, it's crucial that you know more about this therapy before embarking on this journey.

First, let's start by discussing what DBT is.

What Is DBT?

DBT is a cognitive-behavioral treatment initially developed to treat suicide patients diagnosed with BPD. This science-backed therapy has become a gold standard psychological treatment for treating other disorders, including anxiety, depression, eating disorders, substance abuse, post-traumatic stress disorder (PTSD), and self-harm.

DBT is a practical treatment that gives access to skills needed to handle the "extreme" ups and downs of your emotions. It encourages you to face your uncomfortable feelings and learn to manage them instead of avoiding them. With DBT, you will become aware of what's going on in your body; that way, you can be more in control of your brain.

DBT aims to help people live in and enjoy the moment while accessing healthier ways to cope with stress. While cognitive behavioral therapy (CBT) aims to identify and change unhelpful thoughts, DBT teaches skills to manage overwhelming and painful emotions. It also provides strategies to reduce conflicts in relationships.

Psychologist Marsha Linehan originally created DBT to treat individuals with chronic suicide cases who also suffer from BPD (borderline personality disorder). However, this treatment seems to be gaining more attention and popularity daily. As a result, more people are now flexible in adopting this treatment.

The first word, "dialectical," explains the three core beliefs of this philosophy:

- Change is constant and inevitable.
- Opposites can be united to get closer to the truth.
- Everything is interconnected.

This means that two seemingly opposites can be accurate at the same time.

For example, even though I was being shitty to people around me before I got diagnosed with BPD, I still had my good sides. I truly cared about my family and friends and always wanted the best for them. I try to show it whenever I am not experiencing my down moments. So, being a jerk and, at the same time, a caring guy are two opposing facts that are true at the same time.

In DBT, people are taught two opposite strategies (acceptance and change), which means they must make positive changes to manage their emotions and live peacefully.

The History Behind DBT

The founder of DBT, Dr. Marsha Linehan, started researching new alternatives to treat suicidal thoughts in the 70s after her own struggles with mental health. The psychologist knew nothing about BPD at that time but later got to know much about it.

Years ago, Linehan revealed in the New York Times that she struggled with mental illness in her late teens. After overcoming the struggles, she developed a particular interest in helping others who were also struggling with the same issue. In her words, she wanted to "get them out of hell."

When Linehan started working with suicidal patients in the 70s, she realized it was easy to get grant money since she was the only one carrying out randomized controlled trials with suicidal patients. Her team would request that the hospital in the area send the most severe cases of suicide and self-harm to them. She then tried to cure them with behavioral therapy.

When using behaviorism, the patients would respond feeling like they were the problem. This isn't surprising because behaviorism entails a model of change. So, when she gave feedback on how they could change and improve their symptoms, they took it wrongly and assumed she said it was their fault. Their responses were along the line of: "What are you saying? How is this my fault? What about my kids? My spouse? My employer? And the environment I live in? Aren't these making it difficult for me to get better? So how is it my fault?

Based on the patient's response, using only behavioral therapy wasn't enough. The behaviorism approach was already popular during this time, but the humanistic approach also dominated. So, she felt that trying the humanistic approach should be worth it.

Since behaviorism is known for being cut, dry, and sterile, Linehan was willing to consider the other approach – humanism. According to her, it should be a more appropriate stance, and that was how she tried it! But unfortunately, it didn't go as planned either.

Looking at both approaches – humanism, and behaviorism as being at the end of the continuum, they seemed like opposites. So Linehan went from one end to another and found that both approaches didn't give the result she expected.

While researching what would work, Linehan and her team watched through a one-way mirror where they could see patients and study them without being seen. She would study the patients, try out her ideas, and take notes. She later found that certain things she does or tells the patients upset them while other things were more regulating. This discovery wasn't something different or a third theory; it was like a blend of behaviorism and humanism. So, instead of choosing a side and moving back and forth between the concepts, Linehan decided to stay in the fulcrum of both. Dialectics was what seemed to be the balance of the two opposite theories. Linehan and her team were able to see positive results with a bit of practice and patience. Then, as the 90s came around, DBT became a therapeutic choice for BPD.

The origin of DBT involves a non-pejorative stance. Rather than call the patients manipulative or refer to them as the problem, DBT was the approach that equals between client and therapist. This balance she got was also influenced by her Zen training.

You'll notice a similarity if studying DBT and Zen behavior therapy closely. During training, Linehan found many principles she learned in Zen, and her meditation could be applied to her patients to achieve positive results.

HOW DBT DIFFERS FROM OTHER THERAPIES

Despite having basic similarities, DBT and CBT aren't the same. While some patients respond to DBT better, others find that CBT works better for them. This is because the main focus of CBT is on rational thinking, while DBT does the same but focuses more on emotions.

When you understand the definition of DBT, you can quickly know how it differs from other therapies. DBT aims to help patients balance their emotions and improve their behavioral patterns. It starts with identifying these emotions and thought patterns leading to the distress you're experiencing. Then it teaches you how to use the thoughts with healthier ideas to give a more beneficial result. Instead of changing your thoughts and behaviors entirely, DBT suggests that you should adopt a more balanced worldview.

Although some people learn DBT skills independently. (practicing on their own without the help of a therapist) DBT is usually taught in a group setting comprising of four sessions.

CBT focuses on feelings, thoughts, and behaviors as they influence each other. When you apply CBT, you will be learning to see when your thoughts are becoming an issue, and you can then redirect your thoughts using CBT techniques.

No doubt, DBT recognizes dangers just as CBT does. Still, it focuses more on emotions, being mindful, and accepting that pain is part of the human experience. With this acknowledgment, you will feel safer managing difficult emotions, and you can regulate your destructive behaviors more.

Let's quickly discuss some points that reveal how DBT differs from CBT.

Philosophies: The approach of both DBT and CBT differs. DBT focuses on how you interact with yourself and others, using mindfulness philosophies to help you accept yourself and your environment. CBT, on the other hand, is more logic focused as it encourages you to use critical thinking to find healthier ways to think and behave.

Goals: CBT is more goal-oriented than DBT. DBT does have goals. However, it isn't as direct and firm as CBT. While DBT focuses on social and emotional aspects, CBT focuses on your behaviors. The idea behind DBT is to help you find a way to accept yourself, manage your emotions effectively, and regulate the unhelpful behaviors you may have.

Types of Sessions: DBT sessions last longer than CBT. While CBT lasts for a few weeks, a DBT session is usually a months-long process. DBT also involves a group therapy component where you have a safe and supportive environment to practice skills like interpersonal communication.

Uses: Since DBT focuses on regulating intense emotions and CBT focuses on changing unhelpful thoughts, both therapies have different uses. DBT is clinically proven effective in treating BPD, self-harm, eating disorders, emotional dysregulation, anger, substance use disorders, anxiety, and depression. CBT is effective for treating depression, anxiety, Post-Traumatic Stress Disorder (PTSD), phobia, Obsessive Compulsive Disorders (OCD), and Generalized Anxiety Disorders (GAD).

WHAT CAN DBT HELP TREAT

Now that you know how DBT differs from other therapies, especially CBT, we can explore how you can benefit from this therapy.

Even though Masha Linehan initially developed DBT to treat BPD, the techniques have proven to be effective in treating other mental health conditions such as bipolar disorder, depression, anxiety, PTSD, GAD, attention deficit hyperactivity disorder (ADHD), substance use disorders, and eating disorders.

Besides the mental conditions, DBT can help people cope with extreme stress, intense emotions, relationship difficulties, manage challenging situations, suicidal ideation, and self-injurious behavior.

Other notable areas that DBT can be helpful in include:

- Ability to make healthier choices.
- Communication skills.
- Moving toward a solution instead of problems.
- Ability to view things from different perspectives.

- Knowing more about your values and goals.
- Healthier thinking patterns.
- Improved awareness of negative thoughts.
- Have more significant insights into your life.
- Develop skills to face challenges in the present and future.
- Have coping strategies to manage distress.

THE CORE PRINCIPLES OF DBT

DBT aims to reduce the emotional distress that may impact your well-being and how you interact with your environment. It focuses on skills training that includes mindfulness, distress tolerance, emotion regulation, and interpersonal effectiveness. These are the four main components of DBT that, when used right, promises to free you from the shackles of anxiety, and you can go ahead and live your best life! Now, let me explain the component to give you a better understanding.

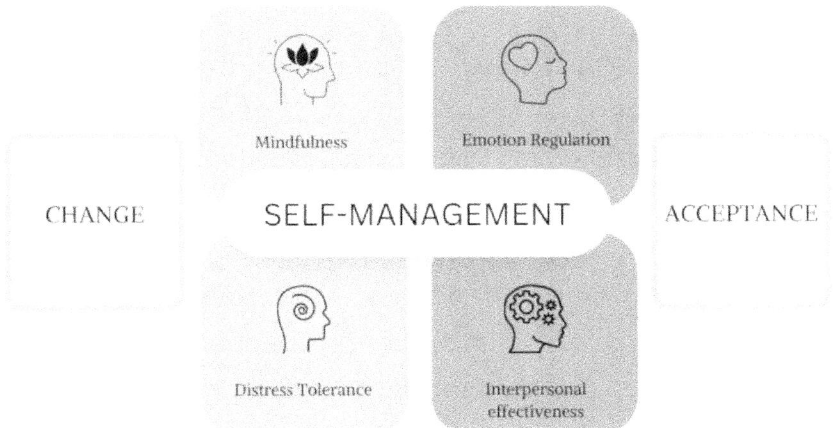

Mindfulness

When dealing with anxiety, it's easy to get worried about what has happened in the past and what will happen in the future. However, with mindfulness skills, you can learn to live in the present and accept what is happening in the present rather than dwell in the past, try not to predict the future, and accept your feelings and thoughts without judgment. Same thing with depression; the condition makes one get stuck in the past, reflecting on what could've or should've happened.

In DBT, mindfulness is grouped into the "how" and "what" skills. The "how" skills teach you to be mindful by taking effective actions while accepting aspects of yourself through radical acceptance, balancing your emotions rationally, and overcoming doubts and restlessness that may be hindering a mindful state. On the other hand, the "what" skills encourage you to focus on your present, emotions, thoughts, and sensations and learn how to separate your emotions from thoughts.

Distress tolerance

When you go through tough times, and you find it challenging to navigate, you can use healthier coping skills like distress tolerance to cope rather than destructive coping skills. Using coping skills such as self-isolating, angry outbursts, avoidance, self-harm, and substance abuse will only complicate issues and won't help. However, with distress tolerance, you can distract yourself until you feel calmer, more relaxed, and feel at peace. This means changing the moment regardless of the challenges and comparing the pros and cons of the available coping strategies.

Emotion regulation

Remember those times when you felt trapped in your emotions, and you couldn't escape them? Where you felt helpless, and nothing seemed to help. With emotion regulation, you can bring all those problematic emotions under your control, regardless of how overwhelming they feel.

As the name suggests, emotion regulation aims to regulate your emotions to prevent them from impacting your thoughts and behaviors. This skill focuses on a few goals: to reduce your emotional vulnerability, understand your emotions, reduce emotional suffering, solve problems in helpful ways, and overcome barriers to emotions that have positive effects.

In addition, with emotion regulation, you can learn to deal with primary emotional reactions that may lead to distressing secondary emotions. For example, anger is a primary emotion that can lead to feelings of guilt, worthlessness, and depression.

Interpersonal effectiveness

Remember how you felt when you had those rapid mood swings and intense emotions? How easy was it for you to move on and relate with others? I am guessing it was difficult. The goal of interpersonal effectiveness is that it helps you to clearly define what you want from how you feel.

When you master this DBT skill, you can confidently ask others about their needs and say "no" when the need arises. You will do these while maintaining self-respect and healthy boundaries with them. Asking questions and asserting one's self in a conversation is essential since you aren't a mind reader and shouldn't be assuming their needs. Assumptions can lead to wrong beliefs.

Interpersonal effectiveness aims to build healthy relationships with others by combining listening skills, social skills, assertiveness training, and setting clear boundaries to stay true to your values. The aim is to learn how to ask what you want the right way and take the necessary steps to get them, build self-respect, and learn how to walk through conflicts more effectively.

When you use these four skills of DBT, they allow you to go into the world and live the healthier, more meaningful, and realistic life you've longed for. In addition, each of the skills discussed strengthens and increases your chance of success as you navigate life.

I believe you now have a solid understanding of DBT and how it can help you regulate painful emotions. Although it takes a little practice, the benefits are very well documented. It's time to discuss one of the essential DBT skills – mindfulness.

See you in the next chapter!

2

MINDFULNESS AND ITS
SIGNIFICANCE IN DBT

ociety is known for taking something old and reinventing it, and a critical DBT skill – mindfulness isn't left out. Mindfulness is an ancient practice that was reinvented with the help of science. However, even before the involvement of science, this practice has been prevalent, and the reason isn't far from the many benefits it possesses.

When I first learned about DBT, I was surprised to know that mindfulness, a practice my closest friend, Ray, had always encouraged me to practice, was a core therapy skill that would end my misery.

Ray was born into a family that encouraged practicing mindfulness daily to maintain a stress-free and peaceful existence. I remember dismissing it when he suggested that I stay mindful of the present rather than worry about the past and future. I assumed the practice was religious or spiritual, and I wasn't down for that. However, I better understood mindfulness after my diagnosis with BPD. Over time, I realized that Ray had been right all along!

Mindfulness is at the heart of DBT as all skills learned through individual or group training start with it. This ancient act is vital in regulating emotions, getting through a crisis without worsening, and resolving interpersonal conflicts. This is because, without mindfulness, it is almost impossible to change the long-standing patterns of thoughts and actions.

To truly capture what mindfulness entails, we will take a brief look at its history, so you know it's not some hippie movement or the latest buzzword. In addition, there will be mention of certain studies to back its effectiveness and the basics of practicing it, including some guided meditation if you're beginning your mindfulness journey.

Just How Old Is Mindfulness

Mindfulness is linked as far back as 2500 years ago. Its origin is rooted in different religious and secular traditions, including Christianity, Hinduism, Islam, and Buddhism, before the interference of modern material practices.

Mindfulness in Hinduism

The history of mindfulness first links with the yogic practices of the Hindu people. This is between 2300 BC and 1500 BC, in Indus Valley, close to modern-day Pakistan. The Hindu scriptures reference acceptance, meditations, and silence; all these are vital elements of modern mindfulness that we practice today. Mindfulness is used as a preparatory practice for raja yoga in Hinduism. With it, you can attain a higher state of consciousness called "Dhyāna" which means contemplation in Hinduism. This exercise is practiced during yoga and aims to attain "Samadhi," which means a meditative state of consciousness. When doing this, your mind will remain and stick to the object of attention. You will gently observe what's happening internally and externally without being lost.

Same thing with the Sanskrit term "Smriti," which means remembering. The aim is to remember to be present in the relationship between yourself and the objects of your awareness.

Mindfulness in Buddhism

Buddhism has been around since 400-500 BC and was founded by Siddhārtha Gautama, the Buddha. Buddhists use meditation to ensure a state of ultimate consciousness, allowing personal attunement with a higher purpose in life. In Buddhism, mindfulness is taught as a way of giving enlightenment.

Sati, the first factor of the Seven Factors of Enlightenment in Buddhism, means mindfulness or remembering to be aware of something. This is a spiritual faculty that's an essential part of Buddhism. To get to the omniscient transcendental wisdom, Buddhists use mindfulness. So to them, it's necessary to be present when engaged in daily activities such as sitting, walking, eating, or working.

Mindful practices in Christianity and Islam

The history of mindfulness goes beyond different practices, even though Hinduism and Buddhism significantly influenced it. Mindfulness also has its roots in Islam, Judaism, and Christianity.

If you're familiar with Christianity, you might have heard the story of Jesus speaking about the "innermost I am." This entails the essence of the identity of every human – every life form. Certain Christian mystics have called this the "Christ within." Another instance is Brother Lawrence of the Resurrection, who served as a lay brother in a Carmelite monastery in Paris. He was known for always emphasizing being aware of the "Holy Spirit" when practicing in the presence of God.

The traces of mindfulness can also be seen in "Muraqabah." This is a Sufi meditation in Islam. Muraqabah aims to uplift the mind, heart, and body into peace, wellness, and happiness, which is the same thing mindfulness does. Through this practice, a person can watch over their heart and have an insight into the heart's relation with their creator and surroundings. In other words, it encourages continuous awareness.

Finally, even though you don't need to have a religious faith to practice mindfulness, it is still important to respect the origin of the important practice.

HOW MINDFULNESS GOT ITS LATEST REVIVAL

Mindfulness was recently introduced to the West in the 70s by Dr. Jon Kabat-Zinn. He taught mindfulness in both academic and medical contexts. Besides teaching mindfulness, he is the founder of the Center for Mindfulness at the University of Massachusetts Medical School. Kaba-Zinn describes mindfulness as "a means of paying attention in a particular way; on purpose, in the present moment, and nonjudgmentally." Even though it wasn't pointed out, his work is rooted in the Buddhist meditation practice.

Other notable people that brought mindfulness practices to the West are Sharon Salzberg, Jack Kornfield, and Joseph Goldstein. They founded the Insight Meditation Society (IMS) in 1975. At almost the same time, Marsha Linehan, the creator of DBT, got curious and wanted to know how helpful mindfulness is to people who were suicidal and had severe emotion dysregulation. So she translated what she learned from Zen principles into skills that aim to increase emotional control and attention.

Since then, mindfulness has been introduced to many institutions, including medical institutions, schools, sports, and wellness.

The latest revival of mindfulness was born after Dr. Jon Kabat-Zinn developed a stress-reduction program in the 1970s. The Mindfulness-Based Stress Reduction (MBSR) program is an 8-week program used in prisons, schools, and various industries, including politics, finance, and professional sports. An article published in time's magazine, *The Mindful Revolution, revealed that mindfulness got popularized, and thousands of MBSR instructors* started teaching mindfulness in over 30 countries. The widespread application and success of MBSR sparked what we know as "The Mindfulness Movement."

Even though there have been different forms of practicing mindfulness over the years, the purpose of this ancient practice has remained the same – to end pain and suffering. In addition, we owe most of the current wave of mindfulness therapies, exercises, and coaching we are witnessing to Kabat-Zinn's stress reduction program.

The effectiveness of MBSR in enhancing one's overall well-being and lowering stress has been supported by much scientific research. Among many is a study where the effectiveness of MBSR was implemented in a community setting as a self-paid course. The study, which included 115 randomized controlled trials (RCTs), suggests that MBSR has beneficial effects on anxiety, depression, stress, quality of life, physical functioning, and other conditions such as chronic pain, cancer, and cardiovascular (Juul et al., 2018).

Kabat-Zinn revealed that MBSR is based on Vipassana. This is a Buddhist type of meditation he engaged in when he got the idea of developing his mindfulness program. Vipassana is a word from the ancient Pali language of India, translated as "insight" or "clear awareness." This technique is based on the teachings of Buddha and was used to attain a deeper insight into ending suffering, referred to as Nirvana. According to Buddha's teachings, mindfulness is among the qualities developed during Vipassana meditation.

So far, we've established the connection between mindfulness and Buddhism, which influenced its latest revival. However, it is more evident in an ancient text Satipatthana Sutta, translated as The Discourse on the Establishing of Mindfulness (the word Sati means mindfulness) in English.

In Satipatthana Sutta, Buddha lays out mindfulness instructions that guide its practitioners to focus on the different aspects of experience. They are; the body, the mind, sensations, and mental contents.

It's important to note that Buddha's first foundation of mindfulness is the body. So it is not surprising to see modern mindfulness practices start by focusing on one or different aspects of the human experience.

Modern mindfulness is now taught with little or no mention of the Buddhist connection, even though a wealth of knowledge of this practice is rooted in Buddhism. Mindfulness is commonly described as a form of mental training, which is a helpful way to understand it. A great deal of research has gone into mindfulness and its benefits. In DBT, mindfulness skills are the core component of better emotion regulation.

THE ROLE OF MINDFULNESS IN DBT

Practicing mindfulness has been a life-changer for me. Even though the process sounds simple, it only works if practiced right.

A growing body of research suggests mindfulness-based interventions (MBIs) as an effective practice for decreasing stress, reducing rumination and emotional reactivity, and encouraging relationship satisfaction.

A study published in the National Library of Science, "Effects of Mindfulness on Psychological Health: A Review of Empirical Studies," showed the effects of mindfulness on psychological health by encouraging reduced psychological symptoms and emotional reactivity, increased subjective well-being, and improved behavioral regulation (Keng et al., 2011).

In another study, 20 novice mediators were tasked to participate in a 10-day intensive mindfulness meditation retreat. The group recorded less rumination, better memory capacity, sustained attention during a task and experienced few depressive symptoms after the retreat (Chambers et al., 2008).

In a newer study, researchers found that people who had been practicing mindfulness for many years could effectively disengage from emotionally upsetting pictures and focus better on the cognitive task than those who don't practice mindfulness (Ortner et al., 2007).

Another study suggests that mindfulness protects against the effect of emotionally stressful relationships by allowing you to express yourself better in social situations and give relationship satisfaction (Barnes et al., 2007).

In a meta-analysis of 39 studies showing the usefulness of MBSR, the researchers concluded that mindfulness is helpful in altering affective and cognitive processes that cause clinical issues (Hoffman et al., 2010).

During the day, many people spend only a tiny portion of their day mindfully engaged. They tend to zone out and get distracted by unhelpful thoughts. Instead of getting involved with reality, they prefer to get engaged with their thoughts and ideas, making it easy to lose sight of what is happening at that moment.

I was guilty of allowing my thoughts to consume me. As a result, I got distracted with tasks instead of staying mindful and enjoying the moment. However, being mindful means noticing your environment, expanding your attention, and enjoying the moment. Practicing this ancient skill is vital in DBT as it plays an essential role in helping people to be mindful, get better, and live the life of their dreams.

My time working as a sales representative in an organization was supposed to be enjoyable and fulfilling because it was one thing I've always wanted to do. I've always wanted to meet people, negotiate with them, and present and sell products or services to them. So, of course, I liked that aspect of the job. However, compiling the weekly and monthly reports was tedious and tiring; I was not too fond of that aspect of the job. Even though I only had to do this once a week and possibly, five times a month, it's still something I didn't look forward to doing. While compiling the reports, I was fond of making harsh judgments and saying difficult things to myself: "This is a total waste of time." "It's so boring and tiring!" "This is terrible." "I am tired of doing this." This continues, and instead of focusing on what I am doing and trying to get it right, my mind will keep wandering, telling me different kinds of unwanted stories about the task.

In hindsight, my actions triggered strong emotions such as resentment, anger, sadness, and despair. And it doesn't stop there! These emotions found a way to affect the rest of my day and even my week. As a result, I experienced a bad mood even when I was done with the task and made mistakes I considered silly because I should know better.

Instead of tolerating this tedious task, I allowed it to get to me and affect my mood. Whenever I am in a bad mood, I start having judgments, and what should be insignificant will cause me great suffering. As a result, I most likely will spend my day in a foul mood and feel worse, especially when I need to carry out my other responsibilities.

This is where mindfulness comes in. If I had been mindful of the dilemma above, I would've done better with the "supposed" unenjoyable task of curating my report. By practicing mindfulness, I should've approached the task with a spirit of acceptance and engaged in it without judgment. Whenever I notice any judgment, I should've turned my mind back to what I was doing, been aware of the sensations I felt holding a pen, and noticed the movements of my hands. By giving more attention to my environment, fully engaging in the task, and repeatedly turning my mind to it, I will provide little or no opportunity for negative attributions. This is how mindfulness can avert strong and unpleasant emotions.

Mindfulness allows you to train your brain and focus on what your senses tell you, calming your mind and body. It teaches you to consider your opinions, validate yourself, help you make better decisions, and avert emotional suffering. Instead of trying to suppress or quash certain emotions, mindfulness encourages permitting yourself to feel them.

When you're mindful, you'll observe what comes with emotions. The emotions will naturally go away the way they came if you don't give them too much attention. For example, you will notice your flushed face, lump in your throat, sweaty palms, and all other experiences without the intention of suppressing them. Since "you can't argue with your emotions," the best approach is to tolerate them without holding or pushing them away.

We've discussed the main reasons mindfulness is used so much in DBT. When you recognize the power of mindfulness, even with a thousand distractions, you will notice them all and shift your attention to where it should be. It's more like fly fishing, where your mind will cast its line too far places if distracted, and then you can gently reel it back when you bring your mind to the present. The process will reoccur as much as needed. It will happen plenty of times in a short duration, and the more you practice, the easier it becomes to know when your mind has wandered. With each practice, you will gain more control and clarity.

THE 7 PRINCIPLES OF MINDFULNESS

Mindfulness encourages you to be more involved in the present moment and be aware of your breath, where you are, and what you're doing.

According to Kabat-Zinn, seven factors constitute the central pillars of mindfulness. Together, these factors can help you cultivate more awareness of the present moment, focus more on important things, and help you calm your anxious mind.

- **Non-judging**

Have you ever sat in a meeting, a classroom, or with someone talking to you and suddenly noticed that you've not been paying attention? If yes, this suggests that your mind has been busy and consumed with thoughts, drifting away from the moment. However, with your non-judging part, you will know when this happens and not be hard on yourself. It's like being an "impartial witness" to your experience by being aware of your experiences and letting the judgments go!

- **Patience**

When you try to incorporate what you've learned – sharpening focus, encouraging awareness and meditating, and you don't seem to get the hang of it, you'll feel frustrated, right? That's where the famous saying "Patience is a virtue" comes in." Don't expect immediate results; remember that mindfulness requires patience and taking small, consistent steps to see results. Understand that you need time and space for mindful practices, and things will happen in their own time.

- **Beginner's mind**

You'll easily lose yourself when you believe everything you hear, see, and experience. You need to be more open to the fact that no moment is the same as another, and with new things comes change. Have a clear, open, and uncluttered mind. Don't allow your experiences, expectations, and beliefs to keep you from seeing things in the present moment. Have a curious mind like that of a child.

- **Trust**

Having trust in yourself and your feelings is an important aspect of mindfulness. Trust your intuition, even if you make mistakes with them. It's better to look inwardly than outwardly for directions. The idea is to find wisdom from within and trust in the unfolding.

- **Non-striving**

Do you find yourself rushing and all charged up to achieve your goals? How often do you strive for the next big thing? If you are used to rushing everything, you need to slow down and focus on where you are. Mindfulness encourages focusing on seeing and accepting things as they are by embracing the moment you are in. Try not to overreact; hold onto your awareness.

- **Acceptance**

What you're doing here is protecting your energy. Many of the battles you're facing result from not letting things be as they are. When you acknowledge and accept such things, you can easily go with the flow without resistance or pushing against things. Although, acceptance can sometimes be misconstrued. Acceptance isn't being content with things you don't like; it's learning to accept things just how they are without being clouded by biases.

- **Letting go**

Is letting go that simple? Of course, letting go and relaxing can be difficult when you're fixated on your ideas and thoughts. However, not letting go will allow you to focus on things that don't matter, alleviating your worries and stress. By letting things go or being as they are, you get freed up from negative energy and do the things that bring you joy and happiness.

As you can see, the seven principles of mindfulness aim to help you find peace within yourself. Following them will keep you more balanced for a healthy and happy life.

There are many ways to incorporate practicing mindfulness into your daily life. This chapter has only covered the basics of mindfulness. The following chapter will discuss different mindful exercises you can start engaging in today!

3

MINDFULNESS TECHNIQUES TO HELP YOU LIVE IN THE PRESENT

Everything happens so fast! One moment, you're struggling to get your sleepy head up from bed, and after a few hours, it's nighttime, and you have to rest in anticipation of the next day's activities.

Rinse and repeat!

Sadly, this is how many people live their lives. They get carried away with what is to come that they forget to enjoy what they have now.

Each day comes with struggles and joys that we fail to recognize. We rush through our everyday activities, never stopping to enjoy the moment. This rush is probably part of what makes us anxious and worried.

During a challenging phase of my life, I found myself just breezing in and out of each day. It then began to accumulate over months. I had goals, but I couldn't achieve them. I woke up every morning feeling grumpy, ate my lousy breakfast, and went to work. At my workplace, I would continuously have disagreements with coworkers and then come home after work feeling angry. Finally, I would go to bed very tired and continue the cycle the next day. I was living my life with nothing to look forward to. My goals were left unattended, and my health suffered from my lack of mindfulness.

Living in the moment is difficult, especially when we have so much going on. Bills to pay, work to do, friends to spend time with, and a family that looks up to you. It's a lot!

People love to emphasize the value of being present in the moment and the various ways that doing so will help us. All of that sounds good, especially the reduced levels of tension and anxiety, but how can we live in the present if our minds are continually fixed on the past and worried about the future?

It is challenging to enjoy the now when regrets about the past or fear about the future consume our thoughts. Thankfully, I got out of that horrible feeling, and I am sure you can do it too.

Many basic techniques of mindfulness are helpful for people who struggle to live in the present. You can do little things every day to help you get over feelings of anxiety.

As I mentioned earlier, I had to figure out everything by myself, so it was hard initially. I used to believe practicing mindfulness meant sitting still with my knees crossed, my teeth clenched, and my hands folded. I used to sit on my balcony every night before going to sleep and do nothing! Although it was boring, I thought that was how I was supposed to feel. One night, I even dozed off on my balcony. The following morning, my body ached, and I was still irritable all day.

After a month of sitting, nothing changed, so I realized I was doing something wrong. So I did more research and finally found the answers I sought. As soon as I discovered that I could practice mindfulness in different and exciting ways, engaging became much easier.

Paying attention to the food while eating is a simple way to practice mindfulness. Focus solely on the food's warmth, crunchiness, and flavor rather than your phone or television. You can also practice mindfulness by taking note of the sound of the sand and you as you walk on it. If you've once tried to pay attention to your body, feelings, and surroundings, then you've practiced mindfulness.

But Why Mindfulness?

It's important to understand that mindfulness is not a fleeting mental state that appears during meditation and disappears for the rest of the day. Instead, mindfulness is a way of life that allows you to take a step back and be in the present in any situation you find yourself in.

Living in the present means letting go of worries about what has already happened and what might happen in the future. It means appreciating the present and living for the day.

Being mindful means being fully present and involved with whatever you are doing at the time, free from distractions, and conscious of your thoughts without becoming sucked into them.

Through meditation, you can develop the skill of mindfulness and practice it daily. By training your mind to be present, you also prepare yourself to live more mindfully – in the moment, breathing and feeling everything.

Mindfulness is an excellent way to reduce stress and increase focus, empathy, patience, energy, and happiness. Although mindfulness doesn't make stress or other problems disappear, it gives us more control over how we respond to them in the present. This increases our chances of responding in a composed and sympathetic manner when faced with stress or other issues. It also makes us deliberate about how we want to react.

HOW TO PRACTICE MINDFULNESS FOR SPECIFIC REASONS

There are countless possibilities every day! Start things off with a happy heart. Every morning, you have control over your attitude; keep it positive and hopeful. Enjoy every moment of the day to the fullest. Embrace as much of today as possible, including all the sights, sounds, scents, joys, and sorrows. These are all around you, but you overlook them or fail to appreciate them fully.

You can practice living in the moment by developing a mindfulness cue, learning to meditate, and engaging in random acts of kindness.

Mindfulness for mood swings

Mood swings are emotions that change quickly and firmly. We all feel agitated and cranky because our emotions can get irregular sometimes. We experience mood swings and lack energy whenever this happens. While mood swings might occasionally be natural, they can also indicate a more serious problem like depression or anxiety.

Fortunately, research has shown that practicing mindfulness helps you control your mood swings, slows down your thoughts, and improves your ability to manage emotional ups and downs by becoming more aware of how your mind works.

Have you ever given it a shot? You should try it!

- Close your eyes, relax, and breathe in and out slowly.
- Try to find your breath slowly. Where can you feel it the most?
- Focus on the breath as though you were just noticing it for the first time. For example, you can focus on your abdomen or the tip of your nose as you breathe.
- Simply notice the air entering your lungs, and as you exhale, notice the air coming out.
- Your thoughts will try to stray, so you should be conscious of this. Gently refocus your attention on where it is supposed to be.
- Say "straying" to yourself when your mind starts to wander. It will help bring your attention back to the breath so that you can just observe it.

- As your mind wanders, gently bring it back to the breath. Then, you can continue until you finally get over your mood swings.

Mindfulness for urges and impulses

Urges and impulses usually peak between 20 and 30 minutes. The temptation will pass if you are determined not to do anything about it. However, by giving in to your urges and impulses, you are making them stronger.

- Take time to think about a recent urge that you felt. Try to take note of every feeling that arises as you think about this urge. Then, pay attention to how these feelings change over time.
- Sit in a peaceful environment, close your eyes and focus only on the area of your body where you frequently experience these urges.
- Pay close attention to it. If more than one part of your body is connected to an urge, focus on the part where you feel the urge the most.
- Keep track of the feelings you are experiencing in this body part. How does it feel?
- For around two minutes, pay attention to your breathing.
- After that, bring your focus back to the area of your body where you are experiencing the urge. Observe whatever feelings arise in these areas.
- If observing the sensations becomes too difficult, gradually bring your focus back to your breathing for a

short while before returning to the areas with the urge again.

- Keep doing these things until the impulse passes.

Mindfulness for anger

In addition to reducing stress, mindfulness improves your relationship with yourself and helps you control powerful emotions like anger. When you're angry, you tend to forget that you have the option to press pause and cool down. Instead, you want to do the worst in a fit of rage.

When you practice mindfulness in the heat of the moment, you have taught yourself how to deal with your anger rather than adding fuel to the fire. It's possible to respond from a calmer, more collected place, regardless of how agitated you feel. You simply have to connect with your emotions.

You may need to use these tips on mindfulness if you experience intense anger that negatively impacts your relationships or escalates into bigger fights.

- Place your hands comfortably at your sides, eyes slightly closed, and sit in a relaxed position.
- Take a few deep breaths to fill your torso with air, and then exhale fully.
- Think of a time when you got angry. Imagine what took place and allow yourself to feel the fury once again.
- When you think back to the incident, other feelings could come to mind, such as sadness.

- The urge to attempt to push it away can come to you. Instead, let the feeling of fury grow intense, though to a safe level. Examine these feelings.
- Allow your emotions to linger before slowly returning your focus to your breath. Take deep breaths.
- Think about your feelings. What feelings did you notice? Did the feelings change while you were observing them? Where did the anger go at the end? Did your anger become stronger or weaker as you became aware of it?

Mindfulness for self-compassion and self-esteem

There will always be someone more successful, wealthy, attractive, intelligent, or powerful than you are. It doesn't mean you should feel bad or be harsh to yourself. This brings us to self-compassion and self-esteem!

Self-esteem is the opinion you have about yourself. Self-compassion makes you feel good about yourself because it does not involve assessing how deserving you are. Instead, you get to give yourself the same compassion you offer others when they fail or feel inadequate.

Practicing mindfulness for self-compassion and esteem will help you make life more manageable and feel better about yourself.

- Sit in an upright position with your hands on your lap.
- Breathe slowly and steadily, taking note of your chest's gentle rise and fall. Do this for five minutes.

- Make yourself happy by imagining things you love, like a smile or the sea.
- Think about someone who makes you feel good and consider what makes you love them.
- Then silently say positive things to yourself out loud. "I am worthy of love. I am gorgeous. I accept myself as I am. I am concerned about my feelings and challenges." As you say these, put your hand over your heart and breathe deeply.
- If you notice that your thoughts are beginning to stray, return to your breath.
- Sit until you start feeling good about yourself.

Mindfulness for fear of abandonment

Going through numerous breakups was tough for me. At one point, I feared that no one would want me. When I eventually got into a relationship again, I was scared that the lady would leave me like the others.

Typically the fear of abandonment can come from a parent, sibling, friend, or lover. Suppose you are going through situations that are similar to mine. Then, this mindfulness exercise would be beneficial for you.

- Sit down and clear your mind of all thoughts. Make sure the area you choose to stay in is quiet and well-ventilated.
- Place your hands on your chest and breathe slowly. Inhale, hold your breath for a while and then let it go,

slowly. Feel the air going in and coming out for about five minutes.

- Think of someone you love so dearly. Let the feeling of love radiate and envelope you.
- While holding your hand on your chest, say things like, "I release all fear to make room for love. The things that leave me aren't meant for me. The things that are meant for me stay with me. I only lose that which I claim to. I release darkness to let light in."
- Always take a breath in after each affirmation. Then, continue this exercise until you feel yourself let go of any negative emotions.

Mindfulness for emptiness

Do you feel incomplete or empty sometimes? This exercise will help you cool off and believe in yourself.

- Sit comfortably and place your hands on your lap.
- Start taking deep breaths, slowly and steadily.
- Think of a part of your body where you feel incomplete or empty. Place your hands on it and breathe.
- Inhale through your nose and exhale through your mouth.
- Make sure you're deep breathing. Be sure that the breath fills your whole body, from your head to the tip of your toes. Then, exhale.
- Do this for at least 25 minutes or until you feel you've had enough

MINDFUL BREATHING

Isn't it amazing that something as small as breathing can hold so much power? Breaths can calm your worries and help you feel better about yourself. The best thing is that you can do these breathing exercises anytime to calm down your emotions.

There are five ways to practice breathing, each with its peculiarities.

- **Mindful breathing**: This exercise focuses on the breath's regular occurrence; it does not include breath manipulation. Focusing on a physical cue, such as the rise and fall of your stomach and the feeling of the breath in your nose, can be helpful. The first step is to start breathing normally while paying close attention to your breath.
- **Counting breaths**: This method of breathing uses another mental cue to keep us focused: counting each breath. You'll find it challenging to keep track of your breath; counting is a way for you to remain focused. Those with highly active thoughts should practice this breathing.
- **Deep inhalation**: To achieve the intended result in this situation, you must deepen your breath. Deep breathing, commonly called belly breathing or diaphragmatic breathing, helps ease anxiety and foster serenity. It helps to deactivate the stress response by inhaling deeply into the belly and exhaling fully.

- **2-4 breathing**: This kind of breath entails lengthening the exhalation such that it exceeds the inhalation. For example, take a two-count inhale and a four-count exhale.
- **Energizing breaths**: You can use your breath to energize yourself if you're feeling lazy. Fill the lungs with air in four equal yet distinct breaths, then let it all out in one long, smooth exhale.

MINDFUL WALKING

Walking mindfully means paying attention to our breath and each step we take as we walk. You can do it wherever you are, whether you're by yourself enjoying nature, in the parking lot, or in your neighborhood. However, it's best to be in nature as it increases the calming effect, ultimately slowing down your brain waves.

The mind becomes distracted when it is left alone. Trying mindful walking helps us gather awareness and be conscious of the environment.

- Walk at a comfortable pace. Place your hands wherever it is most comfortable for you.
- Count up to ten steps and then start over from one again.
- Pay attention to how your foot rises and falls as you walk. Also, take note of how your legs and other parts of your body move. Keep an eye out for any side-to-side movement of your body.

- Your mind will stray, so gently bring it back as much as you need to without getting frustrated.
- Expand your focus on sounds during the next five minutes. Recognize sounds for what they are: sounds. The blaring horns, the chirping birds, notice everything.
- Pay attention to your sense of smell: the wet grass, the smell of wall paint. Pay attention to whatever it tells you without forcing yourself to feel anything.
- Move on to the vision, including the colors, objects, and everything else you see.
- No matter where you are, be mindful of everything around you. Nothing has to be changed, fixed, or done.
- Now, observe your feet touching the ground, and be aware of how it feels. Then stand still for a moment and breathe slowly. Do this until you feel yourself become calm.

MINDFUL EATING

With mindful eating, we can fully enjoy our food at the moment without worrying about our diet or any of the other rules that go along with it.

When we practice mindful eating, we pay attention to our senses and how the food makes us feel.

The goal is not to lose weight. Instead, the goal is to inspire people to enjoy the eating experience fully and to help them relish the present and the meal. This will, in turn, allow them to eat cautiously.

- Sit down and hold a raisin in your hand. Look at the raisin as if it were the first time.
- Be mindful of the raisin's form, texture, color, and size as you observe it. Is it hard or soft?
- Smell the raisin. Don't you just want to throw it in your mouth already? Is it hard to resist the urge to eat it immediately?
- How tiny does the raisin feel in your hand? Take a bite of the raisin and pay attention to what your tongue is saying.
- Bite into the raisin very cautiously. Chew thrice, then stop.
- Describe the raisin's flavor. Which texture is it? What does it taste like? How does it feel on your tongue?
- Swallow it. How does it make you feel?

The raisin experience is a beautiful illustration of what mindful eating is. It lets us concentrate on the experience. In order to practice mindful eating, we need to have these seven attitudes.

- **Non-Judging:** Your preconceived notions about raisins are the first thing you encounter in this experience. Do you approve of them?
- **Patience:** Mindful eating requires patience, and being present moment by moment demands consistent practice.
- **Beginner's mentality:** By approaching your experiences in the same way that a newborn does (taking one taste, one glance, one touch, one smell, one

sound), you can be receptive to whatever their current meaning is.

- **Trust:** We get more tolerant of ourselves and thus more trustworthy by being aware of and enjoying how we feel and how different foods affect us.
- **Non-Striving:** This is obviously in contrast to dieting. Dieting means that we entirely focus on attempting to lose weight. In mindful eating, you, as an eater, are free to be present and truly appreciate the experience because you aren't expecting any particular outcome.
- **Acceptance:** Mindfulness is a practice that involves learning to be willing to observe what occurs and accepting it. It might be accepting the good (the delicious flavor of only one raisin) or the bad (our dislike of raisins). Accept whatever arises in the moment. What is, is what is.
- **Letting go:** To eat mindfully, we must let go of our past experiences with food. When we let go, we can expect new things in the present moment without judging the food by our former beliefs.

BODY SCANS

Our muscles can be relaxed thanks to mindful body scans, which help us reconnect with our bodies and find peace. The scan is divided into three parts: the head, the upper body, and the lower body.

- Sit comfortably and relax.

- For five minutes, observe how your feet interact with the ground.
- Keep an eye on how they make touch with the ground underneath you. Also, observe how your feet are feeling.
- Do your feet need rest? Lift your focus to the lowest portions of your legs, just above your feet. Be conscious of any feelings you may have there.
- Bring your focus gradually to your knees. Observe how your knee makes contact with the chair you are sitting on.
- Pay attention to your buttocks region now. Pay attention to how your body interacts with the chair.
- Your upper body comes next. Feel your abdomen. Is it relaxed, or is it tense? Pay attention to every feeling, no matter how slight. Focus on your lower back now. Observe how it makes contact with the chair's back.
- Now, bring your attention to your hands. Be mindful of any feelings you may experience. Are your hands lying in your lap or on the chair? Feel how your hands and lap connect.
- Move to your head. Pay close attention to your neck and shoulder muscles. Pay attention to how that area is feeling. Do you feel any muscle tension?
- Shift your focus to the top of your head. Pay attention to your lips, nose, eyes, and then ears. Do you have any physical aches or tension? Pay attention to how your head feels. If your thoughts begin to stray, gently bring them back.

And that's it for mindfulness! The next chapter will discuss how to handle intense moments when you encounter a crisis.

WHAT IS DISTRESS TOLERANCE?

You'll likely experience extreme emotional states and crises at some point in life. Sometimes, the crises may be as big as a layoff from your dream job, a divorce, or even the death of a loved one. Other times, the crises may be as minor as missing the bus, a long line at your favorite coffee shop, or heavy traffic during rush hour; those times, you don't know what to wear to a date or when you can't find your keys. Distress tolerance skills can get you to a more manageable place where you can survive crises.

I can still remember a few years ago when my roommate and I heatedly argued over the type of Christmas lights and decorations to get for our minuscule Christmas tree housing in our shared apartment. My friend had simply laughed at a comment I had made. However, what started as a decision over candy canes or globe lights escalated quickly. I couldn't explain why I felt so angry, chest-heaving anger that eventually led to an outburst from me. Sadly, I shouted a rain of not-so-nice words at him, bringing up a few things he had shared with me in confidence.

The situation got so bad he didn't spend Christmas at our apartment that year and eventually moved out a few months later. One of the many failed relationships left me with questions and doubts about myself. I didn't know what came over me, it felt somewhat satisfactory only at that moment, and I couldn't stop myself till I had run out of what to say.

You may have experienced this kind of uncontrollable outbursts, impulses to act irrationally, or felt overwhelming fear when dealing with an emotional crisis. You are not alone in this, and there are scientifically proven ways to deal with the surge of emotions in such moments to achieve safer and better outcomes.

Distress tolerance is a vital DBT skill that can help you make mindful decisions, save you from facing more stress and anxiety and understand what is going on in your own mind.

This chapter discusses how something as simple as deep breaths and counting numbers frees you from the control of your emotions and redirects your mind to work for you rather than against you. It was not until I understood and applied these methods that the happy and fulfilling life I wanted started to look less like a dream and more like reality.

WHAT IS DISTRESS TOLERANCE?

Distress tolerance is the ability to tolerate and survive an emotional crisis without worsening it. It involves a set of skills that helps people handle actual or perceived distress. We all experience a wide range of stress in our lives, from small daily worries such as an annoying boss, an impatient child, or falling out with a friend to significant experiences like the death of a loved one, a business going bankrupt, or a divorce. For some people, a response to stress includes negative emotions that can be overwhelming and unbearable.

When someone has a low distress tolerance, little too mildly stressful situations that translate into emotional stress can overwhelm someone, resulting in potential negative responses or reactions such as self-harm or impulsive behavior. Therefore, learning and practicing distress tolerance skills can positively influence your ability to handle difficult emotions.

In some cases, reality acceptance is the best way to deal with the stress that plagues our thoughts. You can't exactly ignore your emotions but accepting that certain things are beyond your control helps to focus your energy on the things that are within your ability to do. You have to be willing to accept reality because you can't fight it, and to keep struggling leads to more suffering.

In other situations, discovering your triggers and understanding you can't make things better immediately helps you navigate and tolerate painful events, emotions, and impulses easier without making them worse.

In the past, traditional medicine and therapy were centered around stressful situation avoidance to become more stable and equipped to handle stressful emotions, but how much control do you have over that? For some, this increases your misery by forcing you to actively consider what situations may or may not be a trigger. This is why DBT focuses on newer practices and therapies that recognize and accept stressful situations and teaches you to work around them properly. You can take these practices on your own or with the help of a professional.

Now that you know what distress tolerance is and how it affects your stress response let's discuss what goes on in the body when you feel stressed.

The Physiological Effects of Stress

When you feel stress, the body responds the same way it does to threats from predators, aggressors, and harm. This response is adaptive, i.e., changes to prepare the body to handle the threat presented by an internal or external emotional challenge by taking a protective path.

Living in a fast-paced world, we face many attention-demanding activities every day. These activities could be our daily workload, taking care of the family, running an errand, or anything requiring us to put in mental or physical energy. Your body is designed and wired to react and protect itself from external and internal threats, including stress.

Over time, these activities will build up stress, and your body will view these changes as threats and react accordingly. As a result of the counter from your body, you may feel like you're under attack.

Whether it's worrying about relationships, your kids, a mortgage, pressure at work, meeting a deadline, or persistently being under psychological pressure can stimulate your body into triggering a rush of stress hormones that produce physiological changes. For example, stress can fasten your breath and make your heart pound rapidly, sometimes causing beads of sweat, dizziness, and tense muscle.

These intuitive feelings can make life miserable – but you can fight back! You don't have to live in perpetual fear by allowing stress to control your life.

Automatic stress response

When your body feels threatened, for example, hearing a sudden loud sound while you are totally relaxed and unprepared will set off the danger alarm in a small region in your brain called the hypothalamus, alerting your entire system. At the same time, your hormonal and nerve signals will prompt the adrenal glands at the top of the kidney to release a surge of hormones such as cortisol and adrenaline, boosting your energy in return.

It is a complex natural alarm system that communicates with the brain to control motivation, fear, and mood. While adrenaline elevates your blood pressure, increases your heart rate, and improves energy supply, cortisol, on the other hand, increases glucose in the bloodstream, improves the availability of substance-repairing tissues, and enhances the use of glucose in the brain. In addition, cortisol controls harmful or unimportant functions of the fight-or-flight situation, suppresses the digestive system, growth process, and reproductive system, and changes the immune system.

When the natural stress response goes wild

Your body's stress response system can be self-limiting because your hormones will return to normal when a perceived threat passes. For example, when the cortisol and adrenaline levels drop, your blood pressure and heart rate will return to baseline, with other systems resuming their regular routines. However, the fight-or-flight response will stay on stressors and will constantly be present, and you will feel like you are under attack.

Overexposure to cortisol and stress hormones and long-term activation of your stress response can interrupt all your body processes, putting you at risk of health conditions such as:

- Headaches
- Anxiety
- Depression
- Digestive issues
- Weight gain
- Insomnia
- Muscle tension and pain
- Memory and concentration impairment
- Heart attack, heart disease, high blood pressure, and stroke

Due to the risk of having these issues above, you need to learn healthy ways of coping with life stressors.

WHAT DOES THE VAGUS NERVE HAVE TO DO WITH THIS?

The vagus nerve is the longest cranial nerve in the body. It starts behind your ears, runs through your body, and then to the gut. 75% of parasympathetic nerve fibers originate from the vagus nerve. So your sympathetic nervous system will kick in when there's a perceived real or fake threat. The parasympathetic nervous system is tasked with calming your body down.

The function of the vagus nerve is to make you calm when you feel stressed and to alert you when you're no longer in danger. It's like helping you to "rest and digest." This action is a low-tone dorsal activity. On the other hand, the parasympathetic is a high tone activity when you're in freeze mode.

If you aren't emotionally healthy, you are either sympathetic (the fight or flight mode) or parasympathetic (the freeze mode). These aren't the only states of parasympathetic. The two other states are the rest and digest and the ventral vagal branch of the parasympathetic for social engagement (Polyvagal Theory). The function of the ventral vagal is to make you feel less guarded.

According to psychiatrists, the vagal tone can regulate stress responses through meditation and yoga, especially the breathing techniques it encourages. You can resume self-regulating vagal function using mindfulness, breath work, and grounding techniques. This activity will likely improve resilience, mood, and anxiety symptoms.

Vagus Nerve Stimulation (VNS) is a treatment that involves a device looking like a "peacemaker-like" device. When the device is implanted and the vagus nerve is stimulated, you are tapping into being in the present moment and coming home to yourself.

When you're in a difficult situation, you're lighting your vagus nerve and turning inwardly to check in with your true feelings. At that moment that you sing, shout, or speak, you're igniting your vagus nerve. This is why some of these emotions can be emotional for many people.

DISTRESS TOLERANCE AND VAGUS NERVE STIMULATION (VNS)

Distress tolerance is preparing for a stressful event before it happens. Sometimes, you may be unable to overcome the initial shock you feel or the fight or flight response. As a result, the brain can't put coping strategies into place. So, VNS is responsible for restoring the sympathetic system.

When you're experiencing high stress, your body will stay in high gear while stress hormones such as cortisol and adrenaline flow through the body. As a result, the action will create wear and tear on the body and mind, resulting in health problems over time.

Luckily, your body has its own superpower that decreases the fight or flight response. The VNS is responsible for counterbalancing the fight or flight system, triggering a relaxation response.

The vagus nerve is a significant part of how your body and brain function. Without this cranial nerve, your body can't do basic activities. Stimulating it gives many benefits. Some of the ways you can stimulate your vagus nerve include:

- **Breathing techniques**

With breathing exercises such as deep and slow belly breathing, you can shift your focus from the pain or stress you're experiencing. Your mind processes one thing at a time, so when you're focused on the rhythm of your breath, you won't be focused on the stressor or pain.

You can practice deep breathing by inhaling through your nose and exhaling through your mouth. Remember to breathe slowly and deeply from your belly and exhale longer than you inhale to trigger the relaxation response.

- **Cold water immersion**

This involves immersing your forehead (close your eyes) and your cheeks in cold water for a few seconds. This will trigger the vagus nerve, activate the immune system, and decrease heart rate.

- **Laughter**

Who would've thought that having a good laugh can stimulate your vagus nerve, improve your mood, and boost your immune system? In fact, if I were you, I'd make good use of this activity which has zero cost.

- **Massage**

A gentle or firm touch on your body can stimulate the vagus nerve. You can do it yourself or use a professional for this. You can massage your body by applying two pumps of massage oil to your hands, cupping your hands to your nose, and inhaling it. Then you start massaging your neck, starting from the clavicle. Next, move to your ears by rubbing your earlobes, chest, and all over your body until you experience a sensation of a yawn or sigh.

A massage can give you a soothing feeling and bring you to a relaxed state when you feel stressed.

You can make the best out of the techniques for stimulating the vagus nerve by keeping a record or journal of how the techniques make you feel in different situations. This should help you know the right one to implement in a given situation. Write down if one was more effective than the other.

Once you can control the immediate surge of emotions, you will be able to implement some of the distress tolerance techniques we will cover in the next chapter.

MAKE A DIFFERENCE WITH YOUR REVIEW

Unlocking Emotional Balance and Well-being with "What The Heck is DBT"

"Sometimes, the most productive thing you can do is relax."

— MARK BLACK

In life, we often find ourselves caught in a whirlwind of emotions and anxieties, feeling lost and overwhelmed. But there's a way to navigate through this storm, and that's where "What The Heck is DBT" by R.J. Miller comes in.

To make a difference, I have a special request for you...

Would you extend a helping hand to someone you've never met, without expecting anything in return?

You might be wondering who this person is. Well, they're someone just like you were before discovering this book. Eager to learn, ready for change, but unsure where to start.

Our goal is to spread the wisdom of Dialectical Behavior Therapy (DBT) to as many people as possible. Everything we do is driven by this purpose. But to achieve our mission, we need to reach... everyone.

And this is where your help becomes invaluable.

People often rely on reviews when choosing a book. So, here's my request on behalf of someone out there who's struggling, just like you once were:

Please take a moment to leave a review for "What The Heck is DBT."

It doesn't cost you anything and takes less than a minute, but your review could profoundly impact someone's life. Your insights could help...

...another person find peace amidst chaos.

...a parent understand and support their child better.

...a friend manage their emotions more effectively.

...an individual regain control over their life.

...another dreamer find hope and direction.

To share your experience and make a real difference, all you need to do is leave a review. It's quick, simple, and immensely powerful.

Just scan the QR code below to leave your review on Amazon:

If you're moved by the idea of helping someone anonymously, then you're exactly who we're looking for. Welcome to our community. You're one of us now.

I'm thrilled to support you in discovering more DBT skills and strategies that can transform your life. The upcoming chapters are packed with valuable insights that I'm excited to share with you.

Thank you sincerely for your kindness and support. Let's continue our journey together.

- Your biggest fan, R.J. Miller

PS - Remember, sharing knowledge is a powerful way to connect with others. If you believe "What The Heck is DBT" can help someone you know, don't hesitate to pass it along. Your recommendation could be the lifeline they need.

PUTTING DISTRESS TOLERANCE INTO PRACTICE

As I've explained, distress tolerance is the ability to manage emotional situations without feeling overwhelmed. Be it perceived or real; emotional stress can be challenging to manage, especially for individuals with a trauma history. This inability to cope with distress may worsen during a crisis, leaving you helpless and out of control.

Since there is a way out of those times when you feel hated, unloved, and unlucky, we'll be focusing on putting distress tolerance skills into practice. Distress tolerance skills help you learn how to survive a crisis. This chapter will teach you how to handle difficult emotions and learn how to quickly return to a calm state when you encounter stressors.

Imagine this scenario…

You have a big presentation at work tomorrow. You're excited because this could set you up for a significant promotion if you execute it right. But you're also nervous. "What if I mess it up?" "What if it doesn't go the way that I anticipated?"

Your nerves are all frazzled due to excitement and nervousness. To calm yourself down, you decide to hang out with friends and have a few drinks, nothing harmful. You've found that spending time with your closest friends when a major event arises always helps with the nerves. So, you go out with them.

The next day, you wake up half an hour before the presentation. Alarmed, you jump out of bed and fumble through your morning routine. Quickly, you rush to call a taxi and make it just in time for the presentation. "Whew, that was close," you say as you prepare to do the presentation.

Now, imagine this second scenario…

Instead of going out with friends the night before your big presentation, you decide to prepare. So, you get your outfit ready and place it where you can quickly find it and put it on the next day. You also set your alarm to wake you up an hour and thirty minutes before the go-time.

The next day, you wake up and go through your morning routine as usual without rushing or fumbling. You even make it to the office in time to have a coffee and review your presentation once more before going to the conference room to nail it.

Which of these two scenarios seems like the best? The answer is pretty apparent to anyone reading, but one thing I've observed is that crisis management isn't always as easy in practice. Well, unless you hone your skills!

It's one thing to be familiar with DBT distress tolerance skills and another to know how to incorporate them into your daily life. Still, without knowledge of practical techniques, it's not always easy to put distress tolerance into practice. Fortunately, that's exactly what I'll be explaining in this chapter. I should tell you that while the application may take a while to learn, it's always worth it.

This chapter aims to help you learn practical skills for managing disruptive behavior. I'll discuss seven skills, so let's get to it.

TIPP

You're at your breaking point emotionally. Maybe a situation has spiraled entirely out of your control, or this just happened to be the "last straw." In this situation, I recommend the distress tolerance skill called TIPP. TIPP is an acronym for Temperature, Intense Exercise, Paced Breathing, and Paired Muscle Relaxation. It's precisely what you need.

The TIPP skills alter your body chemistry to bring you off the metaphorical ledge. In other words, they reduce your overwhelming feelings in a crisis. I like TIPP because it quickly defuses your emotions and reduces the intensity to a reasonable degree. Usually, I feel a reduction in emotional arousal within a few seconds or minutes of practicing it.

You'll love these skills because they're relatively easy to practice and don't require a lot of thinking or waiting. Another reason is that you can practice them anywhere, even in public. They are easily accessible without the side effects or cost of medication.

With dedicated practice, you can make TIPP skills an adaptive coping technique that you can use anywhere at any time.

• T - Temperature

Ever watched a Hollywood movie where the character suddenly scrambled out of a room to the restroom where they splashed a handful of water on their face? Most likely! You probably don't realize it, but that's a TIPP skill in use.

When you're emotionally aroused, your body might feel hot and feverish. You can change your temperature by splashing cold water on your face, signaling your brain to slow everything down. The brain will then activate the "mammalian dive reflex," which triggers a calming physiological response, such as reduced heart rate. Another way to achieve this is to take a 1 minute cold shower or hold some ice in your hands.

Changing your temperature prevents you from remaining in a heightened emotional state.

• I - Intense Exercise

Like temperature, intense exercise changes your body chemistry adaptively. It releases the stress you're feeling in the moment. This means performing an intense activity that matches the intensity of your emotion.

Intense exercise works because it's impossible to feel distressed and emotionally excited simultaneously. During that exercise, your heart rate increases, and your adrenaline pumps faster than ever. When your brain floods the body with adrenaline, you feel euphoria.

I recommend doing aerobic exercise for 15 to 20 minutes. It helps with releasing pent-up anger or frustration; it's also great to brighten your mood and pump yourself with energy. I have observed that even a few jumping jacks in one spot help with this if I am unable to do a 20-minutes exercise.

- **P - Paced Breathing**

Paced breathing is when you control your breath by exhaling slower and longer than when you inhale. Even something as simple as this can help manage emotional arousal. Breathing exercises are numerous, and anyone will work just fine. If you already have a breathing routine, stick to your usual routine. Otherwise, you can practice the "box breathing" technique, which I find pretty effective.

With paced breathing, each breath interval should be four seconds long. Inhale deeply for four seconds, hold your breath for four seconds, exhale for four seconds, and hold for four seconds before taking in the air again. Continue to use this breathing technique until you feel your body become calm. Consistent breathing deactivates your fight or flight response, relieving your body of tension.

- ### P - Paired Muscle Relaxation

The science behind this technique fascinates me. I tighten a voluntary muscle group, relax it, and allow it to rest - making the muscle more relaxed than before tightening. Relaxed muscles don't use as much oxygen as tensed ones, so breathing and heart rate automatically slow down. When this happens, it's impossible to remain emotionally agitated!

Try the PMR technique on a group of muscles, like the ones in your arms. Or work from toe to head or head to toe - you decide. Tighten the muscle as hard as you can in four seconds. Then, release the tension. Wait for each muscle group to relax before moving on to the next. By the end of the rounds, your entire body should feel fully relaxed.

The TIPP skills will bring you closer to productively coping with your emotions and making constructive decisions during a crisis.

ACCEPTS

The ACCEPTS distress tolerance technique combines skills to cope with a negative emotion until you're ready to deal with it or resolve the situation that triggered the emotion.

Let's say you're at work and you receive a text saying, "We need to have a conversation later today" from your girlfriend. You'll most likely wonder if it's a good or bad conversation you're about to have. That can put you in psychological distress as you wait for the day to end.

Eventually, when you're ready, you'll use skills such as interpersonal effectiveness to meet your needs. In this scenario, the distress tolerance skill you need is ACCEPTS: Activities, Contributing, Comparisons, Emotions, Push Away, Thoughts, and Sensation. These skills will help you to cope with distress until you can appropriately resolve the situation.

- **A - Activities**

Engage in a healthy activity. Take a walk, read a book, watch a movie, do the dishes, bake snacks, call a close friend, immerse yourself in work - just do anything that can keep you busy and take your mind off the upcoming conversation.

Move to another activity if you finish early. You may end up having a very productive day while awaiting the dreaded conversation.

- **C - Contributing**

Providing service to others can relieve distress in more than one way. Contributing distracts you from your distress by keeping your mind focused on someone or something else.

An act of service is any activity that makes you feel good about yourself while keeping your mind off the situation at hand. So, volunteer to babysit your friend's daughter while she's out, help your friend shop for something, bake cookies for a neighbor, or mow your relative's lawn. Simply go out and be of service to someone.

- **C - Comparisons**

Compare the "you" of today to the "you" of five years ago - it helps. The goal here is to put your present into perspective. Remind yourself of a time when you coped with challenges much harder than you do today. You aren't trying to invalidate your distress; you're reminding yourself that you've been in worse situations in the past.

If that doesn't work, compare yourself to someone who's experienced more pain or suffering than you. This skill helps you to gain a different perspective on your current situation.

- **E - Emotions**

Distract yourself from negative emotions by cultivating positive ones. Listen to upbeat music, read an inspirational book, or watch a happy sitcom. By doing this you can evoke the opposite of the distressed feeling you're experiencing.

It would be best if you did something with the opposite emotion for this technique to work. If you're anxious, watch a comedy. If you're angry, watch a romantic movie. Doing so changes your emotion and puts you in a different place.

- **P - Pushing Away**

Leave a distressing situation mentally by pushing it away from your mind temporarily. When you can't deal with an emotion or situation just yet, it's okay to push it away. I find this skill useful when I don't have a solution immediately. The goal isn't avoidance but to find respite, no matter how short.

Every time the situation sneaks up on your mind, block it out mentally. Use this technique to take a break from the pain. Or replace it with another thought, preferably a soothing one. You haven't found a solution to the problem, but you've put it away so that you can focus on more pleasant events in your life for the moment.

- **T - Thoughts**

Replace distressing thoughts with busy ones, such as counting from 100 to 1 or reciting the alphabet backward in your mind. You can even try solving a sudoku puzzle. These distracting thoughts keep your mind busy, preventing you from turning to self-destructive behavior until you achieve emotional regulation.

- **S - Sensation**

This final ACCEPTS skill involves using a strong stimulus (physical) to detach from the feelings of distress and, therefore, distract yourself from the pain. You'll find this particularly helpful if your distress triggers self-destructive or self-harming behavior.

Anything that triggers either of your five senses can help you cope with the pain. You could take a warm bath, put ice on your body, try eating your comfort snack, or watch your favorite show.

IMPROVE

Intense emotions are temporary. Whether it's a big or small circumstance, there will be many instances where you can't control a distressing event. In such situations, you'll need a distress tolerance skill to help you survive the crisis without resorting to unhealthy coping behaviors. The IMPROVE skill can help you learn to tolerate intense emotions until they subside.

IMPROVE is an acronym for Imagery, Meaning, Prayer, Relaxation, One thing in the moment, Vacation, and Encouragement.

- **I - Imagery:** Visualize yourself handling the problem successfully. Imagine the feeling of accomplishment when you're done. In doing so, you may even turn the tide in your favor by changing the outcome.
- **M - Meaning:** Find meaning in a painful situation. What lesson is there for you? Maybe you'll learn to build stronger bonds. Perhaps you'll become more empathetic. Maybe this will set you on the path to healing. Try to see the reason for your present situation.
- **P - Prayer:** You don't have to be religious to pray. Prayer is whatever works for you. If you believe in a higher power, you can pray to God or the Universe. Let go of your problems and ask the higher power to help you tolerate the pain a little longer.
- **R - Relaxation:** Stressful situations trigger the fight or flight response, which makes you tense up. Find

activities to relax to relieve psychological distress. This could be anything from Yoga to deep breathing exercises to taking a relaxing walk in nature.

- **O - One thing in the moment:** Let go of the past and the future by grounding yourself in the moment. Thinking of the past or worrying about the future will only compound the present suffering; it won't solve the problem. Find an activity you can devote yourself to in the moment.

- **V - Vacation:** An ideal vacation allows you to break free from your problems and stressors until you return home, ready to take on the world. But how many of us can take a vacation during a crisis? So, take a mental vacation instead. Visualize yourself lounging on a beach in Ibiza or driving along the Pacific Coast. Stay in that moment for as long as you need to de-stress.

- **E - Encouragement:** Internal encouragement can make a difference in distress tolerance. Encourage yourself with self-affirming phrases that mean something to you. "I got this!" "I am enough." "I can do this on my own!" Say it out loud.

You can use IMPROVE skills anywhere and anytime in a situation you can't control or change. Practice them consistently in minor situations, and they will manifest naturally in major ones.

STOP

STOP is a DBT distress tolerance skill used to ride out a crisis. The mnemonic is pretty easy to remember. Each letter stands for the following

- **S - Stop**

Freeze. Stop dead in your tracks. Don't move. Imagine that there's a red STOP sign right in front of you. Don't react to your emotions instantaneously. Don't let them control you in that heated moment when you're brimming with energy.

- **T - Take a step back**

Take a literal step back, or do it in your mind. Detach yourself from the intense urge to react to the emotion you're experiencing. Once you take that step back, pay attention to your breathing. It may be deep and shallow, or you may be holding it. Whatever it is, take a few deep breaths as slowly as possible.

- **O - Observe**

Observe everything happening within and around you. Pay attention to people in your environment; what are they saying or doing? Notice your thoughts and feelings. In a crisis, we tend to zoom in on a closed perspective instead of seeing the bigger picture. Unfortunately, that restricts us to a slice of information. You must see the whole picture to decide on the best course of action.

- **P - Proceed mindfully**

Use mindfulness techniques to ground yourself in the present moment before making a decision. Consult your wise mind to know what to do, and remind yourself that reacting impulsively won't give you a long-term solution.

Apply the STOP skill in the heat of the moment to ensure you don't do something you'll eventually regret.

RADICAL ACCEPTANCE

You'll often find yourself in undesirable situations that won't change. It's okay if you don't like or approve of the situation, but you must accept it to feel at peace. Before I learned about DBT, I used to try everything possible to change something I didn't like. It took a while before I realized that I couldn't change some things - all I could do was accept and make peace with them.

Radical acceptance is the acknowledgment that you have choices; sometimes, you have to choose whether or not you're willing to accept the reality of a situation. Accept and move forward with your life or choose to stay miserable.

Imagine you're laid off at work. You can't believe it. You try to deny it. So, you continue to do some tasks and forward them to your supervisor. But deep down, you know you've been fired. To avoid the pain, you bury yourself in work you shouldn't be doing.

This feels like it's working out just fine, except that time could have been invested in finding a new job. Instead, you find that you have so many unpaid bills, most of your savings are gone, and you are still unemployed.

With radical acceptance, you can accept that you're afraid you won't get a new job. Getting kicked into the unemployed market will make you miserable, but you need to start working on finding a new job, or forging your own path. Or else, you'll find yourself financially desolate.

So, you fire up your laptop and start applying to jobs you're qualified for or finding new ways to make money. Choosing to focus on the present instead of what may or may not happen will feel genuinely liberating.

Here are ten steps to radical acceptance:

1. Acknowledge that you're fighting or refusing reality.
2. Remind yourself that you cannot change reality, no matter how unpleasant it is.
3. Accept that there are reasons for this new reality. "This is how this happened."
4. Practice accepting reality with your body, mind, and spirit. Use mindfulness, self-talk, imagery, and relaxation techniques to practice acceptance.
5. Write out the things you would do if you could accept the facts as they are. Then, do these things as if you've already accepted.
6. Imagine accepting the unacceptable and practicing in your mind what the next step would be if you did.

7. Notice your body sensations as you imagine that.
8. Allow yourself to feel the associated emotion, grief, disappointment, or sadness. Let it wash over you.
9. Accept that you can still live a worthwhile life even in pain.
10. Try the pros and cons if you're still resisting acceptance.

SELF-SOOTHE

When in a heightened state of stress or anxiety, it becomes challenging to draw upon your natural self-soothing ability. When your levels of distress increase, it helps to have a readily accessible self-care toolkit. That way, you can manage the present moment more skillfully.

Self-soothing skills allow you to calm down and center yourself in times of distress to return to a more grounded place. You can self-soothe effectively during a crisis by utilizing emotional regulation skills and mindfulness with your senses.

- **Sight**

Try sitting outside your porch and gaze upon nature attentively with mindful eyes. Walk to the nearest park or take a leisurely hike up the hills. Sit outdoors at nighttime and feed your eyes with the twinkly little stars.

- **Hearing**

Listen to soothing or vibrant music - depending on how you feel. If you can, play an instrument to calm your frayed nerves. Close your eyes and absorb the sounds around you mindfully. Ensure you immerse yourself in the sounds of your environment.

- **Touch**

Snuggle under your soft, cozy blanket with your loved one or your snuggly little pet if you have one. Pour a warm cup of coffee and feel the warmth on the mug with your hands before drinking. Make a bubble bath for yourself and take as much time as needed to savor the experience.

- **Smell**

Burn a couple of incense sticks or light up a scented candle. Rub essential oils on the inside of your wrists and inhale deeply. Leave your windows open and let the smell of fresh air wash over you.

- **Taste**

Take your time with dessert after dinner and slow down to enjoy the taste. Mindfully, eat a bowl of ice cream; savor the textures, flavors, and tastes. Don't rush anything; take your time.

You can find more creative ways to use your five senses to self-soothe. If you already have self-care activities that you enjoy, continue practicing them for self-soothing. The more you self-soothe in distressing situations now, the better you'll become at self-soothing in the future.

DISTRACTIONS

In the past, I used to believe that distraction was bad for me. I heard many stories about how dividing my attention can affect my focus and leave me feeling frazzled and scattered. While I found this true, I eventually discovered it doesn't apply to every situation. What exactly does this mean?

Distraction isn't mindlessly watching a movie or replaying a kiss in your head as you try to complete an assigned task with your music player on full blast. No, DBT distraction is purposeful. You're choosing to focus on a particular activity instead of doing what your emotions are urging you to do when you're in a crisis. Acting on your emotions in an emotionally charged situation can only backfire.

Sometimes, detaching from an emotional experience with distractions is good for us. You can use this skill when you are:

- Emotionally overwhelmed
- Have an urge to do something you might later regret
- Feel like you have to solve a problem with urgency

Acting on emotional urges often works against our long-term goals - maintaining stable relationships and self-respect and freeing ourselves of addictive behaviors.

Distract yourself with activities. Do anything that takes your mind off the emotion - clean your closet, declutter your home, play video games, or work out. Just choose an activity that doesn't intensify the negative emotions. You can also do something nice for a loved one or stranger. Refer back to ACCEPTS skill.

Distraction is an effective short-term solution to avoid reacting spontaneously to your emotional urges. Distracting yourself works because it puts a distance between you and the thing upsetting you. It helps until you're calm enough to decide on a proper course of action.

Whether it's anxiety, BPD, or personality disorders, your interactions with people will always be a top concern. Sometimes, these tense interactions can be with your family, friends, or co-workers. Therefore, the following chapter explores how you can use DBT skills to improve your relationships with others.

6

INTERPERSONAL EFFECTIVENESS AND YOUR RELATIONSHIPS

Relationships are like plants. They require certain things to flourish, including healthy roots, stems, air, and water. The more a plant gets these things, the more it grows stronger - it may even bear fruits, depending on its kind. Like plants, your relationships require healthy roots, like a foundation. And they must have the necessary social skills to grow stronger.

However, many of us struggle with building healthy social networks. For example, individuals with BPD find social interactions particularly challenging. So do people on the autism spectrum and others with conditions such as ADHD, depression, and anxiety. These are a few conditions that make building a social network nearly impossible. But they aren't the only reasons why people may struggle with social interactions.

UNDERSTANDING INTERPERSONAL EFFECTIVENESS

DBT interpersonal effective skills allow anyone to build healthy relationships with strong roots. They are specifically designed to help you meet your needs in your relationships while maintaining respect across the board.

Emotional instability can make interpersonal relationships more complicated than they need to be. Even when you form relationships effortlessly, you'll inevitably come to need things from people just as they'll need something from you. As a result, many people struggle to form and maintain healthy relationships.

Your exchanges with others about how they can meet your needs and how you might meet their needs can result in tension, confusion, and conflict. Some of us find it very difficult to ask others for assistance. It's also difficult for some to refuse requests with a firm "No." Learning to handle these situations with ease is a core aspect of interpersonal effectiveness. By mastering the skills, you'll learn to get what you need in a relationship without becoming manipulative or codependent.

How you communicate with others significantly affects the quality of your interpersonal relationships and the outcome of your social interactions. To improve communication, you need interpersonal effectiveness skills to take a more deliberate and thoughtful approach to conversations instead of reacting impulsively to strong emotions or stress.

The two vital skills you'll learn are the ability to ask for your needs to be met and how to say no to people when appropriate. Without these skills, you may find it difficult to state requests or get your needs met, behave appropriately with others, or become vulnerable to exploitation.

Go on the internet right now, and you'll find thousands of books on how you can cultivate the proper skills or a specific skill set for personal development. These books provide a myriad of skills to add to your repertoire to make yourself more appealing to the job market or people around you.

But how do you know which skill is crucial?

It's nearly impossible to answer the above question. Still, I will always tell anyone who cares to hear that interpersonal effectiveness skills are some of the best tools you can have in your social kit.

We meet hundreds of people weekly, and we'll probably meet tens of thousands in one lifetime. You don't necessarily need to impress everyone you encounter by choice or chance. Still, it would be best if you built healthy connections with a reasonable number of them.

Whether you struggle with public speaking, are an extrovert, an introvert, or are just a hermit, there's no reason you shouldn't try to improve your communication skills and enhance your social life. This may seem particularly daunting if you struggle with anxiety, depression, autism, ADHD, or BPD. It's doubly challenging for individuals with these conditions to have adequate social interactions. Fortunately, DBT skills can help hone your interpersonal effectiveness.

Why is interpersonal effectiveness crucial?

Interpersonal effectiveness skills are vital because you need them to:

- Cater to your relationships
- Balance your and others' needs
- Balance your wants and shoulds
- Build and maintain self-respect

To some extent, we all do these things naturally. You're somewhat able to say no or ask for things from others as well. For example, you probably find it easy to say no to more wine on a date, but how easy is it when your codependent friend comes asking for another favor?

The importance of interpersonal effectiveness is reflected in how it's one of the primary modules of DBT - in fact; it's the second module. So, many DBT resources and materials focus on improving a client's interpersonal skills because of it.

But if you're wondering just how crucial interpersonal effectiveness is in DBT, let's discuss that. Remember, earlier in this chapter; I stated that how we communicate with others can impact the quality of our relationships. Well, DBT asserts that interpersonal skills are necessary for this very reason. Because, in turn, the quality of your social interactions and relationships affects your well-being, self-esteem, self-confidence, self-image, and understanding of who you are.

So, you can see just how important it is to have adequate interaction skills. If you think you only need basic effectiveness skills to communicate and you're set, I'd like to say that you're wrong. At one point, I was also comfortable with the skills I already had. But it took mastering communication skills at a high level of effectiveness to realize just how crucial they are.

Like all complex skills, reaching the apex of mastery is practically impossible. In other words, you can never completely master a skill. Even the most accomplished public speakers are not master communicators. So, remember that you can continually improve regardless of your level of mastery.

Numerous studies have shown that improving your interpersonal skills will lead to positive outcomes, especially if you struggle with BPD. More specifically, DBT interpersonal effectiveness skills have improved BPD patients' relationship capabilities and overall symptoms while reducing affective instability.

THE GOALS OF INTERPERSONAL EFFECTIVENESS

Maybe you have these skills but are unsure how to apply them in everyday interactions. Or perhaps you simply don't know the right time to use them. In order to understand which skills are suitable for a specific situation and when to utilize them, you should know the goals of interpersonal effectiveness. And that brings me to the three goals:

- Objective effectiveness
- Relationship effectiveness

- Self-respect effectiveness

Achieving each goal in interactions requires interpersonal skills. Although we can apply some skills in different situations, we need specific skills to accomplish any of the goals.

When working toward achieving an objective, you must be able to clarify what you want from the interaction and identify how to get the results you want. If your interaction goal is relationship effectiveness, then maintaining the relationship is your priority. In that case, you need to determine how meaningful that relationship is to you, what you want from the other person, and the necessary actions you can take to move the relationship forward.

And when your goal is to maintain self-respect, i.e., self-respect effectiveness, you need specific interpersonal skills to help you understand how you would like to feel at the end of the interaction and exactly how to feel like that while sticking to the facts and your values.

In most cases, you'll most likely have at least two goals in a situation. And in others, you may have the three goals. For example, suppose you want to obtain something from your partner, keeping in mind that they're an essential part of your life. In that case, you'll want to maintain your relationship while getting what you want. And you'll likely want to retain self-respect in the asking process and apply the skills for each goal simultaneously.

FACTORS THAT BLOCK INTERPERSONAL EFFECTIVENESS

Several factors can act as obstacles to interpersonal effectiveness if you're already skilled at navigating social interactions. These blocks often arise from time to time, so you must continuously work on developing your interpersonal skills.

No matter the situation or the person involved, when you're experiencing distress, it helps to take a step back and mentally review the situation without judgment. Half of the fight to overcome communication blocks is identifying the real problem, not the one you think it is. This requires taking a long, hard look in the mirror and asking yourself how you might have contributed to the problem.

Usually, we acquire the basics of social interactions from the patterns we see in our families growing up. This means that how you relate with others is most likely modeled after your primary caregiver. Obviously, these patterns aren't always the healthiest or most effective.

As you grow up from childhood to adolescence to adulthood, you gradually enact what you've seen in your families with other people - unhealthy or otherwise. If your parents dealt with conflict using unhealthy techniques, you will likely internalize those techniques and re-enact them in your relationships as an adult.

The good thing is that you can unlearn these patterns; they don't have to continue in adulthood. You're at a point where you can identify these patterns and eliminate them. You can choose much healthier ways of interacting with others.

Below are eight aversive strategies for learning or using interpersonal effectiveness skills.

1. **Discounting:** This is when you communicate your needs by telling the other person that their needs are trivial or invalid. *Example*: "You've been on your phone all day - do you expect me to clean after you while you just sit around?"
2. **Withdrawing:** Sometimes, you're so afraid that the other person will abandon or withdraw from you that you preemptively withdraw first, emotionally or in some other way. *Example*: "You can do anything you want - I'm leaving anyway."
3. **Blaming:** You make everything the other person's fault while absolving yourself of all responsibilities. You tell yourself that they should fix it since they caused it. *Example*: "We're only in this mess because of you - fix it!"
4. **Threatening:** This happens when you have so much anger inside that you believe the only way to alleviate your pain is to make the other person suffer. *Example*: "If you don't give me what I want, I will leave you."
5. **Guilt-tripping:** You try to make the other person feel like a failure. Or you make them think they're wrong to ask you to meet their needs. *Example*: "You wouldn't ask that of me if you cared about me."

6. **Belittling**: You attack others to make them feel wrong, stupid, or defective. *Example*: "Why did you insist on coming with me? I knew you wouldn't behave appropriately."

7. **Derailing:** This is a strategy to divert attention from the other person's needs or feelings toward yourself and your own needs. *Example*: "I'm so hurt; I don't care what you say right now."

These are some of the strategies we use to block interpersonal effectiveness. And sometimes, we don't even realize we're doing that.

Other factors that could be blocking interpersonal effectiveness include overthinking or negative thinking, intense emotional arousal, indecision, the environment, and a combination of these factors.

- **Lack of skill**

We tend to dismiss the lack of interpersonal skills as lacking motivation. "I haven't discussed my idea with my boss because I don't want to." But it's probably because you don't know what to say, how to say it, or how to act. If you don't know how to communicate your needs, it won't matter how motivated you are.

Interpersonal skills are acquired the same way we develop other skills: By observing others. You may lack these skills if you don't have anyone to model them for you, you never had the opportunity to observe the skills, or you never had time to practice them.

Like I said earlier, it's possible that you didn't learn healthy interaction skills as a child and, so, have no structure upon which to build them.

- **Overthinking**

Negative thoughts affect our ability to use interpersonal skills. In this case, you have the skills, but you're letting overthinking get in the way of what you want to say or do. "What if my boss doesn't like my idea? I might get fired!"

"I'll end up ruining the task." It's normal to think about potential outcomes for our actions. Still, overthinking makes us hyper-fixate on possible dire consequences. It may push us to worry about being ineffective.

Negative thinking invalidates and creates a cycle of harmful self-talk, making it difficult to achieve our objective in an interaction.

- **Intense emotions**

Emotions are sometimes an automatic response to a situation that has happened in the past, and as you know, emotions impact behavior. In some circumstances, you have the ability to navigate an interaction, but you let your emotions interfere, which causes frustration.

For example, we get frustrated when a situation feels out of control. Or feel guilty because of our reaction to a particular situation.

If you allow them, emotions can become overwhelming and cause you to shut down before or in the interaction process. That's when your distress tolerance skills can aid with interpersonal effectiveness.

- **Indecision**

Negative thinking and intense emotional arousal can cause indecision. This often occurs when we're conflicted about priorities, can't figure out how to balance asking without asking for less or too much, or don't know how to balance saying no or giving in.

In this case, you can't decide what to say or do even though you have the interpersonal skill required.

- **Environment**

In some cases, there could be harmful outcomes to saying no to a request. The other person might take the rejection quite poorly due to their own insecurities, obstructing all chances of salvaging the situation. Sometimes, even those highly skilled at interpersonal interactions simply don't know how to get their way, behave in self-respecting ways, or ensure others continue to like them.

Other times, we consider objective effectiveness, i.e., obtaining our goal, more important than self-respect effectiveness, i.e., retaining our self-respect. In such cases, you'll need radical acceptance to embrace reality as it is.

I mentioned that a combination or interplay of these factors could also block interpersonal effectiveness. The factors play off each other. The more you experience non-giving circumstances (environment), the more you overthink, and the worse you feel. You become stuck in a cycle of ineffectiveness where it becomes impossible to maintain healthy social connections no matter how hard you try.

APPLYING INTERPERSONAL EFFECTIVENESS

There are many things to consider when entering a negotiation with someone else. I use "negotiation" here to refer to the act of asking another person to meet your needs. To successfully use interpersonal effectiveness skills, you must learn how to utilize other DBT skills, including distress tolerance, mindfulness, and emotional regulation.

In interpersonal interactions, we take in a lot of sensory information, such as what the other person says, our physiological responses, thoughts, and present feelings, which are many things to notice and process all at once.

You can only take effective action if you interact with a situation in a mindful manner. Mindfulness is key to interpersonal effectiveness because it allows you to immerse yourself in what's happening so you can notice everything. When you approach your interactions with a mindful attitude, you get too genuinely focus on what's happening.

When I'm about to enter a negotiation, I ask myself a series of questions as a way of utilizing my interpersonal skills. If you learn to ask these questions before making a request of another person or when someone makes a request of you, it'll begin to come naturally. With that in place, you'll be able to make informed decisions on the best way to proceed with negotiations.

Priorities

- How important are my objectives?
- Is this relationship damaged or fragile in any way?
- Am I risking my self-respect?
- Will this interaction injure my self-respect if I refuse this request?

Capability

- Is this person capable of fulfilling my needs?
- Am I capable of giving this person what they want from me?

Timing

- Is this person in the right mood to hear my request?
- When are they most likely to be receptive to my request?
- Is this a good or bad time to turn down their request?

Authority

- Does this person hold authority over me in any way?
- Do I hold authority over them in any way?

Homework

- Am I sufficiently familiar with this request or situation or the person I'm asking for something?
- Do I have the necessary information to present my request to them?
- Am I clear about what I need?
- Am I clear about what the other person is requesting?
- Do I understand what I'm saying yes or committing to?

Rights

- Would accepting this request affect my rights in any way?
- Would turning down this request affect the other person's rights in any way?

Reciprocity

- Have I done as much as I'm asking for this person?
- Have they done as much for me as they're asking for?

Respect

- Do I usually meet my own needs?

- Do I always appear helpless or try to avoid looking helpless?
- Will saying "no" evoke negative feelings about myself?

Long-term vs Short-term

- If I give up on my request right now, will it cause long-term problems later on?
- If I say no to their request, will it cause long-term problems later on?

It's normally impossible for two people in an intimate, platonic, or professional relationship to meet each other's needs every time. Let go of this idea and accept that it's unrealistic. The more realistic thing is that the other person will meet some of your needs most of the time, and vice versa.

When using interpersonal effectiveness skills, think about possible compromises. What are you willing to compromise, and what's non-negotiable? Always find ways to meet the other person halfway to maintain harmony and mutual respect in the relationship.

Combining interpersonal effectiveness with mindfulness practice allows you to attune to your experiences, take a constructive approach to analyzing your thoughts and feelings, and successfully negotiate with the important people in your life.

What should you focus on? Find patterns in how you negotiate with others and determine what needs changing. Don't become overly fixated on fairness in exchanges because that can create a skewed perspective of reality. Also, don't try to be right all the time because that makes it impossible to move forward with harmony and a positive attitude.

Reflect on how attached you are too old communication patterns and take an honest assessment of how you can change your relationships going forward. How would your relationships be different if you gave up on old ways and started approaching interpersonal exchanges with true mindfulness and effectiveness? Change is frightening, but what are you willing to change?

YOUR SOCIAL SKILLS ASSESSMENT

This section has a social skills assessment table to help you understand which areas to work on extensively and which ones need a slight improvement. I recommend taking this assessment as you begin applying the DBT skills you've learned and retaking it a few weeks later.

Rate yourself on the skills below on a scale from 1 to 5 according to the following metric. (don't forget to download your free DBT insider worksheets)

Metric

*In the metric below, 1 means **very bad**, 2 means **bad**, 3 means occasionally good, 4 means **usually good**, and 5 means always **good**.*

1.	I am **very bad** at this skill.
2.	I am **bad** at this skill.
3.	I am **occasionally good** at this skill.
4.	I am **usually good** at this skill.
5.	I am **always good** at this skill.

Here are 20 communication skills to assess yourself.

#	Social Skills	Rating				
1.	Meeting new people	1	2	3	4	5
2.	Introducing yourself	1	2	3	4	5
3.	Listening to I - showing interest in people	1	2	3	4	5
4.	Listening to II - taking in what they say	1	2	3	4	5
5.	Describing your feelings	1	2	3	4	5
6.	Stating your needs	1	2	3	4	5
7.	Dealing with anger, aggression, or hostility	1	2	3	4	5
8.	Receiving praise or criticism	1	2	3	4	5
9.	Receiving negative feedback	1	2	3	4	5
10.	Defusing tension in a conversation	1	2	3	4	5
11.	Increasing the seriousness of a conversation	1	2	3	4	5
12.	Managing silence in a conversation	1	2	3	4	5
13.	Seeking clarification	1	2	3	4	5
14.	Responding to display of apathy or disinterest	1	2	3	4	5
15.	Appreciating people's feelings and needs	1	2	3	4	5
16.	Asking open-ended questions	1	2	3	4	5
17.	Providing relevant information	1	2	3	4	5
18.	Seeking information from others	1	2	3	4	5
19.	Changing the topic or direction of a conversation	1	2	3	4	5
20.	Holding attention or interest	1	2	3	4	5

You can improve this assessment by considering interpersonal communications that aren't included and rating yourself using the above metric. This assessment is an excellent way to figure out where you are and where you want to be.

It's best to use individual values. Still, you can also take the average of all 20 ratings to score an overall "social skill" rating.

To truly improve your interpersonal skills rating, ensure you establish a baseline first. Again, you can do this by taking the assessment at the start of your journey. Creating a baseline gives you something to compare back to. That way, you can observe improvements qualitatively.

The reality is that many of us lack social skills because, in school, our teachers were so preoccupied with teaching algebra, geography, and calculus that they forgot how important it is to acquire practical social skills.

Your interpersonal skills will do more for you than your knowledge of capital cities will do for you - that's a fact. Communication is the most critical aspect of our daily lives as humans because socializing is a priority.

Of course, this isn't to blame the teachers or parents who raised us. Perhaps they lived in a different time when social norms were slightly different. Regardless, you change how you interact and model healthy social skills for the future generation. They'll thank you for it.

In order to learn and model healthy interaction skills for the next generation, it's time to discuss the exact DBT techniques you need in order to improve your interpersonal effectiveness.

STRATEGIES TO INCLUDE INTERPERSONAL EFFECTIVENESS IN YOUR LIFE

I once tried learning a new language on Duolingo. After a few weeks, I started to know the basics. I could do greetings and introductions. But there was nobody around me to practice verbally with. Eventually, due to a busy schedule, I had to take time off from Duolingo practice. By the time I returned to learning this language, I had to start all over! Sadly, I couldn't remember what I had learned so far.

Why did this happen? Well, I had no one to speak the language with. So the only place I could practice was on Duolingo. If I had any other way of practicing it while I couldn't use Duolingo, I most likely wouldn't have lost everything I learned.

This is how social skill learning works. You must continuously practice it to remain prolific. Like a language, if you don't regularly practice your social skills, you'll eventually forget or lose them.

There are three key DBT strategies to help you improve interpersonal effectiveness, i.e., boost your social skills. Let's discuss them one by one.

DEAR MAN

DEAR MAN is an interpersonal effectiveness skill for effective communication. This skill will teach you to respectfully express your wants and needs to all parties involved in the interaction, which increases your chances of getting a positive outcome. Using this strategy, you will learn to take a new approach to assertive communication.

The DEAR MAN strategy works specifically for achieving objective effectiveness in an interaction. To get what you want from your relationships and master the ability to react to situations in a non-judgmental manner, DEAR MAN is the fundamental skill to learn and master.

What does the acronym mean?

- **D - Describe**

Describe your situation clearly and without ambiguity. Don't assume that the other person knows what you want to talk about. State it to them in clear terms. Be as factual as possible. You're trying to set up the conversation with facts instead of expressing your feelings outright.

This is important because the other person might not know what you are requesting until you explain it clearly. By laying the facts on the table, you're ensuring they understand the circumstances leading you to make this request.

For example, let's say your spouse has been missing out on many family events due to work. Instead of keeping your discontent to yourself to avoid conflict or lashing out at them, you can communicate and work out a solution together.

You can describe the situation by saying, "I understand that you have a crazy schedule at work which is causing you to miss a lot of commitments at home. I would like us to talk about it."

- **E - Express**

After describing the situation with facts to support it, express how you feel with "I" statements. An "I" statement allows you to be accountable without sending the other person into defense mode. That way, they're unlikely to see your talk as an attack. This is crucial because you want the other person to know how you feel about the situation you've just described to them. It gives them insight into where you're coming from.

Example: *"Because you've never missed commitments so consistently, I'm afraid the kids will feel neglected. I feel that this is the best time for us to be there for them as much as we can. My biggest fear is that your work will cause a divide in the family, and we won't return from it."*

- **A - Assert**

Assert yourself by firmly stating your need or request. To "assert" means to communicate what you want in a clear and strong manner. Depending on the situation, assertiveness could also mean saying a firm "No" to the other person's request. Be direct - don't beat around the bush, make allusions, or leave it up to the other person to guess what you're asking for.

This is important because you're the only one who can read your own mind. Your partner can't, and you shouldn't expect them to. What you want might seem obvious, but the other person might have no idea. Or, they may be unsure exactly what it is you want. Unclear expectations cause significant conflict in many relationships. Remove the ambiguity and lay it on clearly and directly.

Example: *"I want you to make it to the children's parent-teacher conference this Wednesday."*

- **R - Reinforce**

Relationships are all about reciprocity. If someone does you a favor, you're more likely to return that favor. This usually comes naturally. Reinforce what you just started to ensure the other person knows why they must meet that need or grant that request.

Therefore, this reminds the other person that they get something from granting your request or meeting your need, which can help solidify the relationship even more.

Example: *"I appreciate your hard work to keep our finances afloat and how much time you devote to the kids when you get any opportunity. I'll be happy to take over picking up the kids from school on Thursdays."*

- **M - (Be) Mindful**

Stay in the present moment. Don't be distracted by your environment. Instead, commit to the conversation for as long as it goes on. Even if the other person becomes defensive, try your best to stay on course. Distractions come quickly, especially when you have an uncomfortable discussion. But if you let the conversation steer off course, it becomes unlikely that you'd get what you're asking for.

Remain mindful until you both reach a resolution. This will increase the chance of having a successful and productive negotiation.

Example: At this point in the conversation with your spouse, they'll probably have a lot of rebuttals to what you said. It could be about how they're trying their best or how you have a more flexible schedule. Instead of going down that rabbit hole, stay focused on the situation you're addressing.

You might say, *"I understand that you're working hard, and I also acknowledge that I have a more flexible schedule. We can both come up with a better plan to make the kids feel like you're involved in their lives as much as I am."*

- **A - Appear confident**

Forget how you feel on the inside and maintain a confident exterior. Sit upright with your head held high, make direct eye contact, and speak clearly. Being confident signals to the other person that you expect them to grant your request. It becomes hard to turn you down because confidence shows them you aren't making a request that's too difficult to grant.

Example: Appearing confident portrays an air of finality to your spouse. You can display confidence by maintaining eye contact, staying focused on the topic, remaining calm, and stating your request clearly.

- **N - Negotiate**

Remember that the conversation isn't about making a demand. You're asking the other person for something. If they aren't on board, you might have to make compromises. One way you could do that is to alter your request in a way that makes it more appealing to them. Talk to the other person about how you can work together to resolve the problem, and you'll most likely reach a solution together.

Negotiating is meant to show that you're willing to accommodate each other's feelings, needs, and opinions as much as possible. It's a tactic to show that you care about hearing them and can make compromises.

Example: Listen to your spouse and look for a solution that leaves all parties satisfied, including the kids.

The DEAR MAN technique is an excellent skill for communicating and achieving your objective in any interaction, no matter the relationship.

GIVE

"GIVE" is another interpersonal effectiveness skill designed to help improve your communication skills. I always say that some relationships are worth preserving more than others. The GIVE strategy is designed to help you achieve relationship effectiveness.

Interpersonal relationships can be challenging, especially if you struggle to regulate your emotions or control your reactions. As a result, you can easily damage a relationship without even knowing it. GIVE keeps your relationship intact during a conflict or argument. Also, if you have a particular relationship you would like to improve or maintain, this skill can help you do just that.

A considerable part of interpersonal effectiveness is tending to your relationships consistently. Letting hurt and problems accumulate doesn't help. Instead, it's much better to address them as they happen. You can learn this skill to handle issues before they blow up. It's also practical for ending toxic or hopeless relationships.

Please note that you shouldn't continually use the GIVE technique to address issues on undeserving people. It's for relationships that truly matter.

Before beginning an interpersonal interaction for relationship effectiveness, knowing your specific goal is essential. The general goal is to preserve a relationship. But sometimes, you may want the other person to stop criticizing you or perhaps want them to approve of you.

Below are three things to consider before an interaction aimed at improving a relationship:

1. Act in a manner that makes the other person want to grant your request or meet your specific need.
2. Act in a manner that makes the person react positively to you, turning down their request.
3. Balance your immediate goal with what's good for the relationship in the long term.

Ensure that you balance your objective with relationship and self-respect goals. Do not compromise your self-respect for an undeserving person or relationship. Don't grant a request you don't want just to preserve a relationship. All three things high-lighted above must be coordinated and balanced effectively.

GIVE is an acronym for:

- Gentle
- Interested
- Validate
- Easy manner

(Be) Gentle

You don't want to come across as threatening or aggressive in communication. It'll only put the other person on the defensive, potentially destroying the relationship you're trying to improve or maintain.

A good part of this skill is to avoid criticizing or denigrating the other person. For example, don't make threats, pass judgment, or attack the other person. You also shouldn't name-call or disrespect them in any way, shape, or form.

Humans are more responsive to gentleness. Being gentle is vital because it's a way to get the other individual to do something you'd like them to do, especially if they just won't do it. Anger and threats may seem like more accessible means to your end. Still, they're unlikely to help you achieve the goal of relationship effectiveness. Instead, be open to taking "no" for an answer.

Approach the conversation assuming the other person has reasons for their actions, opinions, or decisions. Even if you disagree with them, it's not a call to disrespect them. Instead, ensure your facial expressions and body language convey respect and your language and actions.

Give the other person time and space to come up with a response. If they request postponing or delaying the conversation or having it in a safer space, accept it and move forward.

(Act) Interested

You feel awful when trying to talk to someone, but they appear more interested in something else, like their phone. It's pretty hurtful, so you shouldn't do it to another person. Instead, when someone is communicating with you, the only right thing to do is listen to them. Show interest in their point of view. No matter how challenging it is, act interested in the conversation - even if it is dreadfully dull.

Humans respond well to interest from the person they're interacting with. So it's okay to wonder if acting interested is dishonest - it isn't. Remember that you're trying to have a pleasant conversation and maintain or improve your relationship with the other person. You can't let disinterest get in the way of that.

Acting interested helps you achieve the relationship effectiveness goal. At some point, you may even find that you're genuinely interested in the conversation. So, maintain direct eye contact, nod occasionally, and let your facial expressions portray interest.

The results may be easier than you think.

Validate

This skill shows the other person that you listened to and understood everything they said. You do this with words and actions. Express that you understand their perspective and why they would feel the way they do. You can validate a person's opinions, feelings, or actions without agreeing with them. Validating doesn't necessarily indicate agreement.

For example, let's say you're upset at your friend for canceling your lunch plans at the last minute. Perhaps he gave an excuse that something came up at work, but you aren't convinced it warranted canceling your plans.

In that case, you may respond with, "I'm sorry something came up at work, and I know how hard you work." Notice that this response doesn't address the problem. This is an excellent example of how to validate, and it's great for maintaining relationships you want to give a second chance.

This skill is handy during disagreements. It teaches you to be more understanding of other people's perspectives, opinions, feelings, etc. Even if you already have a strong relationship, validating can strengthen it.

Easy manner

Smile. Be grateful. Find humor in the situation and throw that into the conversation. Don't make the conversation tense or painful because that will only strain the relationship. Using an easy manner in the interaction allows you to counter potential strains or tensions.

It doesn't matter if you disagree with the other person. However, you shouldn't let the conversation turn sour or adversarial. Instead, make it as light and easy-going as possible. You'll find that soothes the tension.

Nobody wants to feel like another person is guilt-tripping, threatening, or pushing them around. So don't be a bully.

A good attitude increases your chances of getting what you want. However, it can be hard to maintain an easy manner when the other person goes on the defensive or feels hurt by your request. Just remember that their feelings are valid. Try to keep a calm and easy manner as you accept their response or reaction.

Before I use the GIVE skill, I like to think of how I would like other people to treat me during a similar discussion or argument. For example, do I want to be yelled at or spoken to softly? What would either approach look like in words and actions?

Then, I take my answers and use them to practice having the discussion. You can practice with a trusted friend or your adorable pet; ensure you utilize all the tips and tricks given here. Also, don't wait until you have a serious discussion to use these skills. It's easier to remember them if you regularly utilize them.

The DBT GIVE skill is another valuable tool to improve social skills and interactions. Don't forget to put it into practice!

FAST

The "FAST" strategy helps achieve self-respect effectiveness during communication. A long time ago, I embodied passivity; by default, the communication type was passive communication. I tried my best to avoid difficult conversations and conflicts, even at a high personal cost. I never put my needs first; in fact, I often rehearsed things I'd say and how I'd say them to my partner, parents, boss, siblings, or friends, but once the conversation got too intense, I would stay away.

I quite literally felt my self-respect fading away. Thankfully, I became familiar with DBT and learned to shed passive communication for assertive communication. I have learned how to keep self-respect during a disagreement or conflict using the FAST skill, and I want you to do the same.

FAST is an acronym that outlines subskills for maintaining self-respect when trying to get another person to meet your needs.

- **F - Fair**

Be fair, both to yourself and the other person. Fair represents being tactfully honest about your needs and those of the person you're interacting with. It opens up a path to constructive and productive criticism, allowing you to preserve the relationship as you want.

Expressing your needs instead of hiding them or covertly hinting at them requires a degree of assertiveness, which is what "fair" helps you achieve. Being fair also means treating the other person how you would like to be treated.

- **A - No Apologies**

Unnecessary apologies are a no-no. You should only apologize if you've indeed done something that requires apologizing. That is key to rebuilding trust and repairing a damaged relationship. However, if you've done nothing to be sorry for, there's no need to apologize compulsively. You might surprise yourself if you decide to consciously take note of how often you apologize in a day.

Remember that apologizing for mistakes that aren't yours only instills an unnecessary sense of guilt.

- **S - Stick to your values**

The urge to compromise your values to please the other person is usually incredibly high during a conflict. So naturally, you want to please the other person. But don't forget that you also want to keep self-respect, so you mustn't forget what's important to you.

Before the interaction, make a list of your values and explore them. That way, you can decide which values are non-negotiable. You shouldn't have to lose your values to gain the other individual's approval. In fact, if they cannot respect your values, it might be time to reevaluate your relationship with them.

Sticking to your values can help achieve successful conflict resolution.

- **Truthful**

Being truthful means avoiding lies, excuses, and exaggerations. It includes being accountable for your actions while recognizing how to differentiate another person's actions from yours during a conflict.

By demonstrating accountability, you can view your role in the situation from a more authentic point of view. That can help decrease anxiety as you reflect on your actions. But, more importantly, it enables you to identify the areas you can improve on.

Try the FAST skill the next time you find yourself in a conflict and see how it goes.

THINK

Usually, when we have a conflict with another person, we approach the interaction with a negative attitude. This is because your brain naturally interprets the person's words or actions as threatening or attacking. So, you jump to conclusions, causing you to lash out and become defensive or hostile.

Emotions like anger or frustration can make it difficult to control your actions in a tense situation. This defeats your goal of achieving interpersonal effectiveness, especially if you want to improve a relationship, maintain self-respect, or communicate more healthily and productively.

Luckily, the DBT THINK skill can help you reduce conflict and disagreements. You can use this skill to enter the Wise mind, where you can constructively resolve conflicts.

- **T - Think**

Think about the conflict or situation from the other person's point of view. How might they interpret your words, actions, and situation? In other words, put yourself in the person's shoes and think about their perspective.

- **H - Have empathy**

How might the other person be feeling? Are they angry? Sad? Frustrated? Stressed? Anxious? Uncomfortable? It's important to empathize and consider their feelings during the conversation.

- **I - Interpret**

Can you interpret the person's actions in more than one way? Is there an alternate explanation for their behavior? Ensure you seek at least one positive interpretation of the cause of the conflict. That allows you to maintain a productive attitude during the interaction.

- **N - Notice**

Pay attention to how the other person might have been trying to improve or salvage the situation. How are they showing that they care? What skills are they applying to the situation? Are they struggling with stressors or personal problems?

Notice how these affect their behavior in the present moment.

- **K - (Be) Kind**

Treat the other person how you would want them to treat you in a similar situation. Remain kind and gentle during the inter-action. Don't allow powerful emotions or a negative attitude to cloud your judgment during conflict resolution. Instead, pair the THINK, GIVE, FAST, and DEAR MAN skills to develop and maintain healthy relationships with people.

THE IMPORTANCE OF ASSERTIVE COMMUNICATION

Assertiveness is a vital communication skill. It allows you to express yourself more effectively and confidently. More importantly, it helps you do this while respecting other people's beliefs or opinions. Assertive communication can also help cope with stress and anger more productively.

Being assertive can help you:

- Boost self-esteem and self-confidence
- Recognize and understand feelings
- Achieve mutual respect
- Enhance decision-making
- Build honest relationships

You can be more assertive in conversations by:

- Using "I" statements.
- Learning to say "No."
- Keeping your emotions in check

Becoming an assertive communicator takes time and practice. Learning assertiveness may take a while if you've spent years expressing yourself passively. But you'll get there as long as you put in the work.

HEALTHY BOUNDARY-SETTING

Setting healthy personal boundaries is the key to avoiding many arguments, disagreements, and conflicts that lead to stress. The absence of boundaries undermines your identity, values, and beliefs. It ultimately undervalues your true sense of self.

If other people's treatment of you often triggers you, it's time to set healthy emotional and physical boundaries. Boundaries are a measure of self-image and self-esteem. They let people know what you consider acceptable and unacceptable.

How do you do this?

- Write down how important each person in your personal or professional life affects your feelings, mood, etc. Then, think about the motivations behind their behavior.
- Decide on a specific course of action. For example, you may decide to start saying "No" when your boss asks you to stay behind late.
- Write down five things you'd like each person to stop doing to you and around you. For example, you may want your partner to stop ignoring you.
- Write down five things you will no longer allow each person to say to you.

Reevaluate your current boundaries and update them as necessary. Also, be sure to update the new boundaries from time to time. Sometimes, they become invalid.

Establish strong personal boundaries, and people will give you the respect you deserve. The best thing about setting healthy boundaries is it allows you to be your authentic self.

The final step is like the final piece of the puzzle that will help bring all steps together. Our impulses, fears, anger, mood swings, chronic boredom, and self-image all boil down to how we regulate our emotions.

THE POWER OF EMOTIONAL REGULATION

Emotions are mystifying! At some point, we've all been interrupted by some intense emotion, like anger, frustration, or inadequacy, for no apparent reason. That's because our underlying beliefs about emotions affect our ability to regulate and control them when they arise.

This is made even more complex by the beliefs we have about emotions. For example, certain people believe emotions are either positive or negative; some argue that they are a manageable force; and some view emotions, particularly negative ones, as undesired interlopers that corrupt our psyche.

Many of these beliefs are subconscious, meaning we aren't aware of them. We form them based on our experiences and the explicit and implicit messages society passes to us. However, new research has revealed that these beliefs are false or grossly misrepresented. Yet, they impact our behavior in significant ways.

Contrary to popular belief, emotions are neither good nor bad, controllable or uncontrollable, positive or negative. Every emotion is felt for a reason - to alert you of something you aren't paying attention to.

Your ability to regulate emotions and control your responses to them will determine your perception of those emotions. After all, this will ultimately set the foundation for a positive or negative outcome, which is the most important thing.

Imagine that your old friend ignores your invitation to a lunch date after being away for a long time. Naturally, you'd be upset, disappointed, or angry. But if you don't submit to the emotion you're experiencing and instead think about the situation from a different perspective - maybe your friend didn't get the email or the text you sent, or they're just busy with more important things - that would help you regulate your emotions and stop you from acting out in a way you'd regret.

This ability to control how you think about and respond to emotions is called "Emotion Regulation." It is tied to many positive health benefits, including moral decision-making, improved mental health, memory, and general well-being.

Understanding Emotion Regulation

Before discussing emotion regulation, I noticed that many people confuse it with emotional intelligence. As you may already know, emotional intelligence is the ability to understand and manage your emotions.

Therefore, it is similar to emotion regulation. The difference is, that emotion regulation is a subset of emotional intelligence, which is more than the ability to control emotions.

Emotional intelligence is *"the ability to recognize, manage, and understand emotions. It includes the ability to recognize, interpret, and regulate your own emotions and those of others."*

Daniel Goleman, a psychologist who popularized the concept of emotional intelligence, introduced five components of emotional intelligence.

The five critical components of emotional intelligence are:

1. Self-awareness

This is your ability to recognize and understand your emotions. It's one of the critical skills everyone must possess. After all, how can you regulate an emotion you aren't even aware of?

Self-awareness involves:

- Monitoring your emotions.
- Becoming aware of your emotional triggers and reactions.
- Correctly identifying each emotion, you experience.

2. Social skills

Interacting effectively with others is another critical component of emotional intelligence. As you've learned, you need strong social skills to build meaningful emotional connections and relationships with other people. Without this skill, you will live a lonely life.

3. Empathy

Understanding others' feelings is a vital aspect of emotional intelligence. But it goes beyond the ability to identify people's emotional states. Empathy entails how you respond to people based on your knowledge of their emotional state. For example, when you sense that someone is grieving, how do you respond to them?

4. Motivation

Intrinsic motivation comes from within. It is the ability to get motivated by things other than fame, money, accolades, or recognition. Instead, you're driven by a passion for fulfilling your goals and innate needs.

5. Self-regulation

Typically, this comes after self-awareness, but I decided to put it last because it's our focus in this chapter. Awareness of and understanding your emotions isn't enough - you must know how to manage and regulate them.

When people hear self-regulation, they think it's about hiding their feelings away or putting them on lockdown. This is one of the common misconceptions about "negative" feelings - we believe we must suppress them.

On the contrary, self-regulation is about finding the right time and place to express your feelings. Emotion regulation is about suppressing your emotions until you can properly express them.

Once you properly train yourself to regulate your emotions, you become flexible and adaptive to change. You also become better at managing difficult or tense situations and resolving conflict if you cannot avoid it.

The more skilled you are in emotion regulation, the more conscientious you become. In other words, you take responsibility for your actions and become more thoughtful about how your words, actions, and behavior influence others.

EMOTIONAL REGULATION VS. EMOTIONAL DYSREGULATION

While emotions are a regular and constant part of everyday life, some people experience more volatile and intense emotions than the average person. And these higher highs and lower lows subsequently begin to affect their lives.

If you experience volatile emotions, you may feel happy at this moment and intensely sad the next. While we all have occasional periods where our emotions spiral out of control, some people experience this more regularly than others.

Often, the rapidly changing emotions cause them to misbehave, i.e., they say and do things they later regret. Unfortunately, that hurts their credibility and damages their personal and professional relationships.

I defined emotional regulation earlier, but this time, let's look at a more in-depth and academic definition.

"Emotional regulation refers to the process by which individuals influence which emotions they have, when they have them, and how they experience and express their feelings. Emotional regulation can be automated or controlled, conscious or unconscious. It may affect one or more points in the emotion-producing process."

From this definition, it is apparent that emotional regulation is a complex process that involves the ability to initiate, inhibit, and modulate your cognitive state and behavior in response to an internal or external event (trigger).

First, an internal or external stimulus (thinking about a crush or a personal loss) triggers an objective effect, i.e., feeling or emotion. Second, it provokes a cognitive response, i.e., thought, accompanied by an emotion-based physiological response (such as increased heart rate). Finally, a related behavior (expression, avoidance, or physical action) follows.

Emotional regulation is the ability to keep these processes within a socially acceptable proportion. In contrast, emotional dysregulation is the exact opposite of this. It is the inability to control or manage your emotional response to a triggering event or stimuli. With the right emotional triggers, anyone can become emotionally dysregulated.

However, individuals with a history of psychological trauma tend to have multiple triggers; Plus, emotional dysregulation is typically prolonged in some people, resulting in significant rifts in daily functioning and relationships. Emotional dysregulation is also associated with chronic stress, anxiety, and depression.

When an individual experiences prolonged emotional dysregulation, they may react exaggeratedly to environmental and interpersonal emotion-based triggers. For example, they may display intense bursts of anger, cry, create conflict, or exhibit passive-aggressive behavior.

If you find it challenging to regulate your emotions, being in an upsetting situation will cause strongly felt emotions that you won't recover from so quickly. For instance, a simple argument with a friend or family member may invoke such strong emotions that you overreact to the situation in a way that significantly impacts your relationship with the person.

On a national level, you probably know it's time to let go of the unfortunate incident. Still, emotionally, you can't control how strongly you feel about it. You can't stop thinking about what happened, causing you to lose sleep and interest in other things.

That inevitably pushes you to escalate the conflict until your relationship is damaged and difficult to repair. Then, in an extreme scenario, you may turn to substance use to improve how you feel about yourself, thus creating more problems instead of solving the ones on the ground.

Emotional dysregulation has long been identified as a symptom of traumatic disorders. One of the things that may trigger emotional dysregulation is maltreatment in childhood which often leads to Post Traumatic Stress Disorder (PTSD). In addition, there is robust evidence linking childhood interpersonal trauma with emotional dysregulation.

You should know that nobody is born with emotional regulation skills. A newborn baby is incapable of self-soothing due to biological immaturity. It is developed. The infant must have a healthy, nurturing relationship with its primary caregiver in order to develop.

As infants grow, they acquire emotional regulation skills from important adults, including parents, teachers, and close family members. For example, the father or mother may teach the child helpful ways to seek solutions to a problem instead of becoming overwhelmed in the face of challenges.

In contrast, kids with traumatic upbringings, especially those raised by parents with PTSD, cannot learn emotion regulation skills. A traumatized parent or caregiver cannot control their own emotions; therefore, they are unlikely to be able to teach their child.

Sometimes, the traumatized parent may even escalate their child's distress with outbursts or disproportionate emotional responses to the child's problems. In such cases, the child cannot learn vital emotion regulation skills.

Emotional dysregulation is associated with PTSD, BPD, ADHD, Substance abuse, Bipolar Disorder, Disruptive Mood Dysregulation Disorder, and Autism Spectrum Disorders. As you already know, emotional dysregulation makes building healthy, long-lasting interpersonal relationships challenging.

The general idea of emotion dysregulation is that you experience overly intense emotions compared to the event or stimuli that triggered them. This encompasses a range of reactions from being unable to self-soothe or calm down to suppressing difficult emotions or hyper-fixating on the negative. Individuals with emotion dysregulation also behave erratically, irrationally, and impulsively when their emotions are out of control.

Let's look at more examples of emotion dysregulation.

- Your spouse cancels dinner plans, and you conclude that they no longer want you in their life. So, you stay up all night crying and feeding on junk.
- Your waiter at the local restaurant doesn't attend to your order on time. So, you have an angry outburst and fling the tray across the room when they finally bring your meal.
- You attend your firm's luncheon, where everyone except you seems to have the time of their lives. You feel like an outsider because you can't participate in the conversations. After the luncheon, you go home and have a binge-eating session to numb your hurt.

Emotional dysregulation can also make it challenging to recognize the emotion you're experiencing during an intense emotional reaction. You may feel confused, guilty, or overwhelmed due to the emotion. This can make it nearly impossible to make decisions or manage your actions.

Emotional dysregulation in kids may manifest differently, involving crying, outbursts, temper tantrums, refusing to speak or make eye contact, etc.

The inability to manage your emotional reactions impacts your behavior negatively, which, in turn, affects your adult life in the following ways.

- You have difficulty sleeping.
- You hold grudges longer than necessary because you can't seem to let go of past experiences.
- You find yourself in minor disagreements that you exaggerate and blow out of proportion.
- You experience a negative impact on your social functioning, work, school, etc.

In extreme cases, being unable to regulate your emotions leads to addiction or substance abuse problems. It may also cause you to engage in self-harm, binge-eating, restrictive eating, and other harmful behaviors.

Emotional dysregulation is a normal part of the human experience. As I explained earlier, we all experience some degree of dysregulation regarding our emotions. We also exhibit dysregulated behavior from time to time.

However, the prognosis for individuals who frequently experience emotional dysregulation depends on how severe the underlying issue is. Regardless of the underlying psychological problem, DBT addresses most issues associated with emotional dysregulation and can help anyone learn to regulate their emotions better.

KNOW YOUR EMOTIONAL TRIGGERS

Every day, you experience a range of emotions - joy, excitement, frustration, unease, disappointment, and several others. Every emotion you feel relates to a specific event, such as seeing your adorable pet, having dinner with a romantic interest, talking to your boss, or discussing current events with an acquaintance. Usually, your responses to each emotional experience will vary based on your mindset, attitude, and the underlying context of the situation.

Emotional triggers could be anything - such as experiences, memories, or current events - that evokes strong emotional reactions to a situation regardless of your mood at that particular moment. These triggers are typically linked to PTSD.

Everyone has different emotional triggers. Knowing your emotional triggers is key to being emotionally aware. It's crucial to know your triggers and how to cope with them. Please do not overlook this, as it is essential for optimal emotional and physical health.

Emotional triggers look different from individual to individual, and just about everyone has them. For example, some people appreciate constructive criticism and feedback, while others feel slighted by them. While you might laugh at an embarrassing situation and make a joke, another person might feel entirely ashamed.

Your emotional triggers might be associated with unwanted memories, distressing topics, your habits, or someone else's words or actions. Below are situations that typically trigger intense emotional reactions:

- Betrayal
- Rejection
- Challenged beliefs
- Helplessness
- Unfair treatment
- Criticism or disapproval
- Insecurity
- Being ignored or excluded
- Dependence or loss of independence
- Feeling unwanted or unneeded
- Feeling smothered

These are generic emotional triggers. Some triggers are specific to each person, so how do you figure out your emotional triggers?

- **Listen to your body and mind**

To learn your emotional triggers, you must start by paying attention to your mind and body. Notice when a situation evokes an intense emotional response. Next, be aware of the physiological symptoms that often accompany strong emotions: increased heart rate, sweaty palms, dizziness or shakiness, upset stomach, etc.

- **Take a step back**

When you notice the surging emotion and the accompanying symptoms, take a step back from the situation that triggered them. Use that moment to consider what happened and why it activated that particular emotional response.

Say you spent the entire day decluttering your home and rearranging everything to make it more aesthetic. When you finish, you feel satisfied and wait excitedly for your lover to get home and see what you've done. But instead, they return home and go straight to the kitchen for a drink and then settle on the couch to see a TV show without uttering a single comment about the new look of your home.

Naturally, you feel disappointed they didn't acknowledge your hard work, and you feel frustration and anger rising. You can feel your heart racing and your jaws getting clenched. You had to muster everything to stop yourself from snapping and saying something like, "How stupid can you be? Notice anything different about this house?"

- **Trace the origin**

Follow your feelings back to their roots by reflecting on the situation that triggered them. Perhaps you suddenly felt like that teenager that did everything to gain her mother's approval again, without ever getting it.

The emotional trigger here is your partner's indifference toward your effort. When that trigger fired, you felt transported back to a certain point in childhood, when nothing you did was considered good enough.

- **Be curious**

Sometimes, connecting a trigger and the emotion it evoked is difficult. In that case, you have to let curiosity take over and dig a little bit deeper. When you experience intense, overwhelming emotions, don't suppress or ignore them. Instead, use curiosity to get a deeper insight into what triggered them.

Watch out for any patterns. For instance, discussions about romantic relationships might trigger frustration relating to your fear of abandonment.

Once you've learned to identify your emotional triggers, the next step is to know how to manage them.

MANAGE YOUR EMOTIONAL TRIGGERS

Usually, once people can identify their triggers, they think that the solution is to avoid the situations that may fire those triggers. Sadly, it's not as easy as that. Avoiding or escaping from every situation that may evoke difficult emotions is impossible. You're guaranteed to experience unwanted emotions from time to time. Thus, your best step would be to learn how to prepare for and deal with triggers that might arise in your daily life.

Here are some pointers to help you:

- **Own your emotions**

First, you must acknowledge that it's okay to have these feelings - sad, frustrated, angry, or envious. No matter how unpleasant the emotion is, it's normal for triggers to evoke it. I noticed that reminding myself of the difference between the past and the present often helps with embracing my emotions. You can do this with compassion and without judgment.

- **Take a break**

Sometimes, we need physical space to avoid overwhelming emotions. So, take a break - put some distance between you and the situation that triggered your emotions. This should help you avoid impulsively doing something you'd regret later.

Once alone, you can do some breathing or grounding exercises we discussed in a previous chapter. Plus, you'll find more exercises in the chapter after this.

The goal is to delay your reaction to the situation to a more appropriate time when you can handle it productively.

- **Keep an open mind**

In most cases, people in our lives don't set out trying to make us feel bad. Some words and actions that upset you are a byproduct of the other person's emotional triggers and other underlying factors.

When your partner walked in without realizing you'd transformed the home, it could be because they had a hard day at work or received some bad news that made them want to decompress first.

Everyone has their own underlying emotions at all times, and you won't know what's going on with them until you talk about it. It's easier to understand a person's action or behavior when you purposefully seek out a different perspective. .

DEVELOPING EMOTIONAL SELF-AWARENESS

Emotional awareness isn't something you're born with - it's a skill you can learn with practice, patience, and diligence. You learn and develop emotional awareness by knowing how to tune in to difficult emotions and manage them without getting overwhelmed.

The thing about emotions is that they are always there, bubbling beneath the surface, whether you're consciously aware of them or not. They influence your thinking and everything you do, even if you don't realize it.

Emotional awareness is a skill that helps you understand your feelings and why you have those feelings. It is being able to recognize and express what you're feeling to yourself or other people. More importantly, it is finding the connection between that feeling and a resulting action or behavior.

But as I said earlier, emotional awareness is more than just knowing your emotions. It also entails being able to recognize and understand other people's feelings. Again, emotional awareness encompasses two core subskills:

- The ability to recognize and label your emotional experiences.
- The ability to regulate and manage your emotional experiences without getting overwhelmed.

Why does emotional awareness matter?

Instinctive emotional reactions to a trigger typically happen due to a lack of emotional awareness. When you have an outburst, it's usually because you couldn't feel the physiological signs of that emotion rising internally.

Your feelings drive your actions (behavior). A lack of awareness of your feelings culminates in a lack of understanding of your behavior. This results in the inability to appropriately manage that behavior or accurately determine others' wants and needs.

Becoming emotionally aware means you know how to:

- Recognize who you are, how you feel, what you don't like, and what you need and don't need.
- Understand and empathize with other people's feelings and needs.
- Express your feelings and needs effectively.
- Make informed decisions relating to the most important things to you.
- Motivate yourself and take action to achieve your goals.
- Build healthy, long-lasting emotional connections.

Developing emotional awareness can help you create a balance in life. We sometimes think that life is about high highs and low lows. Emotional awareness can moderate the ups and downs, thus striking a necessary balance. If you often end up in situations you regret, becoming emotionally aware can save you from yourself.

Nowadays, it's hard to build new relationships. But you can meet more people and create new, long-lasting bonds if you train yourself to become more emotionally aware than you are currently.

Of course, to become more emotionally aware, you must evaluate your current emotional awareness.

- How many strong emotions can you tolerate, including positive and negative ones?
- Can you feel physical sensations relating to a strong emotion in your body?
- Do you make decisions impulsively or based on instinct?
- Are you comfortable with every emotion you experience?
- Do you find it hard to talk about your emotions - particularly the unpleasant ones?
- Are you comfortable with people being aware of how you feel?
- Are you able to empathize with others' feelings? How easy can you pick up on someone else's feelings without them talking to you?

Answer these questions honestly. Even if you didn't answer "always" or "usually" or "sometimes" to most of them, know that you aren't alone.

The first place to start is to learn to manage stress. The best way to develop or increase emotional awareness is to become friends with all of your emotions and their physical signs. Once you know how to do this, identifying and managing other emotions become much easier.

Emotional awareness is defined by your ability to relieve stress instantly, which is at the core of many unpleasant emotions. Learn how to de-stress and calm yourself down using the DBT techniques we discussed in the last two chapters, and you can begin to explore frightening or disagreeable emotions.

In the final chapter, I will discuss how you can manage and regulate your emotions with Vagus Nerve Stimulation (VNS) and other beneficial techniques.

EXERCISES TO REGULATE AND MANAGE YOUR POWERFUL EMOTIONS

In chapter four, I explained how you could use techniques such as singing, breathing exercises, and massage to stimulate the vagus nerve and soothe agitated emotions at any moment. However, these techniques aren't the only ways to encourage vagus nerve stimulation. There are other ways we'll be focusing on, along with other excellent techniques for mastering, regulating, and managing your emotions.

So far, you have learned that DBT entails four practical steps. But one thing to keep in mind about all four steps to DBT is that they are all interconnected. There is no clear line separating them. Think of DBT as a dish and these four steps as the different parts of the recipe - you need all four to make it a success.

Mindfulness, vagus nerve stimulation, distress tolerance skills, etc., are all excellent reasons for DBT making a great treatment option for different conditions due to its wide range of benefits.

Remember, techniques like STOP can help you navigate a distressing situation or take a step back from intense emotions even when there isn't an immediate crisis.

In the previous chapter, when we looked at how you can return the body to a calm state with various techniques, including vagus nerve stimulation, I mentioned that there is a connection between this nerve and the gut.

And unsurprisingly, how you treat your gut impacts the vagus nerve. So let's briefly examine how probiotics affect the vagus nerve to understand this.

LONG-TERM STIMULATION OF THE VAGUS NERVE

The vagus nerve is the most significant link between the brain and the gastrointestinal tract. This relationship is labeled "the brain-gut axis" by scientists. As you know, activation of the vagus nerve plays a crucial role in influencing the parasympathetic nervous system - including the fight or flight response, digestion, immune function, heart rate, and mood.

Due to this connection between the gut and brain, the vagus nerve can modulate various mental health conditions such as anxiety, depression, PTSD, and others. Research shows that these psychiatric conditions are linked to inflammation and gastrointestinal problems.

Eating probiotics can impart various health benefits. The gut-brain axis is a vital relationship that is furthered with the help of probiotics. Gut bacteria impact brain health; therefore, you can improve brain health by changing your gut bacteria. However, there are varying types of probiotics.

Psychobiotics are probiotics that specifically affect the brain. Some have been proven to improve acute or chronic stress, anxiety, and depression symptoms. In fact, a small study involving people with irritable bowel syndrome and mild depression discovered that symptoms improved using a probiotic called Bifidobacterium longum NCC3001.

This shows that probiotics can be quite helpful in achieving vagus nerve stimulation. As gut bacteria ferment probiotics, they can improve brain health and positively impact conditions relating to brain health.

Another study on the link between probiotics and the cortisol response found that a probiotic called Galacto-oligosaccharides significantly reduced the production of cortisol when taken for three weeks. Cortisol is the body's stress hormone responsible for the stress response, which sometimes induces emotion dysregulation.

Taking probiotics can reduce the stress response, making it easier to regulate your emotions whenever you want to. It's much easier to return the body to a calm state when your cortisol level isn't unreasonably high.

Apart from probiotics, many foods are beneficial to the gut-brain relationship. Introducing more of the following foods into your dietary routine will make a significant difference.

- **Omega-3 fats**: These fats abound in high quantities in the brain but are also available in oily fish. Eating more fish with omega-3 fats can increase the fermentation of good bacteria in your gut.
- **High-fiber food**: Nuts, seeds, whole grains, fruits, vegetables, etc., are all foods with high levels of prebiotic fibers that can help increase healthy gut bacteria.
- **Fermented food**: Yogurt, cheese, sauerkraut, and kefir are fermented foods that can alter brain health and activity. This is due to these foods' healthy microbes - such as lactic acid bacteria.

You can make vagus nerve stimulation much easier if you change the type of bacteria fermented in your gut by changing what you eat or eating more probiotics. Anything that benefits your gut health also benefits your brain health.

LABEL YOUR EMOTION

Earlier, we discussed the necessity of emotional awareness - how you need to be able to identify and label the emotions you're experiencing in order to change or regulate them. Everyone experiences six primary emotions - sadness, fear, anger, joy, disgust, and surprise. Then, we also experience secondary and tertiary emotions.

Primary emotions are the underlying reason for any secondary or tertiary emotion you experience. Sometimes, when we say "I'm tired," it could mean that we're sad, depressed, bored, or lonely. Emotions are interconnected. To accurately label whatever you're feeling in a particular moment, you must figure out the primary emotion underlying it. Questions are necessary if you want to label your emotions accurately.

The following is a seven-step process for identifying and labeling your emotions.

1. Trigger (Prompting Event)

Emotions are reactions to an internal or external event - something that happened within you or in your immediate environment. The event that prompts your emotion is called a trigger, as you learned in the previous chapter. A trigger calls forth emotions, which could be anything from your thoughts, behavior, and physical reactions to another person's behavior or actions. Sometimes, we have intuitive feelings that aren't prompted by any thoughts.

Labeling your emotion requires analyzing the prompting event. It could be an interaction with someone, a loss, financial problems, physical illness, or anything happening to you in the present. It could also be a memory of a past event, a thought, or an underlying feeling (feeling ashamed can prompt anger or rage).

When regulating your emotions, you must be able to recognize the prompting event.

2. Interpretation of the prompting event

Usually, it's not an event itself that prompts a particular emotion. Instead, it's the interpretation of the event that triggers a distressing emotion. The feelings arise after we interpret the event through a specific viewpoint. In other words, the explanation you give for why the event happened causes the rise of negative feelings.

For example, say you see your girlfriend and her male friend laughing together. You immediately conclude that there's something more than a platonic friendship between them. And so, you feel jealousy and anger well up within you.

Or maybe you ended up staying at work later than usual. Then, on your way home, there is a storm, and you feel fear rising within you because you've heard of people getting struck to death by lightning.

Different events can result in the same emotion based on interpretation. Remember that how you interpret a prompting event is determined by many factors, which aren't always factual. Your interpretation may be valid, but that doesn't make it a fact.

3. Physiological response to emotion

I previously explained that the body experiences physiological changes when emotions rise. Unfortunately, many people struggle with noticing these physical sensations. To label an emotion, you have to become pretty good at identifying the physical changes that accompany it.

Emotions often involve physical changes such as relaxing or tensing muscles, rise and drop in blood pressure, and changes in breathing, heart rate, skin color, and temperature.

The changes you want to pay attention to happen in the facial area are:

- Tightened cheeks
- Tightening muscles around the eyes
- Clenched jaws
- Grinding teeth
- Tight forehead muscles

Notice your facial expressions and posture. They are minor changes but can tell you much about your feelings.

4. Urges

Triggers prompt emotions, which prompts behaviors. One function of emotions is to urge us to take action, i.e., behave in a specific way. For example, when you're angry, you get the urge to confront or fight the object of your anger. Or when you feel afraid, you're prompted to run or fight.

A resulting action isn't part of the emotion that prompted it. Still, the urge to engage in that action or behavior is part of the emotional process. For example, when you're angry, you will feel the urge to yell or scream at the person who made you angry.

That urge is part of the feeling, but whatever action you take isn't included in the emotional process.

5. Expressing the emotion

Emotions are your brain's way of communicating with your body. So, emotions are meant to be expressed. Often, we struggle with expressing our emotions. Even when we think we're communicating how we feel, the other person may not understand, which may result in misunderstandings

To accurately label an emotion, you must express precisely how you feel. We communicate our feelings through words, actions, and facial expressions. However, communicating emotions through behavior sometimes causes misunderstandings because behavior is subject to interpretation, like emotional triggers.

6. Name the emotion

If you're not accustomed to labeling your emotions, the first time will be challenging. But, thankfully, you can become good at it with practice.

Many variables interfere with your ability to observe, describe, and name emotions. Secondary emotions are one of these variables.

For example, anger comes after shame. Maybe you found yourself in an embarrassing situation. After the initial feeling of shame, you become angry at yourself for getting in that situation in the first place.

Some feel multiple emotions at the same time - that's quite natural. For example, you may feel sad and angry at the same time if the situation warrants it. The secondary emotion makes it challenging to figure out the underlying feeling, making the emotion harder to deal with.

Always unravel your primary and secondary emotions so you can name them.

7. After Effects

Again, emotions, thoughts, and behaviors exist in a cycle - they affect each other and, together, affect physical function. Sometimes, the after-effects of an emotional experience last longer. One unfortunate after-effect is that a prompting event triggers the same emotion repeatedly, creating a cycle of distress and suffering.

Labeling your emotion will help you understand and detach from the situation prompting that emotion, allowing you to achieve a Wise Mind.

THE EMOTIONAL MIND, RATIONAL MIND, AND WISE MIND

The emotional, rational, and wise minds are the three states of mind we operate in. In DBT, the Wise Mind is a core mindfulness skill. By reaching a wise mind, you can attain inner wisdom and intuition. However, to understand how to achieve a wise mind, you must understand what the other two states of mind entail.

Rational Mind

The rational mind is the traditional thinking mind. It's your practical mind responsible for pragmatic, logical, task-oriented, and rule-oriented decision-making rooted in facts and logic.

Emotional Mind

The emotional mind is a direct contrast to the rational mind. It isn't unreasonable, but it depends on emotion rather than reason. This state of mind does not concern itself with facts or logic. In this state of mind, your thinking is governed by your feelings and moods.

You act based on the action urges prompted by your emotional state rather than a carefully curated plan.

Wise mind

Wise mind is a balance of the emotional and rational mind. It's where they both overlap. The wise mind considers both facts and emotions when making a decision. It's practical yet sensitive to our feelings. Reaching the wise mind enables you to behave rationally while staying true to your very nature.

Think about it this way, the two states of mind - rational and emotional - are cold and hot, respectively. Both play crucial roles in thinking and decision-making, but you need to find a balance, i.e., create something warm by reaching the wise mind.

You can achieve this by using the DBT skill of mindfulness and the techniques we discussed in previous chapters. Still, let's look at more techniques to help find this much-needed balance and attain a wise mind.

OPPOSITE ACTION

Emotions alert us to respond, and our responses are biologically wired. You can choose a different response to the default biological response with the Opposite Action skill. For example, thirst alerts you to hydrate, activating an urge to drink water; hunger alerts you to eat, activating an urge to eat; and fatigue alerts you to rest, activating an urge to sleep.

With certain emotions, your best bet is to do the opposite of what your body thinks it should do. For example, when you're afraid, the biological urge you get is to run. But instead, it can help to face your fear. This helps with extreme phobias.

When you're depressed, the body thinks it should shut down and become inactive. But what if you responded by immersing yourself in more physical activities than ever? Then, your mind and body would greatly benefit.

The opposite action skill is beneficial in controlling the natural urges that come with many emotions. Switch up the following emotion by doing the opposite of what they prompt you to do.

Emotion	Biological Urge	Opposite Action
Anger – alerts us to a perceived or real attack.	Activates the urge to attack or defend ourselves.	Walk away, show empathy, kindness, or compassion.
Fear – alerts us to danger.	Activates the urge to hide or run.	Face your fear, build courage, or stay involved in the action.
Shame – prepares us to isolate.	Activates the urge to hide or recoil from a situation.	Maintain eye contact, and raise your head and shoulders.
Depression – tells us to become inactive.	Activates the urge to withdraw and avoid contact.	Become more socially active than ever.
Disgust – alerts us to avoid something.	Activates the urge to reject or avoid yourself.	Motivate yourself and push through the situation.
Guilt – tells us to seek forgiveness.	Activates the urge to repent and repair damages.	Apologize meaningfully and change your behavior.

If you want your emotions to remain the same, continue to listen to your natural biological urges and do what your body tells you to. But if you want to change your emotions and have them stick around, continue repeating the opposite actions recommended above.

For this skill to truly work, you must engage in the opposite action of your natural biological responses. But, more importantly, you must trust that it'll work.

ABC PLEASE

The ABC PLEASE skill teaches you to attend to your physical and emotional needs and those of the people in your life. This skill can increase emotional resilience and decrease sensitivity to unpleasant emotions.

- **A - Accumulate positive experiences**

You'll naturally feel good about your life when you have more positive experiences than negative ones. Likewise, you're more likely to bounce back from adversity when you have many positive experiences to look back on. It's like taking $10 out of a $200 bank account balance. Still, even the slightest setback can make you feel powerful emotions.

So, incorporate a wide range of activities such as camping, rappelling, rock climbing, etc. into your life. These activities can make you experience positive emotions regularly. When you build positive memories through these, you can find joy and strength by looking back on them in the face of adversity.

For an experience to truly count, you have to be mindful. There is no point in accumulating positive experiences if you don't do it mindfully. We're often physically present but mentally/emotionally absent for an event because our mind was elsewhere. Call it back to the present if your mind starts to wander and fully immerse yourself in it. In time, it'll become a habit to focus entirely on anything you're doing.

- **B - Build mastery**

Learn and become proficient at new activities, skills, or hobbies. Building mastery encourages you to do things that you genuinely love and enjoy. When you accumulate a repertoire of activities and hobbies that you excel at, it boosts your self-confidence and regularly reinforces your talents and capabilities.

The best thing is that it gives you something to fall back on if you ever fall prey to anxiety, depression, or boredom.

- **C – Cope ahead**

Coping ahead means preparing yourself for potentially stressful or strenuous events. This could be a work or class presentation, a test, or a job interview. Whatever it is, prepare yourself emotionally and mentally. Think of the steps you can take to do this.

With a job interview, you might want to research standard interview questions, review your work history, and prepare references to draw upon in case you're asked for them.

Coping ahead prepares you for any distressing emotion that might arise from the event you're about to experience.

- **PL – Physical health**

Take care of yourself when you're sick or miserable. Physical health is key to emotional health. Physical illness makes it hard to be at your optimal best, negatively impacting your emotional state. Practice physical self-care techniques to influence your emotional health positively.

- **E – Eating**

Healthy eating is necessary. Lack of proper nutrition makes you stressed, sluggish, and passive. So, opt for foods that will keep you energetic and active throughout the day.

- **A – Avoid**

Avoid using mood-altering substances. Stay away from non-prescribed medication; they usually have a negative impact on physical and emotional health. Prescribed medications are measured, regulated, and managed to balance the chemicals in your body. It doesn't help to self-medicate; you'll most likely end up with emotional dysregulation.

- **S – Sleep**

Get adequate sleep. Restful sleep energizes the body, making it easy to complete daily tasks and regulate your emotions. Tune in with your body to determine the amount of sleep you need.

- **E – Exercise**

Exercise contributes significantly to physical, emotional, and mental health. It decreases stress, anxiety, depression, and other negative emotions. Many neglect physical exercise because they don't realize how incredibly beneficial it can be. You don't have to do high-intensity exercises - something as simple as a daily run can make all the difference.

POSITIVE SELF-TALK

Self-talk refers to those thoughts that dance around in your head all day. They can be positive or negative. Most times, we engage in negative self-talk without realizing it. Negative self-talk makes you perceive life events as being more stressful than they are. Your self-talk may sabotage your emotional regulation efforts by increasing cortisol production and amplifying stress levels.

Luckily, you can deconstruct negative self-talk and replace them with positive ones. Doing this can relieve stress, boost productivity, and improve self-esteem.

Notice your thinking pattern

Pay attention to how often you think about negative things and how these thoughts affect your experiences. You can try journaling to analyze your everyday thoughts and fish out negative patterns. You can also try these two methods:

- **Stop your thought:** Each time you catch a negative thought in your head, stop that thought by saying "STOP" aloud. It's more powerful when you say it out loud. Plus, that makes you aware of how often you have a specific negative thought.

- **Rubber band snaps:** Go everywhere with a rubber band around your wrist. Every time you catch yourself engaging in negative self-talk, pull the rubber band from your skin and release it - snap! It'll hurt, but it'll also make you constantly aware of your thoughts so you can stop the negative ones in their tracks. Suppose you don't want to experience the consequences of negative thoughts. In that case, you should be more conscious of your thoughts and learn to stop them when they arise.

Replace negative thoughts

An excellent way to stop a bad habit is to replace it with a better habit. For example, once you've identified patterns of self-dialogue, you can change them with the following techniques.

- **Use milder wording:** Change how you talk about pain. Replace "pain" with "discomfort." Pain is much more intense than discomfort. The wordings you use to discuss your pain or suffering can make the experience needlessly intense. Replace words such as "hate" and "anger" with "dislike" and "annoyance," respectively. Say, "I dislike this feeling." not "I hate this feeling."
- **Switch from negative to neutral:** Reframe your assumptions when you find yourself mentally complaining. Don't assume a situation is damaging even when nothing suggests it is. Stop, rethink, and come up with a neutral or positive replacement for any negative thought.

- **Turn self-limiting statements to questions:** "I can't do this" or "I'm not good enough" are examples of self-limiting statements. They increase your stress levels, which makes them particularly damaging. Worse, they discourage you from seeking solutions to a problem. Replace them with "How can I do this?" or "Can I handle this?" and you'll find yourself more productive.

In general, bring more positive energy into your life and routine. If you surround yourself with positivity, your mind will become more optimistic.

PROBLEM-SOLVING

There is an underlying problem behind every emotional trigger. In order to reduce how much a trigger affects you, it's best to solve that problem from a DBT perspective. Once you know that certain situations are potentially problematic for you, work on solving the possible problem before you find yourself in that situation again.

- **Analyze your behavior**

Look back on past situations - what causes you to feel emotionally overwhelmed? Is it something at work, with family, your friends, or kids? Write down the emotions you usually experience in these situations and the behavior they prompt.

- **Reflect on what you can change**

What can you change about situations that trigger distressing emotions and prompt a specific action? Understand that the change you want to make should positively impact your emotional health and immediate overwhelming feeling.

You may not be able to change an internal event. Still, you can work on your internal dialogue during the event. Choose two specific things to try to change during the internal or external event - that could be your thoughts, feelings, or action.

- **Find alternatives**

Now that you know what you need to change, it's time to think of possible alternatives. For example, what would be the perfect replacement for the self-dialogue that happens when your partner arrives late for a date? What can you do differently? Perhaps you need to change the event and take a different approach to your thoughts.

- **Apply this solution**

After you've come up with brilliant alternatives to what you can do to change the unchangeable, choose the best one for your situation and put that into action. Then, actively remind yourself to act in an alternative way or use the alternative self-talk the next time you're in a similar situation. Ultimately, that will change how you respond to the event.

And more importantly, it will solve the underlying problem that triggers the emotion.

JOURNALING

Do you know what Albert Einstein, Charles Darwin, Marie Curie, and Thomas Edison had in common? A journal. Journaling is a form of introspection - a way to communicate and stay in touch with yourself. Keeping a journal of your journey as you navigate using DBT skills to change the way you think, feel, and behave is the best decision you'll ever make regarding improving your emotional and mental health.

Introspection is vital because it helps you find creativity, resilience, and tranquility from within, ultimately improving your performance.

I have tried different formats of journaling. Some were more effective than others. I still use various formats, but my favorite is the LIFE method.

- **L – Learnings:** Write down what you learn about yourself – thoughts, emotions, and actions – each day. Write everything down if you learned something from a book, conversation, podcast, or blog. It reinforces your motivation for personal development.
- **I – Ideas:** Write down every new idea you have. The goal is to nurture your creative imagination, so put it down in your journal, whether it's a nuanced observation or an idea for an invention.

- **F - Feelings:** Write down how you feel throughout each day in your journal. Think of this as keeping an emotional inventory. It'll get easier with practice.
- **E - Experiences:** What did you experience today? Did anything fun or notable happen? Write everything in your journal. I recommend adding a sensory layer to each experience to make it more meaningful. That way, it doesn't feel like a bland grocery list.

Journaling should be a massive part of your DBT journey. It's the best way to track your progress and make improvements where necessary.

Practical Examples of Emotional Regulation

We are almost at the end of this book. But before you go, let me introduce you to three people who found immense power in regulating their emotions: Dan, Lana, and Chris.

Meet Dan.

Dan met Marie at a college function. You could say it was love at first sight. Dan and Marie were immediately taken in with each other. As soon as they finished college, they decided to get married. Marie loved Dan immensely, but she was skeptical about getting married. They had only been together for a few years, yet it seemed like the number of arguments they had doubled with the number of times they had gone on dates. She didn't want a marriage where she'd spend half of the day arguing over the most trivial stuff.

So, Marie sat down and expressed her feelings to him. Dan wasn't surprised, which surprised Marie. He confessed that he's struggled with this since he was mature enough to be in romantic relationships. Dan had tried everything possible to no success. Still, he promised Marie he would put more effort into changing his predisposition for conflict.

He then discussed his situation with a friend who told him how his cousin had used a book about DBT to learn how to take charge of overwhelming emotions. He promised to help Dan borrow the book, and sure enough, he kept his promise.

In reading the book, Dan learned that he constantly got into arguments with his partners because his parents hadn't modeled emotion regulation and good conflict resolution skills to him.

He poured himself into mastering and applying DBT sub-skills such as STOP, DEAR MAN, TIPP, Opposite Action, and mindfulness into his daily conversations. Soon, he began to notice changes. He was beginning to patiently listen to Marie express her feelings and needs without getting defensive and turning it into one big argument.

He used the DBT skill "STOP" whenever he noticed a conversation getting heated. And when he needed to express his feelings or needs, he used the DEAR MAN skill.

Marie was thrilled with Dan's progress. So, a few months later, they got married in a small gathering of friends and family, excited for the journey ahead!

Now meet Lana.

"Would I ever stop sabotaging myself?"

That was the thought in Lana's head as she left the building of her now former workplace. She had been fired. Yet again. She wondered why she couldn't ever control her urges. It's almost like a compulsion to listen to her impulses, even if it gets her into trouble now and then. She decided that it was time to make a change. After all, she can't afford to get fired once again or sabotage another relationship before it's even begun. It was time for a change.

Lana had been seeing a therapist who had told her she could learn to control her emotions and behavior with DBT or CBT skills - she couldn't remember which one. However, she wasn't sure how to do that, so she went back to the therapist to learn more.

Her therapist affirmed that she could transform her life using DBT, a form of therapy focused on regulating one's emotions. First, she needed to learn to control her emotions and limit impulsive behaviors – simple enough.

Lana started practicing everything she learned in therapy. Her therapist gave her homework and worksheets to complete. She learned different techniques that helped regulate her emotions in tense situations, stopping her from impulsively reacting to them.

Lana was happy. For the first time in her life, it seemed like she could think things through and make decisions based on facts rather than emotion. Just the other day, Lana held her breath and counted from 100 to 1 before calmly asking her date why he was late. Usually, she would have snapped at him and probably stormed out in anger.

Knowing how to regulate her emotions made a significant difference in her life. She felt more powerful than ever, knowing her feelings could no longer hold her captive. Now, she's ready to get into the job market and find a new job that she'll hopefully keep for as long as she wants.

What about CHRIS?

Cris has been at his job for ten years - same position, same cubicle. He believed he loved his job, but it didn't feel like it. These days, it felt like he was performing an obligation every time he got up, dressed, and took the subway to work. There was no excitement - He wanted excitement.

He wanted more from life. He had ideas he wanted to present to his boss – ideas that could shoot him to the pinnacle of his career. But each time he thought about showcasing his ideas, he felt a crippling fear followed by distressing thoughts.

"What if she shuts my ideas down?" "What if they aren't good enough?" "I may not be as brilliant as I think I am." "These ideas would probably fail anyway. So what would be the point of presenting them to my boss?"

Feeling discouraged, he decided to keep his ideas to himself and continued to work his lackluster job. Then, one day, he decided to act. He decided that it was time to face his fear of failure if he hoped to leave the darkness, figure out his long-term goals, and make a new positive plan for the future.

In his search for solutions, he stumbled upon a book about DBT.

The DBT book created a turning point in his life. With what he learned in the book, he was able to regulate the feeling of fear that stopped him from pursuing his goals. He learned to face his fears and found power in regulating uncomfortable emotions. Perhaps the best thing the book taught him was how to determine his goals and plan toward them while keeping potential obstructions in check.

He was excited about his future. For the first time in his life, the future held no uncertainties. He knew exactly what he wanted to do and how he wanted to do it.

"Nothing could go wrong. I am master of my emotions and in control of my own life now," he said aloud as he walked into his boss' office to present his ideas.

KEEPING THE GAME ALIVE

Having journeyed through the pages of "What The Heck is DBT" by R.J. Miller, you're now equipped with valuable insights and skills to manage emotions and cope with life's challenges. It's time to share your newfound knowledge and guide others to the same transformative experience.

Your honest review on Amazon isn't just a few words; it's a beacon for others who are seeking help in understanding and handling their emotions. By sharing your thoughts about this book, you're not just recommending a good read; you're directing people to a resource that could change their lives.

Your contribution is essential in keeping the spirit of learning and growth alive in the world of emotional well-being. When we share our knowledge, we not only help others but also reinforce our own understanding and commitment to personal development.

Thank you for being a part of this journey. The path to emotional balance and well-being continues to thrive because of individuals like you who pass on their knowledge and experiences.

Just scan the QR code below to leave your review on Amazon:

Your input helps us reach more people who can benefit from DBT and its life-changing strategies. Together, we're not just reading a book; we're building a community of support, understanding, and growth.

Thank you again for your invaluable support and for helping to spread the word about "What The Heck is DBT."

Let's continue to share, learn, and grow together.

- With gratitude, R.J. Miller

CONCLUSION

Great job!

You're now at the end of your journey with me, and I must commend you for staying with me to this point. It's been an exciting experience for me, and I hope it was for you as well.

I hope you've learned the invaluable skills of DBT that will help you make positive changes in your life. You're ready to utilize them to end your battle with anxiety, calm your raging emotions, and achieve mental wellness. No doubt, we all want a life without pain and one free of overwhelming emotions, but the question is, are you ready to do the work that will get you closer to your wishes?

I've discussed what DBT entails and the four essential skills of DBT. I discussed the different benefits mindfulness offers you and how you can use techniques like mindful eating, mindful breathing, mindful walking, and body scans to stay in the present moment and calm your emotions.

As humans, we'll likely experience extreme emotional states at some point, which is where distress tolerance comes in. With techniques such as IMPROVE, ACCEPTS, TIPP, self-soothing, radical acceptance, and distractions, you can easily handle difficult emotions and quickly return to a calm state when you encounter stressors.

Sometimes, you can have tense interactions with your family, friends, or co-workers, complicating your relationship with them. I discussed strategies such as GIVE, FAST, DEAR MAN, THINK, and other tips to help you improve your social skills.

In the book's final chapters, we discussed the power of regulating our impulses, fears, anger, mood swings, chronic boredom, and self-image using the five critical aspects of emotional intelligence and other DBT techniques (journaling, ABC PLEASE, opposite action, and positive self-talk.

Even though the skills and techniques of DBT are separate, combined practices will lead to a life worth living.

You may encounter challenges as you strive to become better and live a happier life. However, I believe you won't give up or let your hard work go to waste. Get back up and keep moving because your reward is closer then you think.

I've always been passionate about this topic because I understand the pain that comes with intense emotions and behaviors. When it came down to it, putting these newfound skills into practice consistently is what changed my life for the better!

After six months of consistent practice, I had more control over my emotions, and people around me started noticing.

I am happy that I have the opportunity to share this information that has liberated many people in the same rut as you. This book is my special gift to you, and I hope you heal from whatever kind of pain you feel and find peace.

There isn't a hard and fast rule here when it comes to getting started. There are techniques and strategies you will feel more comfortable with and relate to them more easily. You can start with those and commit to them; you will gradually explore others. This book is always here for you to revisit and apply the techniques when needed.

Are you ready to launch into a new phase where you'll live a happier and fulfilled life? I think I got a resounding YES from you.

Everyone deserves the right to a life worth living. While reviews are important to me, it's more important that other people with the same experience as us have the opportunity to read reviews and get the help they need.

Best wishes!

REFERENCES

Ackerman, C. (December, 2017). *Interpersonal Effectiveness: 9 Worksheets & Examples (+ PDF)*. Retrieved from Positive Psychology https://positivepsy chology.com/interpersonal-effectiveness/#dbt-interpersonal-effectiveness

Allied Services Integrated Health System. (June, 2020). *The vagus nerve: your secret weapon in fighting stress*. Retrieved from Allied Services https://www. allied-services.org/news/2020/june/the-vagus-nerve-your-secret- weapon-in-fighting-s/

Barnes, S., Brown, K. W., Krusemark, E., Campbell, W. K., & Rogge, R. D. (2007). *The role of mindfulness in romantic relationship satisfaction and responses to relationship stress. Journal of marital and family therapy*. Retrieved from https://doi.org/10.1111/j.1752-0606.2007.00033.x

Brownne, S.J. (April, 2021). *What The Vagus Nerve Is And How To Stimulate It For Better Mental Health*. Retrieved from Forbes https://www.forbes.com/ sites/womensmedia/2021/04/15/what-the-vagus-nerve-is-and-how-to- stimulate-it-for-better-mental-health/?sh=6d9a83236250

Caballo, V et al. (2014). *Assessing social skills: the factorial structure and other psychometric properties of four self-report measures*. ResearchGate https:// www.researchgate.net/publication/269519251_Assessing_social_skill s_the_factorial_structure_and_other_psychometric_properties_of_four_ self-report_measures/citation/download

CBT Los Angeles. (n.d). *Mindfulness from a DBT Perspective*. Retrieved from CBT L.A https://cogbtherapy.com/cbt-blog/mindfulness-in-dbt

Chambers, R., Lo, B. C. Y., & Allen, N. B. (2008). *The impact of intensive mind- fulness training on attentional control, cognitive style, and affect. Cognitive Therapy and Research*. Retrieved from https://doi.org/10.1007/s10608- 007-9119-0

Cherry, K. (January, 2022). *5 Key Emotional Intelligence Skills*. Retrieved from Verywell Mind https://www.verywellmind.com/components-of- emotional-intelligence-2795438

Cleveland Clinic. (n.d). *Dialectical Behavior Therapy (DBT)*. Retrieved from Cleveland Clinic https://my.clevelandclinic.org/health/treatments/ 22838-dialectical-behavior-therapy-dbt

CACI Research & Education. (October, 2018). *Probiotics and the Vagus Nerve – a New Frontier for Psychiatric Conditions.* Retrieved from CASI https://blog.designsforhealth.com/node/892

Daphne, M.D & Jeffrey, A. (July, 2012). *What are the benefits of mindfulness?* Retrieved from American Psychological Association. https://www.apa.org/monitor/2012/07-08/ce-corner

DBT Selfhelp. (n.d). *Factors Reducing Interpersonal Effectiveness.* Retrieved from DBT Selfhelp https://dbtselfhelp.com/dbt-skills-list/interpersonal-effectiveness/factors-reducing-interpersonal-effectiveness/

DBT Selfhelp. (n.d). *Identifying & Describing Emotions.* Retrieved from DBT Selfhelp https://dbtselfhelp.com/dbt-skills-list/emotion-regulation/identifying-describing-emotions/

DBT Selfhelp. (n.d). *Objectives Effectiveness: DEAR MAN.* Retrieved from DBT Selfhelp https://dbtselfhelp.com/dbt-skills-list/interpersonal-effectiveness/dear-man/

DBT Selfhelp. (n.d). *Relationship Effectiveness: GIVE.* Retrieved from DBT Selfhelp https://dbtselfhelp.com/dbt-skills-list/interpersonal-effectiveness/give/

DBT Selfhelp. (n.d). *Self-Soothe.* Retrieved from DBT Selfhelp https://dbtselfhelp.com/dbt-skills-list/distress-tolerance/self-soothe/

DBT Selfhelp. (n.d). *Self-Respect Effectiveness: FAST.* Retrieved DBT Selfhelp https://dbtselfhelp.com/dbt-skills-list/interpersonal-effectiveness/fast/

EHN Canada. (October, 2021). *The Seven Pillars of Mindfulness.* Retrieved from EHN Resources https://www.edgewoodhealthnetwork.com/resources/blog/the-seven-pillars-of-mindfulness/

Fossas, A. (January, 2015). *The Basics of Mindfulness: Where Did It Come From?* Retrieved from Welldoing.org https://welldoing.org/article/basics-of-mindfulness-come-from

Giang, C.H. (n.d). *What Are The Origins Of Mindfulness?* Retrieved from Thrive Global https://thriveglobal.com/stories/what-are-the-origins-of-mindfulness/

Gelles, D. (n.d). *How to Meditate.* Retrieved from New York Times https://www.nytimes.com/guides/well/how-to-meditate

Gross, J. (September, 1998).The Emerging Field of Emotion Regulation: An Integrative Review. Retrieved from Sage Journals https://doi.org/10.1037/1089-2680.2.3.271

Han, S. (April, 2020). *Your Parasympathetic Nervous System Explained.* Retrieved from Healthline https://www.healthline.com/health/parasympathetic-nervous-system

Harris, A. (June, 2020). *Radical Acceptance in a Time of Uncertainty*. Retrieved from HopeWay https://hopeway.org/blog/radical-acceptance

Headway Clinic. (n.d). *What is DBT?* Retrieved from Headway Clinic https://www.headwayclinic.ca/what-is-dbt/

Hofmann, S. G., Sawyer, A. T., Witt, A. A., & Oh, D. (2010). *The effect of mindfulness-based therapy on anxiety and depression: A meta-analytic review. Journal of consulting and clinical psychology.* Retrieved from https://doi.org/10.1037/a0018555

Juul, L., Pallesen, K. J., Piet, J., Parsons, C., & Fjorback, L. O. (2018). *Effectiveness of Mindfulness-Based Stress Reduction in a Self-Selecting and Self-Paying Community Setting. Mindfulness, 9(4), 1288–1298.* https://doi.org/10.1007/s12671-017-0873-0

Keng, S. L., Smoski, M. J., & Robins, C. J. (2011). *Effects of mindfulness on psychological health: a review of empirical studies. Clinical psychology review, 31(6), 1041–1056.* https://doi.org/10.1016/j.cpr.2011.04.006

Mayo Clinic. (n.d). *Stress management.* Retrieved from Mayo Clinic https://www.mayoclinic.org/healthy-lifestyle/stress-management/in-depth/stress/art-20046037

National Wellness Institute. (n.d). *Understanding Emotional Triggers.* Retrieevd from NWI https://www.ab.bluecross.ca/pdfs/workplace-wellness-resources/Emotional-Triggers-Tool.pdf

M1 Psychology. (n.d). *Developing Emotional Awareness.* Retrieved from M1 Psychology https://m1psychology.com/developing-emotional-awareness/

Osea Malibu. (n.d). *Massage for Vagus Nerve Stimulation.* Retrieved from Osea Malibu https://oseamalibu.com/blogs/wellness-blog/massage-for-vagus-nerve-stimulation

Ortner, Catherine & Kilner, Sachne & Zelazo, Philip. (2007). *Mindfulness meditation and reduced emotional interference on a cognitive task. Motivation and Emotion.* Retrieved from Research Gate https://www.researchgate.net/publication/226504935_Mindfulness_meditation_and_reduced_emotional_interference_on_a_cognitive_task

Psychological Care & Healing Center. (n.d). *Emotional Dysregulation.* Retrieved from PCH https://www.pchtreatment.com/who-we-treat/emotional-dysregulation/

Robertson, R. (August, 2022). *The Gut-Brain Connection: How it Works and The Role of Nutrition.* Retrieved from Healthline https://www.healthline.com/nutrition/gut-brain-connection#TOC_TITLE_HDR_3

Schimelpfening, N. (July, 2022). *What Is Dialectical Behavior Therapy (DBT)?* Retrieved from Verywell Mind https://www.verywellmind.com/dialectical-behavior-therapy-1067402

Sunrise RTC. (n.d). *DBT Interpersonal Effectiveness Skills: The Guide to Healthy Relationships.* Retrieved from Sunrise https://sunrisertc.com/interpersonal-effectiveness/

Tull, V. (July, 2020). *What Is Distress Tolerance?* Retrieved from Verywell Mind https://www.verywellmind.com/distress-tolerance-2797294

Vaughn, S. (October, 2021). *History of DBT: Origins and Foundations.* Retrieved from Psychotherapy Academy https://psychotherapyacademy.org/dbt/history-of-dialectical-behavioral-therapy-a-very-brief-introduction/

Vay, K. (n.d). *What is DBT and How Does It Differ from Other Treatment?* Retrieved from Impact Parent https://impactparents.com/blog/anxiety/what-is-dbt-and-how-does-it-differ-from-other-treatment/

WHAT THE HECK IS CBT?

THE SECRET TO TRAINING AND
RESTRUCTURING NEGATIVE THOUGHTS
USING COGNITIVE BEHAVIORAL THERAPY
SKILLS FOR PEOPLE WHO SUFFER FROM
ANXIETY AND DEPRESSION

FREE SPECIAL GIFT

As a BONUS for purchasing this book,
we would like to give you a
CBT Journal to fastrack your success.

INTRODUCTION

 *"Man is not worried about real problems so much as by his imagined anxieties about real problems."*

— EPICTETUS

You always have arguments with your best friend...

You've just experienced the worst divorce ever...

You broke up with your partner because of your assumptions...

Or perhaps, you've once let go of your dream job because you think you are unqualified for it.

Whatever the case may be, it's normal for everyone to feel sad or gloomy at some point in their life. While it's a fleeting feeling that passes like a storm – the rain clouds clear the sadness. For some people, it's an entirely different story.

For me, when the sadness came, it refused to leave and tagged along wherever I went. Negative thoughts and ruminations were always with me, day and night. Things I used as distractions were no longer working. So, there was no break for me, and life was already a living hell!

With over 6000 thoughts running through the human mind daily, it's not surprising that some thoughts are negative. But why do you give your brain so much work and freedom to accumulate thousands of thoughts? The brain is a mighty powerful organ that becomes incredibly smart when combined with different body systems. However, wires can easily get crossed with a complex organ like the brain, and we end up assuming that the brain knows what it's doing.

Much like when it comes to our problems – the brain will first worry about any problem before there is a chance to create a solution. This typically leads to stress and anxiety way before the potential problem arrives.

So now, let me ask you, what are your biggest fears? Do you have worries that are overwhelming your thought process? Are you worried that your state of mind is blocking you from reaching your goals? Do you find yourself barely coping with a normal life, and when you add criticism from friends, family, or colleagues, bad relationships, burnout, and possibly suicidal thoughts, you can't see a way out of the rut you're in?

All of these questions represent the problems we face in our daily lives. I said "We" because you aren't alone. So many of us have faced similar issues at some point in our lives and are quick to give up the fight and succumb to the effects of ruminating thoughts.

If you are reading this book, you are probably like my old self, who has struggled with negative thoughts. Back then, I was hopeless, and happiness was far away. It was difficult for me to maintain relationships with family members, friends, and colleagues. My symptoms felt like I was being knocked down over and over again. As a result, I lost interest in things I normally enjoyed. And I really didn't have much of an appetite anymore.

Whenever I go through a difficult experience or feel distressed about something, it always feels like my thoughts are running out of control. My mind will start racing, and I find myself constantly dwelling on the past and worrying about what is to come. My thoughts can sometimes be so consuming that it is almost impossible to focus on anything else. Being loving to friends and family, empathic to colleagues, productive at work, or even carrying on a simple conversation seemed impossible. The thoughts were so persistent that nothing could distract me from them… nothing could hold my attention or even try slowing down my thoughts to give me a moment of peace.

My family called me paranoid and irrational and felt I was exaggerating my feelings and problems. Looking back now, I can't even blame them for thinking that way because they had little or no understanding of different mental health conditions.

Since it's natural to want unwanted thoughts to disappear from my head, I always try to push them aside and set myself free from them altogether. But the more I try to fight off unwanted negative thoughts, the stronger they become and take hold of me.

Of course, I tried different types of self-help, including reading books and listening to podcasts, but I didn't get the results I had hoped for. I knew some kind of therapy would be beneficial, but I wasn't comfortable talking to others about my situation. Then, during my research, I came across CBT, which eventually changed my life. CBT has become a healthy part of my daily routine for four years now.

Just like it changed mine and the lives of celebrities like John Green and Ellie Goulding, I believe CBT can change your life too. With CBT, I could retrain my brain, conquer ruminations and negative thoughts, and regain control of my life. Yes! I combatted my PTSD with CBT. But first, you need to understand what CBT entails and how it can help you reconstruct negative thought patterns and overcome physical and mental health conditions such as anxiety, depression, addiction, PTSD, chronic pain, panic attacks, and Attention-deficit/hyperactivity disorder(ADHD).

CBT is an evidence-based treatment that taught me how negative thoughts teamed up with my intense emotions, shutting me down to depress me further. As I recognized the irrational thoughts, I could change them into positive statements. For example, instead of thinking my boss hates me because she assigns the most challenging tasks to me, why don't I see it as she assigns those tasks to me because she believes in me and knows I can handle them?

This was me fighting so hard and taking a fearless inventory of myself over time. By taking this approach, I could confidently talk to my boss and ask for a raise and possibly the promotion I was due for. Little by little, I realized the unproductive thought patterns I was creating. Even though I didn't feel like my symptoms would get better at times, I didn't stop practicing my CBT techniques and skills; I kept going.

This book doesn't promise a magical cure but provides practical strategies to manage symptoms that limit you and empower you to change. It will take you through a journey that guarantees favorable results.

First, we'll start from the foundation by introducing you to the philosophy behind CBT. Then, we'll explore the human thought processes and consequences that follow. We'll also discuss the different health conditions you can treat with CBT and how to apply the strategies to rewire your brain and become more positive. Whether you are in therapy or not, you can gain a lot from this book.

Despite being short-term, CBT is a goal-oriented approach with significant long-term effects and can be done independently. The results can be instant, making it difficult or frustrating for you to see it to the end. You need a support system to ensure you practice for weeks to gain the full benefits. With your collaboration, your negative thoughts and feelings will pass like a dark cloud on a sunny day.

Depression, anxiety, and other problems you may face don't have to last a lifetime. CBT can help you work through your challenges quickly. Since your thoughts, feelings, and behaviors are connected, you can change your life entirely by changing your thoughts. Do you remember the happiness and enthusiasm you felt when you were younger? It will return once again.

Now, are you ready to kick-start your journey for transformative change with your mental health? Join me in the first chapter as I'll introduce the philosophy behind CBT.

THE PHILOSOPHY BEHIND COGNITIVE BEHAVIORAL THERAPY

One in every five people experiences a mental health issue at least once yearly, with anxiety and depression topping the list. Many of us are already familiar with what it means to be sad or excessively worried about something. However, for some, the feelings can be overwhelming and bigger than they can manage. This is where getting help comes in.

Cognitive behavioral therapy (CBT) principles are of great use to those interested in the concept of positive psychology. This psychological intervention has proven effective in treating patients with anxiety, depression, and other psychological conditions.

Becoming increasingly mindful of one's thoughts and learning to interrupt negative thoughts can help you develop a healthier and more positive outlook and a deeper understanding of your power over your behavior. This is the basis of CBT! By seeking to understand your cognition and its link to behavior more in-depth, you can change how you think, and by effect, your life.

Like any relatively new concept, CBT comes with misconceptions – the most prominent being that CBT is all about learning to be positive. In other words, you transform a negative thought into a positive one. While this may appear true to an extent, it doesn't tell the whole story about this popular psychotherapeutic treatment. This misconception is inaccurate, potentially harmful, and a far cry from the truth.

To burst the unfounded myths and misconceptions about CBT and separate what's true from what isn't, let's begin by discussing what CBT is and a brief history of the intervention.

WHAT IS CBT?

CBT is a talk therapy intervention focusing on the relationship between one's thoughts, emotions, and behaviors. It deals with identifying and challenging negative thoughts and self-defeating beliefs. As these are identified, you can now form new thinking patterns, improving your feelings and behaviors.

This type of talk therapy can be described as a combination of psychotherapy and behavioral therapy. Psychotherapy deals with the personal meaning of thinking patterns developed in childhood, whereas behavioral therapy focuses on the intimate relationship between thoughts, behavior, and personal problems.

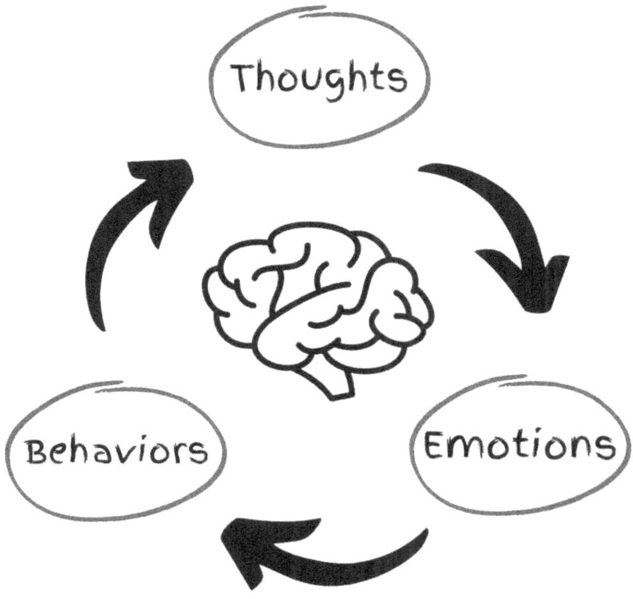

The origins of CBT go back to two different psychology schools: Behaviorism and Cognitive therapy. There has been the behavioral treatment for psychological disorders since the 1900s. Pavlov, Skinner, and Watson were key proponents of behavioral treatments.

Albert Ellis and Aaron T. Beck were two key proponents of cognitive therapy. In the 1950s, Ellis developed Rational Emotive Behavior Therapy (REBT) with the goal of helping patients identify irrational thought patterns. The idea is that emotional distress arises from thoughts. Therefore, by identifying irrational thoughts, you can challenge the pattern and shift to a more rational thought pattern.

Cognitive therapy became popular as a standalone therapy in the 1960s with the discovery of Aaron T. Beck. He noticed a pattern in his depressed patients. He found that they all negatively perceived themselves, the world, and the future. In addition, they also experienced a stream of spontaneous negative thoughts. With his findings, Beck began to form theories on alternate ways of examining and treating depression.

Beck's theory of cognitive distortions and Ellis' theory of irrational thinking offered a better approach to understanding psychological problems individually. So Beck began to use his approach to help clients reevaluate their thoughts. And in doing so, these clients found long-lasting change and became more resilient in handling life's daily functions.

CBT practice grew in the mid-1970s, particularly in treating high-functioning patients. It became stronger through trial and error, further behavioral therapy advancements, and a much-improved understanding of emotional control.

Beck found that there was a critical link between thoughts and feelings. So he came up with the term "automatic thoughts" to describe thoughts that spontaneously popped up in people's heads uninvited.

He also discovered that even though his patients weren't always conscious of these thoughts in their heads, they could learn to identify them. Beck found that people could achieve positive, long-lasting change simply by uncovering these automatic thoughts and challenging them. In essence, Cognitive Therapy helps people to recognize unhelpful thoughts and challenge them. This then makes it possible to find alternatives and open up choices.

Behavioral therapy was used to treat anxiety and phobias effectively. Still, it wasn't until it was combined with cognitive therapy that psychologists could use CBT to treat a wider range of psychological disorders and conditions.

CBT is constantly evaluating its techniques. The result of this is a comprehensive body of research about the effectiveness of this therapy method in treating a wide range of psychological issues. It's necessary to emphasize that CBT techniques have advanced based on research and clinical practice. It is one of the psychological approaches supported with ample evidence that its techniques can actually effect change. In this sense, CBT is different from many types of psychological treatment.

The following are the core principles of CBT:

- Psychological issues are due, in part, to faulty and self-defeating ways of thinking.
- Psychological issues are due, in part, to acquire patterns of self-destructive behavior.
- Individuals suffering from psychological problems can learn to cope with them in better ways, thus relieving symptoms and becoming more functional and effective in daily life.

CBT treatment strategies usually try to change behavioral patterns. They might include:

- Learning to confront one's fears instead of avoiding them.

- Role-playing to learn how to handle potentially problematic interactions.
- Calming one's mind and relaxing one's body in distressing situations.

Not all types of CBT use these strategies. In many cases, the psychologist and client work collaboratively to understand the underlying problem and develop an intervention specific to the client's needs.

CBT emphasizes the importance of helping people be their own therapists, which is considered the most effective approach. Treatment focuses on what's happening in the client's current life rather than past experiences that led to the present difficulties.

Of course, some information about one's past is required. Still, the therapy focuses primarily on getting through the present and going forward in time to come up with better ways of handling life's difficulties.

CBT's approach to treating psychological disorders has pros and cons. Like all therapies, there's a risk of negative feelings returning. Here's a list of advantages CBT offers:

- Unlike other talk therapies, CBT treatments can be completed in a relatively short time frame.
- It can help treat certain mental disorders where medication isn't improving symptoms.
- CBT focuses on modifying thoughts and behavior to change how you feel.

- The strategies are practical and helpful. They can help you learn to cope with future stress.
- CBT is practicable in different formats, including online, in-person, or workbooks.
- It can improve a person's emotional processing skills.

Here's a list of things that one may consider cons of CBT:

- CBT requires you to commit to the process every step of the way. It's not a magic wand that will make your problems go away. You have to put in the work,
- Even if your needs are met through CBT, your environment (interactions, family) can counteract the impact.
- CBT is usually more difficult for individuals with severe mental health disorders.
- Some CBT strategies use exposure to address anxiety sources, which can be uncomfortable.
- Putting in the work in your life will take time, commitment, and patience.

Why Don't We Just Become More Positive?

We said earlier that there are many misconceptions about CBT – the biggest being that CBT is all about having people think positively. Unfortunately, this misconception birthed the erroneous assumption that CBT trains clients to ignore negative happenings in their lives to preserve their experience of positive emotions.

Unsurprisingly, those with this view tend to perceive CBT negatively and may even avoid working with CBT practitioners. In reality, the primary goal of CBT is to help you achieve balanced thinking. Balanced thinking involves evaluating all the information and context in a situation that contributes to your emotional state. This means you must learn to process both positive and negative information effectively. You cannot simply disregard the negative and focus solely on the positive.

Contrary to popular belief, CBT doesn't advocate disregarding negative information or replacing negative information with a positive one. There are many reasons why it's crucial to process both negative and positive information. First, negative emotions exist for a reason – to warn you about a need for change. People often experience stressful life events and challenges, which should be addressed. Disregarding such negative experiences is illogical because it won't help you feel better.

By this same token, CBT helps you to evaluate the positive information and context in a situation. Contrary to belief, the positive information you're encouraged to consider is one supported by evidence, not information based on "positive affirmations," which isn't supported by facts or evidence.

Most people tend to hyper-fixate on the negative when in a distressing situation. This is why CBT encourages us to consider genuine negative and positive information. However, focusing solely on the negative can intensify the degree of distress an individual feels in the situation. Among difficult emotions are anger, frustration, sadness, anxiety, guilt, and embarrassment – to name a few.

In contrast, the intensity of a difficult emotion decreases when you balance your thinking and interpretation of a situation. This approach helps you cope with the emotional aspect of the situation in a better way, which then makes you handle the behavioral aspect more effectively with problem-solving and action.

Adopting a "positive-thoughts-only" attitude makes you vulnerable to the risk of toxic positivity. This over-the-top form of positivity encourages you to invalidate your true feelings. Toxic positivity is the excessive overgeneralization of a happy, upbeat emotional state, no matter the situation. It contributes to the minimization or blatant denial of an authentic emotional experience.

Unfortunately, suppressing negative emotions and masking them with an outward appearance of positivity can only intensify the feelings, increasing discomfort. Like anything done excessively, positivity becomes toxic when it's used to silence the authentic human experience. By dismissing or disallowing the experience of certain emotions, we fall into a perpetual state of denial and repressed feelings.

The reality is that humans are not perfect. Emotions like anger, jealousy, sadness, and greed, as undesirable as they are, make us who we are. So, pretending that it's "positive vibes always" denies the validity of your genuine experience as a human being.

Balanced thinking is important because focusing solely on the positives of a situation prevents you from identifying and addressing negative events in your life, likely contributing to your emotional distress.

Also, focusing solely on the negative gives you a skewed view of the situation, further intensifying your distress. That makes it more difficult to address stressful events and problems in your life.

While it is a misconception that CBT focuses on positivity only, there are times when it's best to process only positive information.

The bottom line is that CBT encourages us to take a balanced approach to critically think and interpret information – a balance of negatives and positives. That is the only practical way to enhance your experience and enjoyment of life.

CBT Compared With Other Forms of Therapy

Before we talk about the difference between CBT and other therapy approaches, it's important to understand the approaches themselves and what they entail. Psychotherapy offers a roadmap for psychologists to understand their client's problems and develop effective solutions. To do this, psychotherapists take five approaches:

- **Psychoanalysis therapy:** This category of psychotherapy focuses on changing unhelpful behaviors, thoughts, and feelings by unraveling the unconscious meanings and motivations behind them. Therapies that use this approach involve a collaborative partnership between therapist and client. As a result, the client (patient) discovers more about themselves as they explore their interactions with the therapist.

- **Behavior therapy:** This psychotherapy approach focuses on the role of learning in developing normal and abnormal behaviors. It is characterized by concepts such as classical conditioning (associative learning), desensitizing, and operant conditioning. With classical conditioning, a therapist could help a patient develop a specific behavior by associating it with something else. For example, Ivan Pavlov trained his famous dogs to drool at the sound of their dinner bell by associating the sound with food. On the other hand, desensitizing involves repeatedly exposing a client to the source of their anxiety. Meanwhile, operant conditioning uses reward and punishment to shape behavior.

- **Cognitive therapy:** As you already know, cognitive therapy focuses on thought (what you think) rather than behavior (what you believe). Building on the work of Aaron T. Beck, cognitive therapists believe dysfunctional thinking causes dysfunctional feelings and behavior. So, by changing your thoughts, you can change how you feel and what you do.

- **Humanistic therapy:** This approach to psychotherapy concerns people's capacity to make rational decisions (choices) and reach their maximum potential. It also focuses on respect and concern for other people.

- **Integrative (holistic) therapy:** Many therapists don't restrict themselves to any one category of psychotherapy. Instead, they combine techniques from different approaches and tailor their intervention to individual clients' needs.

The core difference between CBT and these other approaches is that it is effective for a wider range of conditions.

CBT encompasses four approaches and a broad range of techniques to address one's thoughts, emotions, and behaviors. The practice can range from structured therapy to self-help. Your specific approach will depend on the issue (s) being addressed. Regardless, four therapeutic approaches incorporate CBT.

Dialectical Behavior Therapy (DBT)

Dialectical behavioral therapy is an evidence-based CBT approach that employs problem-solving strategies and teaches clients to find acceptance. In addition, it is used to address distressing thoughts and behavior by incorporating strategies such as mindfulness and emotional regulation.

DBT is effective in treating emotional dysregulation and several mental health disorders. However, clients who benefit from this approach tend to view things from a "black-and-white lens." They regard situations as this or the other, which makes it difficult to see a gray area or find a middle ground.

This type of CBT can potentially help anyone who lacks emotional coping skills and always finds themselves in one crisis or another. In addition, it can potentially allow you to acquire the skills needed to cope with distressing emotions effectively.

DBT can be used to treat anyone with Bipolar Disorder, Borderline Personality Disorder, ADHD, Post Traumatic Stress Disorder, and Eating disorders.

Mindfulness-Based Cognitive Therapy (MBCT)

Mindfulness-based cognitive therapy combines CBT with mindfulness meditation to help cultivate a present-oriented and non-judgmental attitude toward your experiences. It can effectively handle anxiety, depression, and bipolar disorder.

Acceptance and Commitment Therapy (ACT)

Some argue that ACT is purely a behavioral therapy, but it can be classified as a form of CBT. It is a behavior-oriented approach that emphasizes the use of positive reinforcement and counter-conditioning to change how a person responds to their internal experiences.

Internal experiences include:

- Thoughts
- Emotions
- Impulses
- Physical feelings

Acceptance and commitment therapy can help you learn to stop avoiding, denying, and fighting with your inner feelings. With this approach, you learn that certain feelings are appropriate emotional responses to the situations that trigger them. It teaches you to recognize and accept them.

Once you understand that, it becomes easy to accept the challenges and issues that life throws at you. Acceptance is the foundation for making behavioral changes that ultimately improve your life.

ACT can teach you to cope effectively with the following:

- Depression
- Chronic pain
- Workplace stress
- Substance abuse and addiction
- Obsessive-compulsive disorder
- Test-based anxiety

Rational emotive Behavior therapy (REBT)

REBT is a therapy approach that focuses on helping clients to identify irrational beliefs, including negative thoughts and self-defeating feelings. This active-oriented approach will teach you to challenge irrational beliefs until you can eventually recognize and change your unhelpful thought patterns. The ultimate goal is to teach you to swap negative beliefs for healthier, more productive ones.

This type of CBT can be used to help clients struggling with:

- Anxiety
- Depression
- Guilt
- Anger issues
- Procrastination

- Disordered eating
- Aggression

Once again, the type (s) of CBT treatments you'll receive depends on which areas of your life you want to improve with this effective 'talking' therapy.

WHAT IS CBT USED FOR?

Over the past few decades, CBT has been increasingly adopted over other treatment therapies as psychology shifted toward evidence-based practice. Psychology research has established CBT as the most effective therapy for various mental health conditions.

This therapy approach is almost always more effective in treating many mental health issues than medication or traditional talk therapy. Studies have also shown that CBT has the lowest relapse rate of all psychological treatments.

CBT can be used to treat the following range of conditions successfully:

- Anxiety
- Depression
- Phobias
- Panic Disorder
- Obsessive Compulsive Disorder
- Eating disorders
- Addictions
- Bipolar Disorder

- Schizophrenia
- Psychosis
- Anger issues
- Chronic fatigue syndrome
- Irritable bowel syndrome
- Fibromyalgia
- Personality disorders
- Substance misuse

CBT can be a short-term intervention to help you learn to analyze thoughts and beliefs. In addition to these mental health conditions, CBT can also help people cope with the following:

- Chronic pain
- Insomnia
- Serious health issues, such as cancer
- Divorce or painful break-ups
- Grief or loss
- Trauma
- Low self-esteem
- Stress management
- Relationship problems

The fact that CBT is the best treatment available for the afore-mentioned mental health conditions is supported by it being one of the most researched therapy approaches.

Here's some research that proves that CBT is indeed effective for this range of mental health conditions.

- A 2018 review involving 41 studies that looked at the use of CBT in treating anxiety disorders, OCD, and PTSD discovered that CBT could help improve the symptoms of all these conditions. In addition, it was found to be the most effective approach for anxiety, stress, and OCD.

- A 2018 research studying CBT for anxiety found that the therapy produced good long-term results. However, the study focused on young people, and more than half of the participants no longer met the criteria for anxiety two years after the intervention.

- A 2018 study involving 104 participants found evidence that CBT can improve cognitive function in people with PTSD and major depression.

- Recent research from 2020 and 2021 finds that virtual and internet-based CBT practice is promising for effective treatment.

- Studies from 2010 found CBT to be effective in treating substance misuse. The National Institute on Drug Abuse reports that CBT can be used to help cope with addiction and prevent relapse after treatment.

Numerous ongoing research studies are still looking into the efficacy of CBT in treating even more mental health conditions.

IS CBT FOR EVERYONE?

CBT may be more effective than medication or traditional talk therapy in treating many mental health problems, but that doesn't make it suitable for everyone. Moreover, not everyone will succeed with CBT due to a couple of factors we're about to discuss.

CBT has been proven to help adults, teens, and kids. However, it is one form of therapy that emphasizes structure. If you struggle with structure, you may find it harder to use CBT to address your issues.

Additionally, it requires you to take an active role in the therapy process. While your therapist can help break down your thoughts and feelings so you can examine them more closely, you'll most likely end each session with some type of homework that teaches coping skills you're expected to apply in different aspects of your life.

Also, CBT requires you to closely examine your thoughts and feelings, which can be incredibly hard for some people. The process takes time, commitment, and dedication. You must be willing to do the work required for change to happen. Some people may find this hard or outright impossible.

The techniques involve lots of homework you must be willing to get done if you don't want to risk impeding your progress or success. Therefore, commitment and dedication are crucial for a successful CBT treatment.

One thing about CBT is that it tends to look a lot different for clients, depending on the mental health condition they are treating. For example, someone treated for bipolar disorder or schizophrenia will have an entirely different experience than someone using CBT to address anxiety or panic disorder.

In many cases, CBT emphasizes the therapy process over the relationship between therapist and client. However, suppose you would like to build an emotional rapport with your therapist. In that case, this approach may not deliver in some cases.

As stated previously, CBT uses a shorter treatment time frame than other treatment methods. In some cases, it is limited to just 6-12 sessions. Therefore, if you want a therapy that goes in-depth into your issues and covers the bases, this one may not suit you.

It's important to acknowledge and accept the reality that CBT may not work for you. Otherwise, you'll end up blaming yourself or the therapist when it doesn't solve your issues. You might think, "Oh, there must be nothing that can help me if even CBT fails. I am a real lost cause." That is far from the truth.

If you've tried CBT for a while and didn't notice any improvement in your life, you might need to consider a different type of intervention.

There are various approaches to psychotherapy. For example, if you're doing CBT with a therapist rather than by yourself, you might ask them for other interventions you can do along with or combined with CBT.

Or, you might check the self-help section on Amazon or a local bookstore and find workbooks that offer a different therapeutic approach to your problems. For example, if your problem is connected to relationships, you might find family or couples therapy more effective.

Sometimes, what you need to do for CBT to work is to increase your "dosage." Building momentum is difficult if you aren't working hard enough between sessions, as this therapy boils down to commitment and consistency to achieve your end goal.

In many cases, all it takes to unlock the effectiveness of CBT is to create more time between sessions to practice the skills you learn. Then, reflect on your current therapy "dosage" and see if you need to adjust it.

Remember, there is solid research supporting the use of CBT in helping a wide variety of people with an even wider variety of mental health symptoms. The approach is an excellent place to start if you're entering therapy, but that doesn't make it a cure-all. If CBT doesn't help you or isn't effective for all of your symptoms, you have numerous options.

By now, you should be motivated by everything you've learned about CBT. It shows that there is hope ahead of the road. Yes, you might feel slightly abashed by the idea of having to do plenty of homework during this journey, but don't let that demotivate you. If you commit to your homework as much as you did in high school, you'll find success with CBT.

In the next chapter, we will discuss how the brain functions in relation to thoughts and the ease with which it can be confused or distorted.

Chapter One Highlights

- CBT is an established treatment for chronic stress, anxiety, depression, pain, and other mental health conditions. Compared to other therapy approaches, it is the best-studied psychotherapy for treating psychological issues relating to cognition and behavior.
- CBT techniques can change how you feel and behave by addressing faulty or self-destructive thoughts and replacing them with positive ones. As a result, you can learn to cope with your psychological problems in healthier ways by changing how you view and respond to them.
- The key to overcoming psychological issues is to adopt a balanced view of positive and negative information rather than focusing on positivity alone. Negative emotions exist to help you navigate life's many challenges, so you cannot completely disregard or suppress them.
- You are not perfect; nobody is. It's normal and acceptable to experience unpleasant emotions because they make you who you are. Don't deny or repress the validity of your "negative" emotions because that impairs your outlook on life and makes it difficult to address stressors and challenges in life.
- CBT is more effective than traditional therapies and medications, but it may not be suitable for you. If you want to be successful with this approach, you must be willing to take an active role in the treatment process.

2

THE THOUGHT PROCESS AND CONSEQUENCES

For an organ roughly three (3) pounds in size, you'll agree with me that the brain has extensive responsibilities – from body movement, to your senses, organs, speech, and the regulation of the entire body system. The brain is also responsible for cognitive processes, i.e., thoughts and emotions. Like any part of your body, your cognition won't function as it should if you don't take good care of the brain.

Your brain processes nearly 80 000 thoughts daily. But have you ever wondered where these come from? Or what are they made of? And if you can measure them? Do you think while doing something else, or is this part of the brain on auto-pilot? In other words, do we form thoughts automatically?

The big question should be, have you ever thought about your thoughts? Oops… now you're thinking about them.

Okay, the first thing I aim to help you understand in this chapter is how thoughts form. And I'll do that by explaining how the brain creates a neural pathway for thought processes. Heads up! This chapter might seem a bit more technical since we'll be discussing the thought processes which relate to the brain. However, I will ensure I make it as simple as possible.

WHERE DO OUR THOUGHTS STEM FROM?

What were your assumptions when you started reading this book? You probably thought, "Alright, it's time to see what there is to know about CBT" or something similar. But first, let's deconstruct this thought to determine exactly what it is.

The first step to understanding where thoughts come from is determining what a thought is. You would probably define a thought as "something I tell myself."

Phew, that's quite something. And, depending on who you pose the question ("what is a thought?)", you'll get different answers.

Of course, from a psychological perspective, we'll focus on the reductionist theory that describes thoughts as *"physical entities that chemical changes in the brain can explain."*

Although the science of neuron communication is well-studied, scientists have yet to accurately define the complexity of cognitive processes.

The brain contains approximately 100 billion cells called neurons. These neurons produce what you may know as neurotransmitters – a bunch of chemicals that create electrical signals in the neurons, allowing them to communicate with one another.

Thoughts are electrochemical reactions that take place in the brain. When neurons release neurotransmitters, they generate these electrical impulses, which travel like waves to thousands of neighboring neurons, leading to thought formation. But that's just a single thought formation, right? If so, how do thought patterns then form?

One theory is that thoughts form when neurons fire. External stimuli create repeated neuron firing, reinforcing the circuitry and producing a thought pattern. If you find yourself in the same situation twice, your neurons will fire similarly, reinforcing them. As noted, that's why we react to similar situations the same way, since the neurons responsible for our response fire again and again.

Often, we repeat certain actions (driving, cooking, or singing a favorite song), which activate the same neurons until they become familiar to us. This creates a reinforced circuit related to these activities. The same applies to situations that trigger a reaction in us.

This is fascinating, as it means you can shift from a negative thought pattern to a positive one or change a behavior. Now, note that tracking a particular harmful thought will trigger a change in how neurons fire, essentially leading to the formation of a new thought process.

Thoughts are your perceptions, beliefs, and ideas about your environment. It is the lens by which you see your entire existence. In addition, they are a filter for how you perceive the world. We're all familiar with the word "attitude," which often has a negative connotation. A long-lasting thought transforms into an attitude, whether positive or negative.

The complexity of the brain's chemical processes of thought formation is why our thoughts are so hard to track. A single neuron firing can range from 1 to 1000 signals per second. As a result, we tend to underestimate the capacity of our brains. Think about the number of neurotransmitters fired as you read this line. Trust me; it's a lot!

As you're reading this, the letter photons go straight to your retina, from where the light-detecting cells detect them – turning them into electrical signals. The electrical signals are then transported to the nerve cells, which quickly spread to neighboring nerve cells. You don't even realize it, but that electrochemical signal activates billions of neurons in seconds. Incredible, right?

Sometimes, you notice a catchy tune from your favorite artist replaying in your head over and over, and you're constantly humming along. You often don't pay conscious attention when you drive home from work, but you take a right turn anyway. You might even be lost in your thoughts while driving, and you won't make mistakes.

Cognitive neuroscience says that only 5% of our cognitive activities are done consciously. That means 95% of these activities, including thinking, are done subconsciously. In essence, your brain has adapted to making you perform many activities without being constantly aware. Scientists call this "adaptive unconscious."

The "adaptive unconscious" ensures you don't make tedious calculations every time you're driving. And you can be more attentive as you engage in that activity like the first time you tried it. Once you learn something, you don't forget it.

As you might have figured, this is the same as automatic negative thoughts. They are in your subconscious, shaping your behavior and attitude toward life, and you don't even realize it.

In the past, we believed that once neural connections were formed, they remained for good. But today, we know that neurons create synapses, which are like branches. So we use some regularly, thereby strengthening them. Meanwhile, the ones we don't use are eliminated. This is called neuroplasticity.

According to Dr. Celeste Campbell, a neuropsychologist in the Polytrauma Program at the Washington, DC Veterans Administration Medical Center, "From the time the brain begins to develop in utero until the day we die, the connections among our brain cells reorganize in response to our changing needs. This process allows us to learn from and adapt to different experiences."

Every time you learn something new, the brain creates new connections between your nerve cells. Every day, the brain rewires itself to adapt to new experiences and circumstances. That is how remarkable this organ truly is. But you can also stimulate and encourage neuroplasticity without waiting for your brain to do it. In other words, you're capable of changing your brain and the way it thinks.

HOW THOUGHTS, EMOTIONS, AND BEHAVIORS ARE LINKED

Have you ever wondered why you can't stop repeating a particular behavior or why you can't help feeling a specific way no matter how hard you try?

Awareness of your thoughts and feelings is vital for your mental wellness. As humans, we're hardwired to think and feel. However, the range of thoughts and feelings you experience can make it hard to understand how they may affect your life.

Thoughts and feelings have a profound impact on your daily life. They help you make sense of your environment and connect you with the world.

Recognizing that thoughts and feelings are two distinct things is key to processing them. To become better at processing and understanding your thoughts and feelings, know what they are, what they aren't, the relationship between them, and how they differ from each other. Note that it can take time and patience to differentiate between your feelings and thoughts.

You might feel confused if you try to understand thoughts and feelings on your own, partly because of how you refer to them. Many times, we say, "I'm feeling this way," even though it's, in fact, not a feeling.

For example, you might say, "I feel stupid." This isn't a real feeling. The correct statement is, "I think I am stupid," because it's a thought. And you probably have that thought because you feel sad, hurt, or ashamed. Therefore, "I feel sad because I think I am stupid" is more accurate.

Many of us aren't aware of the impact of our thoughts and feelings on behavior. The way you think about a situation affects how you feel about it. Your thoughts and feelings influence your behaviors, choices, and outcomes. Thoughts, emotions, and behavior are interconnected. Your thoughts can trigger certain feelings, which, in turn, can trigger specific behaviors.

To understand the connection between all three, let's define them individually. When you understand that connection, you'll be able to modify your thoughts, emotions, and behavior to improve your mental and emotional wellness – which is the whole point of learning CBT.

Since you already know what thoughts are, let's briefly explain what emotions and behaviors are.

Emotions

These are feelings triggered by your thoughts or experiences – from happiness to sadness, anger, anxiety, fear, surprise, and other feelings. You experience these feelings in varying intensity, usually with associated physiological signs. For instance, when you're anxious, you may feel like there is a pit at the bottom of your stomach. And when you're angry, you may feel tightness in your chest.

Strong emotions can make it difficult to think logically. This is due to the impact of emotions on how you think and make decisions. For example, anger can make you react irrationally and do or say something you would never say in a normal state of mind.

Emotions are universal experiences, and you need to learn to express them. There is no such thing as a "bad" feeling. Every emotion exists because it serves a purpose.

Behaviors

These are the actions you take as a response to your emotions. They are the way you present yourself to others. Your behaviors are an outward expression of how you feel internally. If someone finds communicating their thoughts or feelings hard, you can look to their behaviors for clues.

When you experience a strong emotion, you're prompted to act on it, sometimes without thinking. Unfortunately, this can make you behave in ways you might regret later. For instance, you might yell or scream at someone if you're experiencing an emotion like anger. Or if you're feeling sad, you might withdraw from others or cry alone in your room.

Behavioral changes typically indicate an internal struggle. They are signs that someone may be struggling with a mental health problem. If you want to know whether someone you know finds it hard to discuss their thoughts or feelings, compare their behavior before and after stress. The more significant the difference in their behavior, the greater their internal struggle.

The Connection Explained!

The connection between thoughts, emotions, and behavior is pretty straightforward: your behaviors are directly tied to your feelings, and vice versa. Because of this, you can change your behavior by changing your feelings; and you can change your feelings by changing your behavior.

This is why clinical psychologists say that we can fight depression by actively changing specific behaviors. It's the most direct way to help many people struggling with depression improve their mood.

Also, work on identifying the emotions that trigger certain behaviors. Then, you can learn to manage your behavior by handling your emotions better.

In all of this, you might be wondering where thoughts fit in. Thoughts encompass words, pictures, speech, and even smells. Thoughts in this context refer to different mental activities, such as plans, hopes, wishes, judgments, predictions, and memories.

You don't notice your thoughts most of the time – but they are there in the background, helping you to complete tasks automatically and shaping your decisions. Sometimes, you become aware of these thoughts – for example, when you try to remember something that happened a few years back or learn a new skill.

Thoughts and feelings are intricately linked, as thoughts can evoke strong emotions. For example, if you find your work quite stressful, you might start to experience anxiety anytime you're at work. In turn, the feeling of anxiety could cause you to have automatic negative thoughts (ANTs). Such as thinking you aren't good enough or that you'll lose your job if you can't handle the pressure. Of course, this does nothing but reinforce your negative emotional state, keeping you in a cycle that's hard to break out of.

Another example is if you enjoy swimming or being near water outdoors. The mere thought of going to a pool can evoke feelings of happiness and excitement. In turn, those feelings can prompt you to plan activities that include being around water.

However, if you're afraid of large bodies of water, such as a river or pool, or the thought of swimming scares you, you'll naturally avoid plans that include such activities. Depending on your thoughts, the same experience can evoke different feelings (excitement or anxiety). In this case, there is no right or wrong – you simply have different views of the same situation or experience.

Try the exercise below to know whether automatic thoughts profoundly and immediately impact your feelings and behavior.

Imagine that you're walking home from the theater on a dark Saturday evening. It's quite late, and you're wondering whether you should still have dinner by this time. Your thoughts are interrupted by a quiet, rustling noise a few steps away from you. What is it?

Thought 1 – "It's a stray cat."

What do you feel immediately when this thought pops into your head? How does it affect your emotions? What do you do at that moment?

It's a cat, so you relax and keep walking toward the metro. And you return to thinking about your dinner.

Thought 2 - "It's a mugger."

What do you feel when this thought pops into your head? How does it affect your emotions? What do you do differently at that moment?

This will probably evoke a different feeling and reaction from the first thought. You may tense up in fear or anxiety. Your hands start to sweat, your heartbeat might increase, and your tummy churns.

What do you do? Maybe you increase your steps or look for a place to run or hide. Then, you see a cat come out from your left and instantly relax.

This scenario highlights how a simple thought (not fact) can change your feelings and actions. That is an excellent example of the link between your thoughts, feelings, and behaviors. Aaron T. Beck emphasized the importance of this relationship. He proposed that changing one of the three (thoughts, emotions, and behaviors) would change any of the others.

The essence of CBT is that changing cognition, behavior, or both can change emotion and improve symptoms of specific mental health problems.

While you might be tempted to ignore your thoughts or suppress difficult feelings in order to cope with them, by doing this, you risk making irrational decisions that may lead to unhealthy results.

For example, if someone close does something to hurt you, the secondary emotion you'll experience is most likely anger. But you may try to suppress the anger because it's painful and not in line with what you feel for the person who hurt you.

You may feel conflicted about your anger and, in that case, decide to suppress the feelings rather than cope with the pain. However, pushing those feelings down can trigger more negative feelings, making you feel worse.

Now, you're going around with difficult feelings and a wound caused by the original experience, combined with other distressing feelings from trying to avoid your original feelings.

Unfortunately, you end up interacting with your external environment with unwanted feelings below the surface. And you risk them coming out toward another person at the wrong time.

Please don't push your feelings down and ignore them like they don't exist. You'll have to deal with them in another way that may be out of your control – like feeling angry to the point where self-awareness and understanding become difficult or impossible.

EXAMINING YOUR COGNITIVE DISTORTIONS

We all experience cognitive distortions daily. Cognitive distortions are negative thoughts, irrational beliefs, and habits that skew our perception of things. They play a crucial role in our cognitive processes. You aren't alone if you feel like you're in a loop of negative thinking.

Cognitive distortions make us exaggerate or view reality in a warped and unhealthy way. This can damage our relationships, mental health, and overall well-being. Let's discuss the different forms of cognitive distortions and how they affect you.

Aaron T. Beck was the first person to introduce us to the concept of cognitive distortions when he noticed dysfunctional thinking in his patients. But David Burns was the one who popularized the approach of identifying, correcting, and changing distorted thinking patterns to treat patients struggling with depression.

Negative thoughts and feelings exaggerate cognitive distortions. They convince you that your skewed thoughts are true, blinding you from reality. Unfortunately, these thought patterns are common and occur automatically in your everyday thoughts. This makes them hard to recognize and challenge, especially as they are wired into the brain.

One thing about the brain is that it likes shortcuts. Your brain remembers events from your past and will form a connection when you have similar thoughts or emotions in the present. Ordinarily, this is a good way to remember things (memory), but it's potentially dangerous for negative thoughts and feelings.

Habitual thinking can reinforce cognitive distortions, leading to increased anxiety, depression, and dysfunctional relationships. The following are four facts about cognitive distortions:

- All cognitive distortions are habitual ways of thinking or beliefs.
- They are false, exaggerated, and often inaccurate.
- They manifest as negative emotions or feelings.
- They can increase stress, anxiety, and depression, possibly causing psychological disorders.

There is no evidence that anxiety or depression causes cognitive distortions. Still, they are more common in people struggling with anxiety, depression, or other severe mental conditions.

The dysfunctional thought patterns are a product of the complex relationship between your thoughts, behaviors, and emotions. They don't have a specific root cause or an underlying reason. Instead, numerous factors, including social, cultural, and environmental factors, could contribute to these dysfunctional thinking patterns.

Social factors:

- Our social network and media can influence our beliefs, ideas, thoughts, and perceptions of ourselves and others.

- Dysfunctional social relationships can make us cultivate an "Us vs. Them" attitude.
- Parental guidance plays a key role in our mentality and attitude.
- Positive communication can promote healthy relationships and mental well-being.
- Active participation in social events may contribute to emotional and mental wellness.

Cultural factors:

- Customs, beliefs, religion, moral values, and language influence behavior.
- They influence how we communicate, behave, and handle our emotions.
- Culture impacts our willingness to express our emotions, speak up about our mental health, or seek help for a mental health issue.

Environmental factors:

- Accessibility to health care (physical and mental) services decreases stress and improves mental wellness.
- Genetics, financial status, and educational background influence our attitude, sense of security, persistence, and resilience.

These factors influence our upbringing, influencing our thoughts, emotions, and behaviors toward life events.

As noted, everyone experiences dysfunctional thinking patterns in their everyday thoughts. The mind operates on autopilot when we have cognitive distortions. Most people aren't negatively impacted; some can immediately recognize the unhelpful thoughts.

You don't realize that you are having these negative thoughts, making it incredibly hard to recognize that they are illogical and inaccurate. If you can't recognize faulty thinking, you reinforce them, which increases stress, anxiety, and depression, causing relationship problems and triggering other unwanted health issues.

We tend to assume that our feelings are caused by an event or something that happened to us. However, you don't jump from experiencing an event straight to emotion. Something plays a role in how you feel about the event or thing that happened to you – and that's your interpretation (thought) of the event. For example, "This thing happened and made me feel this way."

Below, we briefly discuss some of the most common cognitive distortions you might be experiencing.

- **"All or nothing" thinking**

This is also called polarized or "black and white" thinking. A person with this distortion believes that things are either this way or that way – no middle ground or a gray area. This cognitive distortion makes you think in extremes.

For example, a student used to being at the top of their class might feel like a failure if they fall to second place. The mentality is, *"If I'm not at the top of my class all the time, I am a total failure."*

- **Overgeneralization**

Overgeneralization is a pattern of thinking where you focus on a single event that you experienced and conclude based on that one piece of negative evidence. Then, since your conclusion is from that single event, you erroneously conclude that all similar events in the future will have the same negative outcome.

For example, a student falls to second place in their class for just one semester. Based on that, they conclude that they're a failure and will remain in second place for the rest of their life.

- **Mental Filtering**

This occurs when you focus solely on the negative aspect of a situation. This distortion is categorized into negative mental filtering and disqualifying the positive.

Negative mental filtering involves filtering out all the positives of a situation and fixating on the negatives. You magnify the negative details of the situation and dwell on the feelings they evoke. This can prevent you from seeing things as they are since you're focused on what went wrong rather than what worked.

For example, a subordinate receives an excellent review from their supervisor at work. Still, the person focuses on a single negative comment in the review.

Disqualifying the positive, on the other hand, acknowledges the positive aspect of the situation but rejects it. It is an absolute rejection of one's positive experiences. This cognitive distortion makes you invalidate and dismiss the positives as you try to find ways to make them negative.

For example, the subordinate who got an excellent review at work overlooks their manager's pause and tries to explain it away as a fluke rather than a product of their hard work.

- **Mind reading**

This occurs when you think you know what another person is thinking. It is based purely on your assumptions with zero physical evidence. You assume you know people's intentions and reasons for doing what they do and conclude that is the only valid reason. You also fail to acknowledge the other possibilities.

For example, you're on a lunch date with your friend, but they seem disinterested. You automatically conclude they don't want to spend time with you. In reality, it could be that they feel discomforted or have hundreds of other reasons that have nothing to do with you.

- **Fortune telling**

This distortion is similar to mind reading because it's also based purely on assumptions. You jump to conclusions or make predictions with little to no evidence. The conclusion or prediction almost always has a negative outcome.

For example, you're about to go on a date with someone you like, but you're pretty sure the date will go horribly. You make predictions that aren't based on actual evidence.

- **Catastrophizing**

You catastrophize when you exaggerate or minimize the magnitude of an event. Exaggerating (magnification) escalates negative thoughts and makes you assume the worst-case scenario. It occurs when there are unknowns about a situation you can't control.

For example, you're meeting someone for a date. However, that person is running late, so you start assuming the worst – "Maybe they don't like me after all" or "They are probably out with someone else." But there are other reasonable explanations for your date's lateness.

On the other hand, minimizing the magnitude of an event occurs when you diminish your positive experiences.

For example, you are promoted at work but fail to acknowledge the accomplishment. You diminish the importance of the promotion because *"It's not a big deal; other people were promoted."*

- **Labeling**

This is a more extreme form of overgeneralization. Instead of recognizing it as a mistake or a one-time thing, you label the person involved. This kind of thinking makes you judge yourself and others based on a single negative experience.

For example, you label your coworker a "selfish jerk" because they couldn't help you with a task, even though they might have been occupied with their work.

- **Personalization**

Ever met someone who takes everything personally? If yes, that's due to a cognitive distortion called personalization – the tendency to take things personally. This negative thinking pattern makes you feel directly or personally attacked by other people's words and actions, even when unrelated to you.

For example, you attend a work luncheon where everyone interacts with others except you. As such, you feel like everybody at your workplace hates you. This makes you think your coworkers are discriminating against you.

- **Blaming**

This faulty thinking occurs when you blame others for your problems. It's similar to personalization, but the difference is that you award blame to external factors. Rather than taking responsibility, you assume the victim role and blame others for your pain.

For example, you blame your partner for a conflict instead of sharing the responsibility for things you both did. You assume you're the victim and your partner intentionally hurts you.

- **Emotional reasoning**

Whatever emotion you feel in response to a situation must be true. Unfortunately, this distortion makes you treat your feelings as facts by blocking your ability to reason logically. As a result, you incorrectly assume that the negative feeling evoked by your emotion is the only truth that matters.

For example, you feel lonely because your friends are at a resort for the weekend, and you can't go. But from this feeling, you conclude that people don't want to be around you. Your thought: *"My friends would have stayed here if they cared about me."*

There are other cognitive distortions, but the ones I've just discussed are commonly addressed with CBT.

Becoming aware of cognitive distortions and their impact on your thinking is the key to overcoming negative thinking.

Now that you're well familiar with how the brain is wired, you are one step closer to learning how to rewire your brain and overcome negative thoughts. But, more importantly, it will be easier to learn how to change your emotions by addressing your cognition and behavior.

Chapter Two Highlights

- Thoughts, emotions, and behaviors are linked, and they all affect each other. You can change how you feel by addressing how you think and act. Learn to identify the thoughts that trigger your behaviors, and you'll be able to handle your feelings better.
- Cognitive distortions (faulty thinking patterns) are often false, exaggerated, and inaccurate. However, paying attention to them can result in chronic stress, anxiety, and depression and possibly cause other psychological issues. Therefore, figuring out faulty thinking patterns to eliminate them is a part of the CBT program.
- Cognitive errors disrupt your perception of life experiences, giving you an irrationally negative outlook on life. This can damage your mental health and well-being. However, you can overcome negative thinking by eliminating distortions in your cognitive processes.
- Culture influences how you handle emotions, act, and interact with people. Cultural factors, such as language, customs, religion, etc., affect how you express yourself and your willingness to speak to others about your mental health issues. Examine any factor that may be hindering the treatment process for you.
- Don't ignore or push your feelings down, as that can make them spiral out of control, thus increasing your distress. Instead, emotional self-awareness should be a regular part of your daily life.

HOW TO EFFECTIVELY REWIRE THE BRAIN

Back when I struggled with negative thoughts, it felt like I was constantly dipping my feet into quicksand and sinking deeper and deeper until I was completely buried under. That is how I felt, especially with how the thoughts weighed on my mind daily. All it took was a single negative thought for my mind to spiral out of control. Before I could even say Jack Robinson, I found myself in a negative loop.

I felt hopeless and didn't see a way out of my situation. I was like a spider caught in my own web, except this was a web of strong, self-defeating beliefs and intense distress. Naturally, most people in my social circle withdrew from me. Nobody wanted to be around me, thanks to the demons in my head as I constantly lashed out.

At one point, I was convinced that I was fighting real demons. In a way, you could say that I was, but I didn't know that they were pesky little thoughts in the subconscious of my mind. Of course, I tried to deal with the thoughts by pushing them to the back of my mind. The more I tried this, the harder it was for me to fight them off – and they eventually took hold of my mind.

That was until CBT taught me to recognize my dysfunctional thinking patterns. And subsequently, using CBT techniques, I rewired my brain to overcome automatic negative thoughts and reframe my thought processes into producing healthier thinking patterns.

WHAT ARE AUTOMATIC NEGATIVE THOUGHTS (ANTS)?

How many negative thoughts pop into your head daily? How many have sneaked into your mind since you started this journey? Would you have a specific number if you paid attention and counted? Perhaps you've thought, *"This book won't help me. Nothing will help me. I am destined to be depressed all my life."*

Automatic negative thoughts come out of nowhere. For example, you're minding your business one minute, and out of nowhere, you're thinking:

"I'm a failure."

"I could have been more productive this week."

"I won't achieve my goals."

"I'm destined to be unsuccessful."

You probably wouldn't allow a friend or a random person to sneak up behind you and say these things to you. But every day, you let these dysfunctional thoughts rule your head and dictate your mood, decisions, and life. Unfortunately, the longer you give them power over your thought process, the harder it is to seize back control and rewire your brain to approach life with a positive outlook.

Automatic negative thoughts are self-explanatory. They are unwanted and negative thoughts that disturb your mind without a conscious effort. This is why you don't even realize they are there unless you deliberately look for them. One thing about ANTs is they don't even have to be related to your current situation to appear in your head.

ANTs are involuntary responses based on your core beliefs about yourself, others, and the world. They can influence your mood in such a powerful way and create self-doubt, irritability, anger, anxiety, and depression.

Individuals struggling with anxiety and depression experience automatic negative thoughts, but these thoughts vary from person to person, depending on their cognitive distortions.

Generally, though, all automatic negative thoughts are:

- Negative
- Self-sabotaging
- Invasive and uninvited
- Biased because they distort your view of reality
- Easy to believe

Coincidentally, the "ANTs" acronym is undeniably appropriate because, like ants, automatic negative thoughts are intrusive, unwanted, and capable of ruining your picnic or, in this case, your life. Buddha once said, *"Nothing can harm you as much as your thoughts."* And for people dealing with ANTs, this is undoubtedly true.

First, I should make it clear that it is perfectly normal to have negative thoughts. One of the mistakes I made when I started practicing CBT techniques was trying to erase all of my negative thoughts all at once. I eventually learned just how unrealistic that was.

The earlier humans survived the jungle by constantly looking out for threats, attending to problems as they arose, and learning from their mistakes. Imagination is one of the best qualities of your mind, and it exists for you to imagine potential problems and threats. That allows you to solve problems before they spiral out of your control.

But this quality of imagination also works against you by making your mind a *"random negative thought generator."* Your mind will use cognitive distortions to convince you of things that aren't true and make you believe them. So, guess what... It's all in your mind.

Automatic negative thoughts overwhelm your mind when negative thinking becomes habitual. Stats show that 90% of our daily thoughts are repetitive. That means you recycle the same thoughts over and over each day; you'll have almost similar thoughts today as you had yesterday and the day before.

When you have a negative or positive experience, your brain remembers it. If you have a similar experience another time, your brain triggers a negative response believing there's a threat. That response is what evokes anxiety, anger, depression, or agitation. And it can create a downward spiral toward a never-ending cycle of negative thoughts, emotions, and dysfunctional behavior.

If you indulge in negative thinking often enough, your brain creates a neural pathway. The more you engage in it, the stronger that connection becomes. That is how we form habits and why breaking a bad habit can be difficult.

But since I said automatic negative thoughts are normal and exist to ensure our survival, why are they so toxic and harmful?

Negative thinking patterns induce stress, which changes the brain in many ways. Every negative thought your mind produces alters the chemical composition of your brain, causing a cascade of negative effects that extend to emotion and behavior.

Some of the negative effects of ANTs include:

- Depleting feel-good brain chemicals such as dopamine and serotonin
- Slowing the release of brain-derived neurotrophic factor (BDNF), a protein involved in forming new brain cells
- Enlarging the size of your amygdala (the brain's fear center) while shrinking the size of your brain
- Accelerating the aging process
- Increasing your risk of psychiatric and neurodegenerative conditions

Automatic negative thoughts put the brain under chronic stress, changing it to its DNA level. You might not know this yet, but chronic stress is directly linked to anxiety, depression, and other mental health conditions.

Suppose you're struggling with anxiety. In that case, you might have negative thoughts about the future. You might tell yourself:

- *"I will make a fool of myself at the interview."*
- *"The company is going to reject me."*
- *"My whole class will laugh at me when I fumble my presentation."*

These thoughts, usually set in the future, are about things that haven't even happened yet. Although you don't know what the outcome of your situation will be, ANTs convince you that things won't go well with zero or illogical evidence. Your thoughts aren't supported by reality or logic, yet they compel you to live in fear and avoid certain situations.

For example, if you have social anxiety, you might have automatic negative thoughts that convince you to avoid social situations.

Not all ANTs are based on predicting the future. Many negative thoughts focus on the self and the past. Some of these ANTs may pop up like:

- *"I'm unworthy and unlovable."*
- *"I don't deserve to be happy."*

- *"Everyone hates me."*
- *"I make everything so much worse."*

These thoughts can overwhelm you with feelings of helplessness and hopelessness and can be exhausting.

Automatic negative thoughts aren't productive. They don't do anything except make you feel bad about yourself. So why does your brain keep allowing them to pop into your head? Like ANTs themselves, the answer to this question varies.

You're a meaning-making creature. You want answers and make decisions pretty quickly. Sometimes, the easiest way to get an answer is to blame yourself or others. You might find it easier to attribute guilt to yourself rather than put the blame on a larger history.

The mind also wants a quick fix or answer. You may find it easier to "predict the future" than to wait for it to arrive. It's much easier to dismiss yourself as a failure rather than accept that you, like everyone else, are bound to make mistakes. Unfortunately, you can't magically make ANTs disappear. Remember, when a negative thought pattern is repeated long enough, it metamorphoses into rumination.

THE RELATIONSHIP BETWEEN ANTS AND RUMINATION

We all enjoy music. You can probably relate to the hook of a catchy song getting stuck in your head. Even though you may not like the song or artist, you find yourself thinking about it for longer than you'd like – an earworm, as we say. This can be a pleasant experience for the most part.

However, when it's a thought, specifically a negative one, the experience is far less pleasant. When automatic negative thoughts begin to spiral, you can get stuck in a loop of repetitive negative thinking, otherwise called rumination.

Rumination is the habit of continuously engaging in repetitive negative thought processes without end. The cycle can be distressing, difficult to break, and often involves thinking over and over about a negative thought or evasive problem.

Rumination consumes much mental and emotional energy, which can negatively impact your mental well-being. It can present itself as worrying about the future, obsessing over the past, or trying to forecast how a situation might play out. But, sometimes, it's just you experiencing the same thought in a loop without variation.

Rumination is a co-occurring symptom in many mental health problems like anxiety and depression. It is a defining symptom of Obsessive Compulsive Disorder (OCD). You could say that rumination is a compulsion because you can't help yourself, despite being unaware of the thoughts.

For a depressed person, the rumination theme usually borders on being inadequate. However, when rumination is based on anxiety, you get stuck because the recurring negative thoughts encourage you to pursue questions you can't answer and truths you don't know.

Rumination is usually addressed from an OCD perspective. By definition, compulsion is something you do to reduce the distress caused by unwanted, intrusive thoughts. But rumination is often misinterpreted and rarely addressed as a compulsion.

This is because we erroneously assume that compulsions can only be observable actions or behaviors, like washing hands or checking the gas repeatedly to ensure it's switched off. However, rumination is a mental compulsion that happens internally, which is why other people can't observe it.

For example, someone with contamination OCD gets the compulsion to wash their hands repeatedly – that is an observable action. Conversely, someone with OCD relating to existential themes gets the compulsion to ruminate on things such as life, meaning, etc. In both cases, the compulsions (ritual hand washing and rumination) are responses to an unwanted, intrusive thought.

Although rumination exists to solve a problem, it can become problematic in its own right. Rumination can sometimes feel out of control. Those who ruminate may only realize what they are doing once a significant amount of time has passed, and they have spiraled far down the rabbit hole.

In fact, you may not be aware that you are stuck in that spiral of negative thinking. Still, it's an act you compulsively engage in rather than just an automatic negative thought that conveniently pops up.

The key to stopping rumination is recognizing the difference between actively thinking about something and simply "having a thought" about that thing. A negative thought becomes "rumination" when you turn that thought over in your mind and over-engage with it to a fault instead of leaving it in your subconscious.

STOP FALLING FOR NEGATIVITY BIAS

Negativity bias is a cognitive bias that makes the brain focus more on negatives than positives. The human tendency is to register negative events more readily than positive ones while dwelling on them. You feel it more intensely when someone criticizes rather than praises you.

As humans, we are wired to:

- Remember negative experiences more accurately than positive ones.
- Recall criticism better than praise, even if it is constructive.
- React more intensely to negative stimuli.
- Ruminate about negative events more frequently than positive ones.
- React more strongly to negative experiences than to equally positive ones.

Negativity bias is why bad impressions are much more difficult to overcome than good ones. It is also why traumatic experiences from our past have such lasting effects throughout our lives. In your interactions, you're more likely to notice the negative bits and recall them more vividly in the future.

For example, I remember having a great day at work due to the reception of my contribution to a group project. It was great until a coworker who was also part of the project gave me a backhanded compliment that I found pretty insulting. I was already struggling with recurring negative thoughts, so I spent the rest of that workday and the week fixating on the offhand comment.

When I met a friend later that day for dinner, she asked how my day was, and my reply was "pretty awful" – even though it was a good day by all ramifications.

When I began my CBT journey, I learned about negativity bias and how it can lead us to pay more attention to the seemingly bad events in our lives, magnifying their importance and making them much bigger than they should be.

Psychological research has established that human beings tend to focus more on the negative as we explore and try to make sense of the world. This is because we are wired to believe a negative piece of news over a positive one.

Your human nature makes the risk of losing seem greater than the chance of winning – even though, in reality, the potential benefit outweighs the cost. For instance, if I gave you a chance to win $150 or lose $100 with equal probability, you would most likely choose to pass on the opportunity. But why?

This has to do with the link between negativity bias and loss aversion. This cognitive bias outlines how the pain of losing something is twice as powerful as the joy of winning or gaining something.

Negativity bias makes us:

- Pay more attention to negative events
- Seek lessons in negative experiences and outcomes
- Make a decision based on negative data rather than positive information

"Bad things" grab our attention more and stick to our memories for a long time. And in many cases, they influence our perceptions of the world and our decisions.

Psychological research shows that negativity bias drives motivation to complete tasks. You are less motivated to complete a task when the incentive is framed as something you gain than when it's framed to help you avoid losing something. For example, your job.

This affects how motivated we are to pursue our goals. Rather than think about what you'll gain if you work toward something, you're likely to focus on what you might have to give up to achieve that same goal. Plus, research shows that we're more likely to accept negative news as truthful.

This human tendency to focus more on bad things and dismiss or overlook good things is understandable from an evolutionary point of view. In earlier times, paying attention to threats and dangerous things was the thin line between life and death.

Our ancestors, who were more attuned to danger, had higher chances of survival than others. This is because constant awareness of threats and danger was necessary to stay alive. But even though we no longer face the same threats or dangers as our early ancestors, our brain still pays extra attention to "danger" to keep us safe.

Today, we no longer need to be on constant alert to survive, but that bias toward the negative still plays a vital role in the functioning of our brains. Research has shown that bias can have a range of effects on how we think, feel, and respond to stimuli.

Your relationships are some of the areas of your life where you might feel the impact of negativity bias. It can prompt you to always expect the worst from people, especially in intimate relationships where you've known the other person for a long time.

For example, I used to anticipate negative reactions whenever I had something to discuss with my partner. This made me approach our conversations defensively, leading to arguments and resentment.

Regarding your interpersonal relationships (family, friends, lovers, coworkers, etc.), it helps to remember that negative comments hold more weight than positive ones. It also helps if you're aware of your tendency to preoccupy yourself with the negative.

Negativity bias also affects your decision-making process. Kahneman and Tversky, two Nobel-winning researchers, found that humans tend to place greater weight on the negative aspect of an experience than the positive, especially when making a decision. Also, when forming an impression of other people, you're likely to fixate on negative data.

The good thing is negative biases are no different than ANTs and rumination. You can overcome all three by reframing how you think. So, how do you do that?

HOW TO REFRAME NEGATIVE THOUGHTS IN NINE STEPS

You can reframe negative thinking patterns in nine steps. Over time, you'll find that your mind has switched to a more rational way of thinking.

- Stop the cycle
- Breathe
- Recognize that you are not your thoughts
- Distract the mind
- Interrupt the cycle with self-care
- Challenge the thought
- Know your triggers
- Journal
- Practice gratitude

Now, let's take a deeper look at each step.

1. Stop the cycle

If you find yourself stuck in a loop of negative thoughts, pay attention to when the thoughts sneak into your mind and stop them. Awareness is a vital first step for stopping a negative thought on its track and then challenging it. So, pause for a moment and observe what you're thinking – you'll find it isn't right. Then, isolate that thought and focus on it. This is called metacognition. You realize, "Hey, this thinking isn't quite accurate." Remember to breathe and relax in your body. ANT can make you disassociate from your body.

2. Breathe

Once you're aware of your dysfunctional thought and isolated it, separate it from who you are. Empowering yourself to challenge negative thoughts by taking small, brave actions would be best. In this second step, that action is to slow down your breath by inhaling more deeply. The goal is to interrupt your sympathetic nervous system, which is in charge of your body's "fight or flight" response.

Deep breathing activates the parasympathetic nervous system, inducing a sense of calm and relaxation. So, inhale deeply and exhale slowly to release the tension in your body. Pay attention to the sound of your breath. Visualize it flowing into your body and lighting up your cells.

3. Recognize that you aren't your thoughts

Remember that thoughts are not facts. You are a separate entity from your thoughts. Rather than succumb to the negative thinking pattern, use the sense of discomfort to remind yourself of your true strengths.

When you practice deep breathing, you'll become painfully aware of the internal chatter, the noise, labeling, and narrating by that voice in your head. I learned to be a passive observer of my thoughts, and you can do the same. It helped me become more aware that I am not my thoughts.

But you'll also realize that you aren't your thoughts. So the next time you feel overwhelmed by negative thoughts, remember that you're capable of streamlining the process because you're in charge. The moment you do that can be very powerful.

4. Distract the mind

The intensity of automatic negative thoughts can be quite frightening. The frustrating thing is these thoughts are on auto-pilot, so you aren't consciously aware of them. By focusing on problem-solving, you can distract your mind from the buzz and chatter of negative thoughts.

Don't believe your thoughts. You may be depressed, but you are also a problem solver. Remember that you can break the cycle by finding a healthy distraction to keep your mind occupied.

5. Interrupt the cycle with self-care

Automatic negative thoughts put the body in a constant state of stress and hypervigilance. And depression can make all sorts of unreasonable demands from the body. When you fixate on a negative experience, seize that opportunity to do something engaging and enjoyable.

Respond to that by breathing. Find something that can make you feel good; do something nice for yourself. Practice self-care and self-compassion regularly.

6. Challenge your thoughts

"Where is the evidence?"

This is an important question you must pose to your mind when an automatic negative thought pops up. There is power in questioning your thoughts. ANTs trigger powerful emotions, but that doesn't make them true or logical. Interrupt your thought to assess if it's factual to stop the cycle of rumination.

Suppose a thought such as, "I am going to fail," arises in your head. Instead of letting that thought go on unchallenged, interrupt it with a "huh?" Then, look within to see if any evidence supports the negative statement.

If you look into that thought, you'll probably find no substance.

7. Know your triggers

Work on identifying your triggers so you can know when a negative thought is about to arise. It prepares you to challenge and question the thought. Perhaps you're alone or with someone. What time is it? Did something happen in particular that you can point to? Or is there an event preceding an influx of negative thoughts in your daily life?

That leads to the next point.

8. Journal

Journaling is an excellent way to track your negative thoughts' triggers. Keeping a journal is straightforward. Make it simple and go straight to the point. Be as detailed as possible when you write down the things that trigger you.

9. Practice Gratitude

Create a list of things you're genuinely grateful for, particularly activities you enjoy. You don't have to make it complicated – even the simplest things matter. Your gratitude journal can uplift your mood when you feel low and depressed. Be sure to include a ton of uplifting activities and memories.

Exercise for Challenging Negative Thoughts

Below is a list of questions to challenge intrusive and unhelpful thoughts. Use this list alongside your *"Thought journal."*

- *Are there facts to support this thought? Is there contradictory evidence to refute it?*
- *If this thought were true, what would be the worst possible outcome?*
- *Am I generalizing based on a past event?*
- *Can I view this from a positive perspective?*
- *How can I deal with this scenario effectively?*
- *Am I ready to accept aspects of this event or situation?*
- *Is this still within my control?*
- *Are my thoughts aggravating the situation?*
- *Besides myself, who or what else might affect my reaction to this situation?*

You can also come up with some questions on your own.

As mentioned earlier, stress is the primary source of many people's anxiety, depression, and other mental health problems. Unfortunately, you might have grown up believing that stress is something you should just put up with as a part of everyday life. But the consequences of accepting that can wreak havoc on your physical and mental health.

Before you begin to address your problems with CBT techniques, you must learn healthy ways to cope with stress. And that's precisely what I'll be discussing in the next chapter.

Stay with me!

Chapter Three Highlights

- Negative thoughts are automatic and intrusive. They are based on the beliefs you have about yourself, the people around you, and the world at large. Allowing negative thoughts to run in your head unopposed can destabilize your feelings and behavior. Therefore, it's important to constantly challenge negative thought patterns.

- Anxiety and depression are characterized by rumination – a habit of repeating negative thought patterns endlessly. This can cause distress and consume your emotional and mental energy. However, you can stop rumination by making a conscious decision not to engage with negative thoughts.

- Negativity bias wires you to commit negative experiences to memory far more often than positive ones. Breaking this bias can change your attitude toward your positive or negative experiences. It also teaches you to react to them in healthier ways.

- A vital part of the CBT program is learning to reframe negative thoughts into more rational and positive ones. Your thoughts are just thoughts – they are neither factual nor accurate. It's OK to challenge and question them instead of just accepting them.

- Journaling can help you track negative thoughts and monitor how they trigger unpleasant feelings. In addition, it can make it easier to challenge or support these thoughts based on available evidence. Essentially, this is how you rewire the brain.

4

GETTING A GRIP ON STRESS

Stress may not technically be a disease, but it can impact your physical and mental health in ways you could never imagine. And it may shock you to know just how prevalent stress is in America and around the world. Unfortunately, despite how hard we try, stress remains part of life, something we can only learn to tolerate.

Stress is a response – your body's way of physically, emotionally, and mentally reacting to stressors. Often, stress is triggered in response to change – a new job, a big move, a divorce, a wedding, etc. But the source of stress may also be a person's environment, such as a toxic workplace or a relationship conflict.

When a perceived threat confronts the brain, the body releases cortisol (the stress hormone), epinephrine, and norepinephrine, increasing stress levels. This also increases blood pressure, tense muscles, and alertness. You may know this as the "fight or flight" response. However, in many cases, the source of stress isn't a physical aggressor, which can cause headaches, lack of sleep, increased muscle tension, and several other symptoms.

I had no idea how common stress was until I discovered many stats that blew my mind. There's barely anyone who can completely escape stress. We all deal with stress in our way.

Short bursts of this response can help us boost productivity or improve focus. For example, stress enables you to get that due assignment done right before the deadline. It makes you think, "I work better under pressure."

In contrast, chronic stress contributes to health problems such as high blood pressure, anxiety disorders, depression, heart disease, and gastrointestinal disorders.

So, how common is stress in the United States?

- 49% of U.S. adults report that stress negatively impacts their behavior.
- 80% of American employees report feeling stressed on the job.
- Over 75% of Americans reported headaches, fatigue, sleep disturbances, and other stress symptoms.
- 63% of American adults are stressed about the economy. Yet, ironically, workplace stress robs the economy of over $300 billion annually – which doesn't help the economy.

It's tempting to believe that stress is only an annoyance that visits and leaves with some events. But the reality is that short-term and long-term stress can have an immediate and prolonged impact on a person's overall well-being. So stress should not be dismissed, and you're about to learn why.

WHY STRESS SHOULD NOT BE DISMISSED

The effect of stress on your health and well-being cannot be overstated. A 2013 study published in The Journal of the American Medical Association (JAMA) suggests that 60-80% of primary care hospital visits are linked to stress. Every condition and symptom can be worsened by stress in the body. And if you want to know what part of the body stress is experienced, the answer is straightforward: every part. You'll agree that this doesn't seem like something anyone should want to dismiss.

Your nervous system is connected to every tissue in your body. Thus, when the stress side of your nervous system becomes overactive, it affects every part of your body. If there is already a disorder going on in a specific organ system, it could be aggravated by the stress response,

Unfortunately, that makes the list of diseases and conditions that can be worsened by stress as long as the complete list of diagnoses – thousands of medical conditions. Common conditions can be present at all times, whereas other conditions happen, depending on the time of year.

For example, gastrointestinal disorders can be diagnosed all year round. Meanwhile, respiratory illnesses become prevalent in the winter because stress impairs the immune system.

Stress naturally occurs when we cannot cope with specific events or demands. Often, these demands come from relationships, work, financial troubles, and other situations. But it's caused by anything that poses a real or perceived threat to your well-being. Ultimately, stress is a natural response that is integral to survival.

The fight-or-flight response is your body's way of telling you that something needs attention or action as soon as possible. It tells you when and how to respond to danger. So, being in tune with that part of you is crucial.

But it becomes too easy to trigger when the body remains in fight-or-flight mode for a long time. This also happens when there are too many external stressors at a time. The result is that your mental and physical health becomes vulnerable to attacks.

You should be familiar with the two types of stress below:

- **Acute stress:** is the type of stress we all experience. It is short-term, and it goes away as quickly as it comes. That is the stress you feel when you find yourself in traffic on your way to work or when you have an argument with your spouse. Acute stress exists to help us cope with dangerous situations. We also experience it when we do something exciting. But, again, everyone experiences acute stress at one time or another.
- **Chronic stress:** is long-term stress that negatively affects the body. Any stress that remains for weeks or months is considered chronic stress. For example, you

may struggle with chronic stress if you have financial troubles, an unhappy relationship, or work troubles. It's easy to become used to chronic stress to the point where you don't even know it's a problem. And that's how it always eventually leads to health complications.

One thing about stress is that it manifests differently in everyone. We all react differently to stressors. Personally, simply thinking about a stressor can trigger stress. However, something that is a source of stress for you may not affect another person in that same way, and nearly any event can act as a stressor.

Science does not yet have a reason why the same stressor may induce different degrees of stress in two people. However, it's been established that anxiety, depression, and other mental health conditions can make some people more susceptible to stress responses than others.

Past experiences may influence how you react to triggers. Common events that can serve as stressors include:

- Employment issues
- Lack of money or time
- Illness
- Moving to a new home
- Unhappy relationship or marriage
- Divorce
- Grief or bereavement
- Family problems

Other commonly reported stressors are:

- Pregnancy or becoming a first-time parent
- Pregnancy loss
- Fear of accidents
- Fear of crime
- Problematic neighbors
- Excessive noise and overcrowding
- Uncertainty about the future or outcome of an important event

One may experience ongoing stress in response to a traumatic event, such as abuse or an accident.

When the body triggers a stress response, it slows down bodily functions, including the ones performed by the digestive and immune systems. This happens so that the body can focus on alertness, breathing, and blood flow and also prepare (tense) the muscles for emergency use.

Some of the changes that occur in your body during a stress response include:

- Pulse and blood pressure rise
- Increased breathing
- Decrease in immune activity
- Delayed digestive function
- Decrease in sleepiness due to hyperalertness

Your reaction to a difficult or uncomfortable situation determines the impact of stress on your overall health. Some people don't have a severe stress response even when exposed to multiple stressors simultaneously, whereas others react strongly to a single stressor.

A person who feels like they don't have the resources to cope effectively with stress will most likely react strongly to stressors, potentially causing health problems. Stressors affect everyone differently.

Some generally acknowledged positive experiences can cause stress, such as traveling, getting a promotion, getting married, having a baby, or moving to a bigger, better home.

This is because these positive events are rooted in significant change. They involve new responsibilities, extra effort, and adapting to new environments. They also require you to step into new territories. As you probably know, the unknown can be terrifying.

While you're looking forward to your promotion at work, you may be excessively worried about your ability to handle the new responsibilities that come with the promotion. So, a situation does not have to be negative to harm your health and mood.

It's not helpful to dismiss stress because it can adversely affect your overall health and well-being. Stress can make life's usual hassles more challenging to manage. You realize the importance of your mind-body connection when you examine how stress impacts your life.

When the brain (mind) experiences significant stress levels, the body responds accordingly. Feeling stressed over money, interpersonal relationships, or your living condition can create literal health problems. The inverse of this is also true. Dealing with health problems like diabetes or high blood pressure can skyrocket your stress levels.

Here are examples of stress-influenced conditions:

- Diabetes
- Heart disease
- Obesity
- Ulcers
- Sexual dysfunction
- Hyperthyroidism
- Alopecia (hair loss)
- Tooth and gum disease

CHECK YOUR STRESS SYMPTOMS

The body's reaction to a stressor is to release hormones. And as I noted earlier, these hormones make your muscles tense, increase your breathing, and make you more alert, which causes different physical, emotional, and behavioral symptoms within. The scary part is that you may not even realize that these symptoms are affecting your health.

Perhaps you think that your nagging headache or lack of focus, or decreased productivity at work is being caused by your illness. In reality, stress may be the actual true cause. But you will only know that if you're familiar with the different symptoms of stress.

Stress symptoms affect your thoughts, feelings, and behaviors, and if left unchecked, it can result in many of the health problems I outlined previously. Learning to recognize common symptoms is the first step toward managing them.

Physical symptoms of stress include:

- Headaches
- Sweating
- Back or chest pain
- Muscle cramps or spasms
- Stomach upset
- Weight loss or gain
- Constipation or diarrhea
- Aches and pains in different parts of the body
- A decline in sex drive
- Sleep problems

Emotional symptoms of stress include:

- Anxiety
- Lack of focus
- Irritability
- Anger
- Restlessness
- Sadness or depression
- Feeling overwhelmed
- Forgetfulness
- Burnout
- Fatigue

- Feeling insecure

Behavioral symptoms of stress include:

- Food cravings (undereating or overeating)
- Angry outbursts
- Social withdrawal
- Tobacco misuse
- Alcohol and drug misuse
- Frequent crying or whining
- Reduced exercise
- More relationship conflicts

You can watch out for these signs to know when you're dealing with prolonged stress. If you notice these symptoms, taking steps for effective stress management is essential. There are various stress management strategies that you can use, and I'll be discussing a few of them.

DIAPHRAGMATIC BREATHING

The diaphragm is a muscle at the base of your lungs, regarded as the most efficient organ for breathing. There is breathing, and then there is diaphragmatic breathing. As you can probably tell, the two are worlds apart.

Diaphragmatic breathing involves utilizing the diaphragm more accurately when you breathe. These benefits reduce blood pressure and heart rate and promote relaxation. In addition, it manages the physical symptoms of stress, which also improves your emotional and behavioral symptoms.

This breathing technique:

- Strengthens the diaphragm
- Slows your breathing to make it more impactful on the body
- Decreases oxygen demand
- Utilizes less energy and effort to breathe

Our normal breathing doesn't utilize our lungs to their full capacity. But you can achieve this with diaphragmatic breathing and ultimately increase lung efficiency. Diaphragmatic breathing requires you to take deep breaths with your diaphragm consciously.

You may or may not already be familiar with diaphragmatic breathing through other names such as abdominal breathing, belly breathing, etc.

This breathing technique offers many benefits, including:

- Inducing relaxation
- Improving muscle function during a workout
- Increasing oxygen presence in the blood
- Improving the ease of passing gas waste from the lungs
- Reducing heart rate
- Reducing blood pressure

Diaphragmatic breathing can help you manage any condition that affects your breathing, such as stress, anxiety, asthma, COPD, etc. You can combine the technique with any treatments recommended by your doctor or healthcare provider.

There are two ways to do the diaphragmatic breathing technique: lying down and sitting. Let's look at these individually.

Here are four steps to try diaphragmatic breathing (lying down):

1. Lie flat on your back in bed or on a flat surface, with your knees bent and your head supported with a pillow. You can place a pillow beneath your knees to support your legs.
2. Put one hand on your chest and the other under your rib cage. That will allow you to feel the movement of your diaphragm as you breathe in and out.
3. Take a deep breath slowly through your nose. You should feel your stomach move out and the hand on your chest rise. Ensure your hand remains still on your upper chest.
4. Tighten the muscles in your stomach to push your belly back in, ensuring your hand lowers as you breathe out through pursed lips. Your hand should remain firmly on your chest.

You might want to practice the "lying down" technique a few times before you try it while sitting down.

To perform diaphragmatic breathing while sitting, follow these instructions.

1. Sit in a chair that makes you feel as comfortable as possible, with your knees bent. Relax your shoulders, neck, and head.
2. Place one hand on your chest and just under your rib cage to feel the diaphragm's movement as you inhale and exhale.
3. Take a deep breath slowly through your nose. Ensure the hand on your chest stays firmly in the same place. You should feel your stomach move out and your hands rise.
4. Tighten the muscles in your stomach to push your belly back in as you breathe out through pursed lips. Your hand should remain as still as possible on your chest.

Diaphragmatic breathing becomes easier the more you practice. At first, it will take a lot of effort, and you'll get tired easily. But it will become automatic if you keep at it. You can start with 5-10 minutes of practice about three or four times daily. Gradually increase your practice time and make it harder by placing a book on your stomach if you're up to it.

Stress breathing is another technique you can use to relieve stress or anxiety. It can help induce instant relaxation in any distressing or uncomfortable situation. It's also a great way to heat your body. With this strategy, you can pull in and store energy in your body on demand.

Here is the stress breath exercise in four steps:

1. Breathe in slowly and deeply and make it audible. You should feel the sound vibrating at the back of your throat.
2. Hold your breath and slowly bring your chin toward your chest. Now, count back from five.
3. Breathe out (audibly through the nose) as you slowly raise your head back up.
4. That's one complete cycle. Now, repeat steps 1 to 2 twelve times in a row.

Practice the stress breath daily during the day and at nighttime.

PROGRESSIVE MUSCLE RELAXATION (PMR)

The benefits of PMR are endless. PMR helps release tension buildup in the muscles and body. In turn, helping you manage stress and anxiety, all while relieving you from insomnia and reducing chronic pain symptoms.

This relaxation technique involves the simple exercise of tightening your muscle groups one at a time and then relaxing them to release the knots and tension in those muscles. Healthcare providers typically combine progressive muscle relaxation with standard treatments to relieve symptoms for conditions such as headaches, high blood pressure, digestive problems, and cancer pain.

I learned to use PMR to relieve acute stress instantly, so it doesn't build up and become chronic stress - you can too. My favorite thing about this technique is that you only need 10 to 20 minutes of daily practice to check your stress levels.

The best way to practice PMR is to tense and relax one muscle group at a time in a linear order, beginning with the lower part of your body and moving up to the abdomen, chest, and face. Like diaphragmatic breathing, you can do this seated or lying down. Ensure you wear comfortable clothing and practice quietly with no distractions.

Here's how to perform progressive muscle relaxation:

1. Take a few deep breaths to relax your body and prepare your muscles.
2. While breathing in, tighten the first muscle group (perhaps your feet) as much as possible. Wait for ten seconds, then exhale and suddenly relax that muscle group.
3. Stay in relaxation mode for 10-20 seconds before moving on to the next muscle group (for example, your legs).
4. When you release the tension in your muscles, focus on the changes within the affected muscle group. You could visualize the tension flowing out of your body as you do each group.
5. Work your way up until you've contracted and relaxed all muscle groups in your body.

As a beginner in progressive muscle relaxation, I found the following tips helpful.

- Set aside 15-20 minutes to practice every day. Choose a quiet, comfortable part of your home.
- Switch off all your gadgets to avoid being distracted during the exercise.
- Do not hold your breath, as that will only cause unneeded tension.
- Inhale deeply when you tighten your muscles and exhale deeply when you release them.
- Follow any sequence that works best for you. For example, you can start at the head and move down the body if you find that more effective.
- Practice this exercise even when you're calm and relaxed. That will make it easier to master stressful or difficult times.
- Finally, wear loose clothing to ensure you're as comfortable as possible.

In the beginning, listening to PMR recordings during the exercise is helpful. That way, you can follow instructions without thinking about them constantly. But, of course, that also helps you avoid distractions.

Research has shown that PMR has many benefits, including stress and anxiety relief. The best thing is you can practice in the comfort of your home or even in your car. So be sure to practice regularly. Over time, you'll feel more relaxed and calmer physically and mentally.

GUIDED MEDITATION FOR STRESS

If stress is affecting your behavior and health, then consider trying meditation, which science has proven to relieve stress. When I first began studying meditation, I was surprised to learn that as little as 10 minutes of daily practice can help improve my health and well-being.

My teacher then explained to me that the most important thing is the frequency of meditation, not the length. So, it's more helpful to meditate daily for ten minutes than for an hour weekly.

I integrated that into my routine and later became extremely good at meditating. Now, it's just like any other thing I do automatically every day. And I have also been teaching others how to integrate meditation into their everyday life successfully.

Meditation is popular as a treatment for stress and other mental health challenges. It allows you to enter a deep state of relaxation while becoming more aware of your thoughts and surroundings. You can alleviate chronic stress by meditating for just eight weeks, which science has proven.

The best thing about meditation is that it isn't just a treatment for mental health problems but also a way to bring out your best qualities. That's why you shouldn't just apply the exercise for occasional stress or anxiety relief but also make it a part of your lifetime self-care routine. It will help you become a healthy, compassionate person capable of forming deep, meaningful connections.

Guided meditation will help:

- Make your mind more focused and stable
- Increase your experience of positive emotions
- Increase your ability to open up yourself and connect with others
- Help you let go of regrets about the past and worries about the future and immerse yourself in the present moment

You can practice meditation at any time of the day, but I have found that the best time is when you wake up or right before you go to bed. Meditating right before bedtime helps me sleep more deeply and soundly.

Meditating isn't to eliminate stress – you can't do that – it's to manage it. Meditation teaches you to observe your mental patterns, isolate them, and be less physically and emotionally affected by them. It helps you change your perception of stress and, by effect, your reaction to it.

Stress creates negative stories in the mind. If you allow yourself to get caught up in those stories, you'll keep yourself in the cycle, ensuring that you feel that way for far longer than necessary.

Meditating creates curiosity about your thoughts and feelings, as though you're examining stress from a new perspective. In other words, you deliberately reframe your experience of stress and how you react to it.

Your perception of stress can either aggravate or minimize your physical and emotional responses. With meditation, you learn to step back and observe how your mind fuels stress-inducing thoughts and narratives.

So how do you meditate?

Generally, meditation requires calming your mind and body, quieting your senses, and turning inward to get in touch with who you are beneath the negative thoughts and feelings, and worries of daily life. You can make meditation sessions as short as 10 minutes, but here are the steps involved.

1. **Posture**: Your posture is extremely vital to meditation. Sit upright in a cross-legged pose on the floor or in a chair with your feet flat on the floor. You can place your hands flat on your knees and purse your lips to open your mouth slightly.
2. **Breathe**: Practice the diaphragmatic breathing technique to stabilize your mind. Focus on the rise and fall of your belly or the air passing in and out of your nose.
3. **Motivation**: Find motivation for your meditative exercise. Your motivation may be to address a mental problem you're struggling with.
4. **Release your thoughts**: Meditation practice stresses the importance of letting your thoughts go. This means allowing your thoughts to float naturally without suppressing, ignoring, or paying attention to them. This is how you attune with the deeper part of yourself.

5. **Gratitude**: At the end of your meditation, think about the kindness you've experienced from the universe, family, friends, and strangers. End your session with gratitude.

Distractions come easily during a meditation exercise, especially for beginners. So, it's best to practice guided meditation. You can find guided meditation audios on YouTube, Headspace, and apps made specifically for meditation. And you can use the audio to create your version of guided meditation that applies to your situation.

TAKING A MORE MINDFUL APPROACH

Mindfulness is about grounding yourself in the present moment. It's about taking deep breaths and becoming aware of your thoughts and feelings. By doing this, you will learn more about your body's needs. Being mindful means sitting with an uncomfortable situation for a while instead of reacting to it immediately. This allows your mind and body to cultivate inner strength so that stressors no longer affect you strongly.

These practices will help you take a more mindful approach to daily living.

1. Mindful wakeup

Begin each day with a purpose. Set an intention to make your words, responses, and actions more mindful and compassionate every day. The first thing you should do in the morning is sit in your bed, close your eyes, and tune in to your physical sensations. Then, take three long, deep breaths – in through the nose and out through the mouth. Let your breathing fall into a rhythm as you focus on the rise and fall of your belly.

Ask yourself: "What is my purpose for today?" or "What do I need to feel more connected and fulfilled today?" Then, set your intention – for example, "I will be kind to myself; be generous with my words and actions; be patient with others; remain grounded in the moment," or anything else that matters to you.

Check in with yourself as you go through your day. Pause, breathe, and remember your intention. As you practice this each day, you'll notice a shift in the quality of your mood, communications, and relationships.

2. Mindful eating

Eating can be much more than that bland sensation of "bite, chew, and swallow." Most times, we eat without paying attention to the activity itself. You can make eating a richer and more pleasurable experience by engaging in it mindfully. When you eat, don't do anything else. Focus on the food and how it interacts with your sense of taste and smell. Be in touch with your hunger to avoid eating more than necessary.

3. Mindful walking

Walking can be more than what it is if you take a more mindful approach. Mindful walking means being aware of every step you take and your breathing as you walk. You can practice it anywhere, whether in nature, in the comfort of your home, or at work.

To walk mindfully, focus on the point in front of your feet. Begin by walking slower and more meaningfully than usual. Pay attention to the sensations in your feet as you touch the ground and lift it again. The goal is to pay attention to how you walk, so do just that. Then, shift your attention to whatever you're experiencing in the present moment. Do not engage with it; acknowledge it and let it go.

4. Mindful movement

This involves practicing Yoga techniques to reduce stress. Techniques like child's pose, forward bend, and legs up-the-wall can help with stress relief and gentle body stretching. The different poses can be practiced in the mornings and evenings for relaxation.

Additionally, it helps to quit multitasking – it affects your ability to do things mindfully. Other ways to promote a mindful approach include:

- Body scans
- Listening to relaxing music
- Play

The goal is to create a lifestyle of healthy habits that reduce stress and its effects. I advise starting only some of these strategies at a time, as it may cause stress. However, to make lasting change, starting with one strategy for 10-15 minutes daily is best to cultivate a habit. For example, try 10 minutes of guided meditation when you wake up and PMR before bed. Then, rotate the activities until you successfully integrate them into your daily life.

Of course, for many, chronic stress has taken a toll to the point where it has developed into anxiety and depression. So, in the next chapter, we will discuss how you can take control of anxiety and depression by learning more about triggers and emotional regulation.

Chapter Four Highlights

- Stress is a non-negotiable part of life. It is your body's response to change. But left unchecked, stress leads to anxiety, depression, and other mental health problems. You may not be able to get rid of stress, but you can control and learn to tolerate it.
- The stress response signals you to pay attention to something or take action about a situation as soon as possible. You have to be in tune with this response at all times. Otherwise, you risk getting stuck in fight-or-flight mode, leading to chronic stress or anxiety.
- Stress symptoms affect your thoughts, feelings, behavior, and body as a whole. Knowing your stress symptoms is part of staying in tune with the stress response. You can manage stress by learning to cope with the signs effectively.
- Diaphragmatic breathing is an excellent technique to manage your stress response and symptoms. It can help

with any condition connected to breathing, including stress, anxiety, COPD, asthma, etc. Practice the recommended breathing exercise for at least 10 minutes daily.

- Mindfulness can help you learn more about your body and its needs. It teaches you to stay in the moment and tune with your thoughts and feelings. Practice mindfulness daily to cultivate inner strength and break the power stressors have over you.

5

TAKING CONTROL OF ANXIETY AND DEPRESSION

Anxiety is one of the most common mental health conditions. It is connected with many disorders; surveys reveal that a third of people have experienced anxiety at some point in their lives.

I have also dealt with anxiety in the past. I know that it is a feeling of fear and distress. However, I did not know then that anxiety is the body's response to stress. You experience anxiety when your body struggles with chronic stress, danger, or a threat.

This response is normal for everyone. But anxiety becomes a disorder when it's present at all times or if it starts interfering with everyday functioning. If left unchecked, anxiety can lead to major depression. This chapter discusses the link between stress, anxiety, and depression.

Many people are unaware, but approximately 121 million people globally suffer from depression. This may seem like an insignificant number when you consider the global population. However, according to statistics, a yearly 850 000 deaths are linked to depression. As the world improves at discussing mental health disorders, we all must become more aware of the consequences to reduce this heartbreaking number.

Before I explain the link between anxiety and depression, let's first look at the difference and similarities between stress and anxiety.

STRESS VS. ANXIETY

Stress and anxiety are both normal responses, but they sometimes overwhelm us. Like stress, anxiety is a natural part of the body's "fight or flight" response – a way of reacting to perceived danger. As noted, this response's purpose is to ensure you're alert, focused, and prepared to deal with any perceived threat.

As I explained in the previous chapter, external factors primarily trigger stress. The trigger could be anything, from work to family or illness. Stress is typically short-term unless it becomes chronic. Once you resolve the source of your stress – like a work issue, for example – it naturally disappears.

On the other hand, anxiety is when the source of stress has been resolved, but the feelings of fear and unease persist. In other words, it is your body's response to stress. You may recognize the unease, distress, or dread you experience before significant events. That feeling is there to help you stay alert, focused, and aware.

The anxiety response can be helpful because it kicks in when you face a physical or emotional threat, real or perceived. However, for many people, it interferes with their daily life.

Stress and anxiety have many similar symptoms. When you're anxious, you might experience the following:

- Increased heart rate
- Faster breathing
- A feeling of dread or worry
- Sweating
- Nervousness
- Restlessness
- Tense muscles
- Diarrhea or constipation

Since stress and anxiety are part of the same response, which makes them have similar symptoms, it can be challenging to distinguish them from each other. As a result, you might be unable to tell when you're experiencing stress or anxiety.

Anxiety manifests differently in people and therefore has varying patterns. When present all the time, it is referred to as Generalized Anxiety, which is different from anxiety or panic attacks – described as intense bouts of anxiety, usually without an observable trigger. But some people also deal with phobias – where specific situations trigger their anxiety. For example, some people have a fear of heights.

I mentioned earlier that anxiety is common in many mental health disorders. It is a hallmark feature of Obsessive-Compulsive Disorder, Post Traumatic Stress Disorder, and other conditions. Individuals suffering from depression often deal with regular bouts of anxiety, and as you've learned, anxiety can cause depression.

It's difficult to pinpoint a specific cause of anxiety. However, many seem to lean towards it due to childhood upbringing and family history. Some research has also indicated that there might be a genetic element to how we experience anxiety.

For many, a life experience of an anxiety-triggering event may lead to the development of an anxiety disorder. Also, some report that a distressing event triggered their first anxiety episode, but then it was followed by other episodes to the point where the disorder appeared to sneak into their lives on its own.

Some common physical and mental symptoms of generalized anxiety include:

- Sleeping troubles
- Incessant worrying
- Feeling stressed and irritable
- Inability to focus, forgetting things
- Poor appetite
- Muscle pains
- Shaking
- Dizziness

Some common symptoms of anxiety attacks:

- Happen suddenly and come on intensely
- A feeling of losing control
- A crippling sense of fear or dread
- Sudden trigger of the physical symptoms highlighted earlier

You experience anxiety when exposed to the trigger event for phobias, but the feelings reduce at other times. Also, you feel compelled to avoid the anxiety-triggering situation.

There are risk factors for anxiety disorders, and they can vary. For example, women are the prominent demographic for generalized anxiety disorder and phobias. In contrast, men and women are equally affected by social anxiety.

But, in general, some risk factors for all types of anxiety disorders include:

- Specific personality traits include being shy when meeting new people or withdrawing in new situations.
- Traumatic experiences in early life or adulthood.
- A family history of mental health disorders such as anxiety.
- Certain physical health conditions, such as arrhythmia or thyroid problems.

UNDERSTANDING ANXIETY TRIGGERS

In the past, when I suffered from anxiety, I sometimes knew what set me off, and other times, I didn't. There were days when my panic seemed to appear out of nowhere. This particular problem made me struggle. How could I hope to manage my anxiety successfully if I couldn't identify the triggers? It's important to know what ticks your anxiety off. Being aware of this is necessary for effective anxiety management.

Science suggests that anxiety is caused by genetics and environmental factors. Many events, situations, and emotions we experience daily may trigger anxiety symptoms or amplify them. These are the things that we refer to as triggers.

Anxiety triggers vary from individual to individual, but people who suffer from anxiety disorders generally experience the same triggers. Most people have numerous triggers. But for some, anxiety can be set off without an obvious trigger.

For these reasons, you must unravel your anxiety triggers. Being able to identify them is the foundation for managing anxiety symptoms successfully.

One thing I learned was that my anxiety largely depended on the type of anxiety I suffered from and the stressors in my daily life. In some cases, knowing the type of anxiety you suffer is key to identifying your triggers.

And in other cases, it's vice versa: identifying your triggers is all you need to determine the type of anxiety you struggle with.

If, for instance, taking the bus makes you incredibly anxious, you may have a phobia or agoraphobia. However, if your anxiety is more of a persistent, low-level feeling of unease or worry, that may be a generalized anxiety disorder.

You might think that you have no anxiety triggers and that your anxiety comes out of nowhere – but this is rarely the case. Unfortunately, a lack of self-awareness usually drowns out the events or emotions that precede anxiety in many cases.

For example, you may be unaware of the connection between the caffeine you drank last night and the heart-racing, dreadful feeling you're experiencing today. That's right – caffeine triggers anxiety in many people.

If you struggle with anxiety, triggers may include life events, habits, and other stressors that seem out of control.

Tracking your anxiety is important if you want to be able to identify triggers. When you feel dread or panicky feelings sneaking up on you, note how you feel and write down what may have preceded that feeling. I started doing this when I learned how to use CBT to tackle my negative feelings. It helped me recognize patterns and think more critically about the elements driving my panic and worry.

On that note, let's talk about common anxiety triggers that I became aware of in my quest to unravel and take control of anxiety.

1. **Physical health issues:** Health issues can be difficult and upsetting. A diagnosis of a chronic illness such as

cancer may trigger or amplify anxiety symptoms. Health problems are powerful triggers because they evoke immediate and personal feelings.

2. **Medications:** Some over-the-counter and prescription medications may trigger anxiety in certain people due to their active ingredients. Many of these ingredients can cause unease or make you unwell, setting off a series of negative thoughts in your mind. But, of course, that only intensifies the symptoms of anxiety. Examples of medications that trigger anxiety are birth control pills, weight loss pills, and cough medications.

3. **Caffeine:** Many people are addicted to caffeine and don't know it. A 2022 review reveals that drinking five cups of coffee daily can increase anxiety and induce panic attacks in individuals with panic disorders. If you need that morning cup of joe to wake up, you might unknowingly trigger or worsen anxiety.

4. **Financial troubles:** Being in debt or worrying about money can make you anxious. Money fears are real, and they can trigger anxiety, too. Additionally, paying an unexpected bill can also induce anxiety in many people. You might need professional help from a financial advisor or a guide to coping with this particular anxiety trigger. A feeling of companionship in the financial process may help you handle the unease better.

5. **Social events:** Many don't find parties or rooms full of strangers fun. And for some, that can induce anxiety. This is referred to as social anxiety disorder. If social events that require interacting with people and making

small talk make you feel uneasy or unwell, you might be dealing with social anxiety disorder.

6. **Conflict:** Disagreements, arguments, and relationship problems are examples of conflicts that can trigger or worsen anxiety. If you find that arguments and disagreements particularly trigger you, learning effective conflict resolution strategies may be the solution to controlling your anxiety.

7. **Stress**: As you've learned, stress is the precursor to anxiety for most people. Everyday stressors such as getting stuck in traffic or missing an appointment can cause anxiety. Stress can make us skip meals, drink more coffee, or miss bedtime – and these factors can also trigger or compound anxiety. Chronic stress is also known to trigger long-term anxiety, worsen symptoms, and cause other health problems.

8. **Public speaking:** Having to speak at public events, partaking in a competition, talking in front of a superior, or even reading aloud in public can lead to anxiety. If your job requires public speaking or performances, you might struggle daily with anxiety.

9. **Negative thinking:** Unpleasant thoughts evoke unpleasant feelings, and that is especially true for anxiety. The thoughts in your head and the words you speak to yourself can trigger anxiety if they are negative. Likewise, language might influence your feelings if you tend to think negatively.

10. **Personal triggers:** These are anxiety triggers that are specific to you and your situation. They are more difficult to identify, but you can work with a trained

psychotherapist to figure them out. Personal triggers may begin with a location, a smell, a song, or even a taste. They consciously or unconsciously remind you of past traumatic events or bad memories.

Other anxiety triggers to watch out for include:

- Lack of sleep
- Substance or alcohol abuse
- Isolation
- Excessive screen time
- Fears and phobias
- Worrying about the future

Here is a detailed list of potential anxiety triggers. Rank them on a scale of 1-10 to determine how anxious these triggers make you feel.

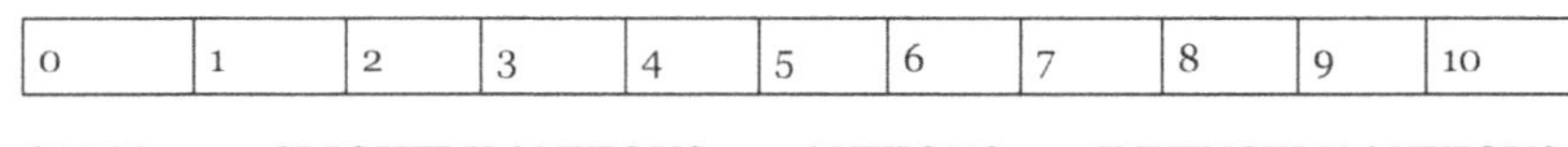

- Meeting new people
- Relationship conflict or drama
- Going to new places for the first time
- Speaking to a group of people
- Performing in front of many people
- Interacting online
- Unavoidable confrontation
- Texting people on social media

- Having to complete so many tasks
- Communicating with peers or adults
- Working in a team or group
- Having to change your routine
- Leaving your phone unattended for a long time
- Stress from grades or schoolwork
- Raised voices or loud noises
- Being by yourself for a long time
- Giving a presentation in front of your coworkers
- Disappointing friends or family members
- Pressure to behave in specific ways
- Interacting with a crush
- Having too many responsibilities
- Changes in your weight or appearance
- Not being able to pay your bills
- Uncertainty about the future
- Being in tight spaces
- Being in open, public spaces
- Being around some people
- Having to make an important decision

Think about other things that make you anxious and use the scale to rate your anxiety levels.

CBT STRATEGIES FOR ANXIETY

Any strategy that helps you cope with stress successfully can help with anxiety too. Remember the stress management techniques we discussed in the previous chapter? They are also effective for dealing with anxiety. You can also handle anxiety by challenging and reframing your negative thinking patterns using the steps highlighted in Chapter Three.

Other than these, there are specific CBT techniques to better manage your anxiety or anxiety disorder. Let's look at four important ones below.

Journaling for Anxiety

Keeping a journal may seem like something you do as a child or teenager, but there are physical and mental health benefits to journaling in adulthood. Writing is an excellent way to lay out the thoughts in your head. I find that it helps me reflect and fish out patterns in places that I ordinarily wouldn't.

If you're wondering, "Will journaling help me deal with my anxiety?" The answer is yes. The purpose of journaling is to reduce feelings of distress and anxiety and increase your well-being. Not only is it a straightforward technique, but it is also enjoyable. I would go as far as saying it is the CBT technique I find engaging the most.

There are different ways to journal and hardly any limitations on who can do it or benefit from it. You can make it a daily, weekly, or monthly task or do it on an as-needed basis when you feel overwhelmed with stress or anxiety. Choose the journaling method that you think would be most effective for you.

Anxiety left unchecked leads to rumination. But journaling can help you minimize this – it is a powerful technique for examining and reframing your thinking patterns from ruminative to focused and action-oriented.

Another thing journaling is excellent at is helping to monitor stress and anxiety symptoms. It is my favorite way to record my experiences and determine the proper steps toward improving my mental health and relieving anxiety.

Suppose you haven't been able to successfully narrow down the root cause of your anxiety or the feelings it evokes. In that case, keeping a journal is quite effective. It's a good way to identify patterns and possible stressors.

Also, understand that journaling feels different for everyone. We all experience anxiety differently, so it makes sense that we would also journal it differently. I usually stop at a few paragraphs when I journal, but it's okay if you want to write down pages and pages of your thoughts. Just let everything out as it comes.

So, here are the steps I follow:

1. **Write down your thoughts, feelings, and worries:** Start by writing for at least five minutes. Write down whatever you have on your mind, and continue until you feel like you have written enough without developing into rumination. Be as descriptive as possible when writing about specific events causing difficulties in the present. Remember that with anxiety, it's not always about what is presently happening that causes stress, but also worries about what could happen.

2. **Read and reflect:** Review what you have in front of you once you're done writing. Reflect on your thoughts and

feelings, and explore possible options. Could you do anything to change or improve your situation – or your thoughts about the situation? Could things improve for the best? For example, how likely will it happen if you have a particular worry? Can you be sure? If your worry turns out to be true, could you put a spin on it and make it more of a neutral or positive experience rather than a negative one? Is there a way to get a better outcome?

3. **Reframe your thinking:** For every fear or concern in your journal, write down at least one alternative to see it from a different perspective. Create a new narrative and a new set of possibilities. Then, write them down next to the fears and concerns you have. You could also examine cognitive errors to see how you can benefit from reframing anxiety-inducing thinking patterns.

4. **Create a plan:**It helps prepare you for the possibility of your fear getting realized. So if it did happen, what would be your first step? You don't need to have a complete plan; you can jot down steps that you would take and the resources you'd need. Creating a plan will minimize whatever fear you have about the unknown.

Ultimately, it always helps to choose one thing you could do right now to prepare your mind for the future. For instance, you could develop the necessary skills to help you deal with the challenge. Or you could continue to work on your stress and anxiety management skills to increase your emotional resilience.

Role-Playing

With role-playing, you learn new behaviors to help overcome your phobia. In therapy, this is one of the most effective treatments for phobia patients, who usually believe that the situation they fear is dangerous by default – even if it isn't. Unfortunately, this is not a strategy you can do on your own because it involves a patient and a therapist acting out difficult scenarios that the phobia patient fears.

Therapists believe that phobias are caused primarily by learned behaviors and environmental triggers. They believe that phobias are ultimately learned responses to stimuli. Role-playing helps to "unlearn" your response and substitute it with a more rational one, effectively curing the phobia.

In a role-playing session, your therapist assumes the role of that thing you fear, such as a boss or parent. You then interact with them, using behaviors previously learned in therapy. At the end of a role-playing session, there is always a debriefing in which you and your therapist discuss the interaction and find new ways to improve it. This technique will be particularly helpful if you struggle with social or interpersonal phobias.

Essentially, role-playing can help work through learned behaviors in potentially distressing situations. It can lessen your fear and help:

- Improve problem-solving skills
- Gain confidence and familiarity in specific situations
- Acquire better social skills

- Increase assertiveness
- Improve communication skills

Successive Approximation

This aims to help you learn how to tackle challenging goals. This is when you break down complicated or overwhelming tasks into smaller, more practical steps to make them easier to complete. One successive step builds on the previous step, and it helps to gain more confidence as you progress, bit by bit.

For example, suppose you're anxious about a meeting at work. In that case, you can begin by preparing – fire up your laptop, open up the report you need for the meeting, etc. Once you complete these seemingly small tasks, you can progress to other things.

Build upon each task with a bigger one. Each completed task will make you feel like you have a "win" before the big task itself.

Exposure Therapy

Like role-playing, exposure therapy is used specifically to treat phobias. It helps you to confront your fears and phobias. It involves being gradually exposed to your anxiety triggers while your therapist offers guidance on the best way to handle them. This should be done gradually in small increments. Eventually, you should feel more confident and less vulnerable in coping with the things that provoke anxiety.

Exposure therapy is based on the idea of making fear "extinct." When you force yourself to confront a specific fear for a sufficient period, your mind eventually adapts to the stimulus that triggers that fear until it stops evoking stress altogether.

Let's say you have a fear of something ridiculous, like shoes. Pretend you're deathly afraid of shoes to the point where you avoid them entirely and go everywhere barefoot.

Imagine your therapist locks you in a room with one pair of shoes, and there is no way out. At first, you'd be scared; terrified even – the situation would induce a strong anxiety response. But, after maybe 30 minutes, your mind will begin to adapt when nothing happens. You'll eventually get used to being around the pair of shoes, and it will stop inducing fear and anxiety.

How does that happen?

The human brain does not enjoy being under stress. And so, if no danger occurs by being around the thing that causes you to fear, your brain purposely reduces the stress by decreasing the feeling of anxiety it is experiencing by being around the stimulus.

That is how you can use exposure therapy to extinct anxiety by slowly introducing you to a feared stimulus until it no longer makes you afraid.

THE DEPTHS OF DEPRESSION

Depression is an intense sadness accompanied by other symptoms affecting how you think, feel, and behave. It can make you lose interest in activities that once brought you joy. If left unchecked, depression can cause various emotional and physical problems. It can even impair your functioning in your everyday routine, both at work and at home.

Since the brain is such a complex organ, we cannot simply say that depression results from chemical imbalances in the brain. But, sometimes, it is your brain's way of regulating moods, specifically if caused by chronic stress.

The symptoms of depression vary from mild to severe and are as follows:

- An intense or crippling sense of sadness
- Loss of pleasure or interest in favored activities
- Fluctuations in appetite and, by effect, weight
- Sleeping too much or not getting enough sleep
- Loss of energy and rise in fatigue
- Slowed movements and speech
- Feelings of guilt and worthlessness
- Inability to think, concentrate or make decisions
- Thinking about death or suicide

To be diagnosed with depression or major depressive disorder, these symptoms must last at least 14 days, and there must be an observable change in your usual level of functioning.

We often confuse depression with sadness or grief. Loss is a harrowing experience. It can be difficult to endure a loss – of a job, a relationship, or a loved one. In situations like this, it is normal to have feelings of sadness or grief in response. So, we might describe ourselves as being "depressed." But depression is much more than sadness, even though it involves intense sadness.

Anyone can suffer from depression – even those who appear to live a relatively ideal life. Genetics, personality, environmental factors, and biochemistry are typically significant factors that influence the severity of one's depression.

HOW TO START LIFTING YOUR DEPRESSION

First, I'd like you to know that stress and anxiety management techniques such as journaling and cognitive reframing are just as effective for depression. With that said, you can use the following CBT techniques to deal with depression.

- **ABC Analysis**

This method is similar to journaling. However, it focuses on helping you break down behaviors associated with depression, like withdrawing from people or sleeping all the time. The ABC model follows the structure below:

1. First, you analyze the "activating" event, i.e., the trigger.
2. Second, you analyze your "beliefs" about the event. In short, how does the trigger make you feel? And what do you think about it?
3. Third, you analyze the "consequences" of the trigger, including how you feel about it and your behaviors in response to it.

By analyzing triggers and consequences, you can explore possible outcomes and try to explore the underlying causes of your depressive events.

- **Fact-checking**

Fact-checking can help you recognize which behavioral responses are based on emotions or opinions rather than facts. This technique is similar to challenging negative thoughts. It encourages you to challenge your thoughts and understand that they are not rooted in facts. Rather, they are opinions based on your emotions because you're stuck in a harmful thinking pattern.

- **Behavioral experiments**

If your depression is caused by fear and anxiety, you can conduct behavioral experiments in which you imagine the worst possible outcome for a scenario. Then, let this scenario play out in your head to recognize that you can manage any outcome, even if your worst fears come to pass.

To test your behavioral responses to a thought, you can explore the possible outcomes that different thoughts can produce. For example, you can test the thought, "If I am kinder to myself, it will motivate me to work harder," versus "If I harshly criticize myself, it will motivate me to work harder."

Start using criticisms when you need to work harder on something and write down the results. Also, when practicing using kindness and self-compassion, track your results by writing them down. Next, compare the results to see which statement is more accurate.

Behavioral experiments can help test beliefs to determine how to become your best self.

- **Behavioral activation**

This has proved to be an effective treatment for depression. This is when you use certain behaviors to influence your emotional state. For example, losing interest in activities you once enjoyed can intensify depressive symptoms. Still, you can counter that with this technique.

You can activate a positive emotional state by deliberately engaging in specific behaviors – even if you don't feel up to it. So, engage in fulfilling and healthy activities that make you feel good even if you suffer from depression. That will make you more likely to keep participating in meaningful activities that boost your self-worth and self-confidence.

For example, suppose you like playing the keyboard. In that case, depression may cause you to struggle with motivation for playing. As a result, you may stop playing altogether, unknowingly reinforcing the feeling of hopelessness and depriving yourself of an activity that makes you feel good about yourself.

However, if you push yourself to play the keyboard for just five minutes daily, you prove to yourself that you still got it. That can improve your mood, keep you active, and remind you of the things that make you happy.

- **Writing self-statements to counter negative thoughts**

When you notice negative thoughts plaguing you, counteract them by writing down the opposite of that thought – specifically something positive. This method may be difficult if you're a CBT newbie, but it is also extremely effective. So, it's worth trying out, no matter what.

For example, if a negative thought like, "I am a failure," keeps popping into your head, write down something like, "I am a person with great potential," or "I have great prospects." Of course, it might be difficult to replace dysfunctional thoughts initially. Still, the more you practice, the easier it will be to create an association with those positive self-statements.

Journaling is challenging for everyone, so I have developed five prompts to help you start writing and expressing your thoughts and feelings. Choose one from below.

1. What is a situation that made me sad today?
2. What feeling is most dominant today? Which part of my body is it concentrated in? What emotion would I like to replace it with?
3. When I have the energy, what would I like to do?
4. If I could change something in my life right now, what would it be? How can I start working on making that change?
5. My inner critic needs to quiet down because …

Please see a professional immediately if you struggle with severe depression and suicidal thoughts.

As I have established, stress, anxiety, and depression all have physical symptoms. But when the body cannot cope with a perceived threat, these physical symptoms can become panic attacks. The next chapter will explore what it feels like to experience panic attacks and how you can cope.

Chapter Five Highlights

- Anxiety is the cumulative result of persistent, unresolved stress. Just as stress is the body's response to change, anxiety is the body's response to stress. It is a nagging feeling of fear and unease that arises to help you stay alert and focused before a significant event. Anxiety isn't inherently harmful, but your reaction to it can be.
- Anxiety triggers are different for everyone. Anything can be an anxiety trigger. Changing how you react to

anxiety begins by figuring out your triggers. Self-awareness is the foundation for tracking anxiety triggers.

- CBT techniques can help you manage anxiety by tracking and reframing negative thought patterns, which change how you react to them. You can also cope with anxiety better using the stress management techniques recommended in the previous chapter.
- Depression is often confused with sadness or grief, but they are different emotions. Depression can impair functioning and cause various physical and mental health problems. However, you may be able to fight depression by tackling chronic stress or anxiety.
- Journaling, cognitive reframing, and other CBT anxiety management techniques also work effectively for depression.

MAKE A DIFFERENCE WITH YOUR REVIEW

Unlock the Power of Generosity

"Altruism is the best source of happiness. There is no doubt about that."

— DALAI LAMA

Hey there, awesome reader! I've got something super important to ask you, and it's all about spreading kindness and making a big difference.

Have you ever thought about helping someone you've never met? Like, someone who's going through tough times, trying to figure things out, just like you might have been before. Well, guess what? You totally can!

Our big goal is to make sure everyone knows about the good stuff in "What The Heck Is CBT?" by R.J. Miller. This book is packed with helpful tips and tricks to make life easier and happier. But to reach as many people as possible, we need your help!

Here's the deal: lots of folks decide which book to read based on what other readers say about it. So, I'm asking you a super special favor on behalf of someone out there who really needs these CBT skills:

Could you please leave a review for this book?

It won't cost you a penny, and it'll only take a minute, but your review could change someone's life in a huge way. Your words could help:

...another kid understand their feelings better.
...a parent find new ways to help their family.
...a friend feel less alone in their struggles.
...someone find the courage to chase their dreams.
...a bunch of people feel happier and more confident.

Ready to get that awesome feeling of helping someone out? It's easy-peasy! Just leave a review by scanning this QR code:

If you love the idea of helping someone you've never met, you're totally our kind of person! Welcome to the club! We're super excited to have you on board.

And guess what? By leaving a review, you're not just helping others – you're also making your own journey through the book even more amazing. You'll love the good stuff coming up in the next chapters!

A big, big thank you from the bottom of my heart. Now, let's get back to our awesome adventure in the book.

- Your biggest fan, R.J. Miller

P.S. - Did you know? When you do something nice for someone, they remember it and think you're even cooler! If you think this book could help someone you know, why not share it with them? Spread the love and make someone's day!

6

HOW TO COPE WITH PANIC ATTACKS

"A panic attack goes from 0 to 100 in an instant. It's halfway between feeling like you'll faint and feeling like you'll die"

— UNKNOWN

Have you ever experienced an episode of intense anxiety that lasted quite briefly but had you feeling like your world was ending or your chest was closing in on itself? If yes, you're familiar with panic attacks. However, even if you've never experienced one personally, you have probably watched a TV or movie character go through that brief episode.

A panic attack is a sudden and brief episode of intense fear and anxiety that triggers strong physical sensations and reactions without an external cause or real danger. It is the same as anxiety but crippling on an entirely new level. Physical signs of a panic attack may include increased heart rate, shortness of breath, trembling, dizziness, and muscle tension.

Panic attacks are often unexpected and usually unrelated to a visible external threat. They occur quite frequently and can last up to half an hour. However, the effects of a panic attack last for a few hours. And for someone who experiences them regularly, the effects can last a lifetime.

Many people have experienced one or two attacks in their lifetime, which tend to go away, usually when the source of stress ends. According to available data, approximately 35% of the American population experience panic attacks at one point in their lives. That is how common they are. Panic attacks are also referred to as anxiety attacks.

I have never had an anxiety attack, but I have witnessed a few episodes of friends who struggle with them. The experience can be frightening. When a panic attack happens, a victim might think that they're having a heart attack or dying, feeling that they are losing control. However, for many, the crippling feelings of panic only arise during periods of stress or illness.

If you experience recurring episodes of anxiety attacks, that means you have a panic disorder – which, as you've learned, is a type of anxiety disorder. People with panic disorders generally have unexpected and recurring anxiety attacks and a never-ending fear of repeated episodes.

But panic attacks aren't always caused by anxiety. Some symptoms of panic attacks are associated with some medical conditions. Certain medications and drugs, including caffeine, alcohol, and tranquilizers, also induce symptoms of panic attacks.

A panic disorder isn't life-threatening, but it can significantly affect a person's quality of life. Unless you learn to control them or seek treatment, prolonged panic attacks can severely destabilize your life. You may even be forced to avoid going outside or being alone for fear of having an attack.

Symptoms of Panic attacks

A panic attack typically happens without warning. It can attack at any time – when you're in the middle of a presentation, driving home, at the mall, or even sound asleep while having a beautiful dream.

Panic attacks vary, but the symptoms peak within minutes. A panic attack's aftermath may leave you tired and worn out.

When an anxiety attack begins, you may experience some of these symptoms or reactions:

- Fear of loss of control
- Fear of death
- Tightness in the throat
- Shortness of breath
- Rapid heartbeats
- Trembling
- Headache
- Chest pain
- Nausea

- Numbness
- Cold or chills
- A feeling of detachment from reality

Perhaps the worst thing about having a panic attack is the crippling fear of a repeated attack. I mentioned earlier that a panic attack is the same as anxiety and can be triggered during periods of stress. Does that mean it has a connection to the body's fight-or-flight-or-freeze response? You are about to find out.

GETTING ACQUAINTED WITH THE FIGHT, FLIGHT, OR FREEZE RESPONSE

I explained a few chapters back that the fight-flight-freeze response is how your body naturally reacts to danger, which may or may not be real. It is a stress response to prepare you for perceived threats, such as a lurking shadow in the dark streets of your neighborhood or a growling dog.

When the body is threatened or faced with possible danger, the brain instructs the automatic nervous system to activate the 'fight-flight-freeze' response. The activation floods the body with various chemicals, i.e., neurotransmitters, triggering physiological changes.

However, you don't necessarily have to be in real danger for your body to activate this response. This means the response can activate in situations where it isn't needed. This is what triggers panic attacks.

An anxiety attack occurs when this stress response is activated with no real threat or danger in sight. Your body can enter the fight-or-flight mode and induce panic attack symptoms in the most stress-free situations, such as sleeping or watching TV.

People also react to perceived danger differently, which is how the name "fight, flight, or freeze" originated.

The stress response is involuntary and includes some physiological changes that prepare you to:

- Fight – take action to get rid of the threat
- Flight – flee away from the threat
- Freeze – become immobile in the face of the threat

Some include a fourth reaction, "fawn," which involves trying to please the individual representative of the threat to stop them from harming you. We also have a fifth potential reaction: tonic immobility. Some refer to this as a "flop." It is when you become entirely unresponsive, both physically and mentally. For instance, fainting in response to a perceived threat is a "flop" response.

Together, scientists refer to fight-flight-freeze as the acute stress response.

One by one, let's discuss what happens when your body is in fight, flight or freeze mode.

What happens in "fight or flight" mode?

The autonomic nervous system (ANS) is the part of your nervous system in charge of rapid, unconscious responses, including reflexes. For example, when you're faced with a threat, the brain contacts the ANS, which sends the body messages to prepare for danger in a specific way.

If you experience the "fight or flight" response, your body will instantly experience physiological changes such as:

- **Increased heart rate and rapid breathing:** This happens so your body can send more oxygenated blood to your brain and muscles in case you need to escape danger physically. It also triggers a rise in blood pressure.
- **Flushing:** As your body sends blood to vital areas, your skin may become flushed or paler than usual or alternate between flushed and pale.
- **Dry mouth:** The blood vessels around your mouth constrict, causing the salivary glands to halt saliva production, leading to a dry mouth temporarily.
- **Dilated pupils:** Your pupils dilate to make more room for light to enter the eyes. This allows you to see better so that you can observe your environment.
- **Tense muscles:** As your muscles prepare for physical action, they tense up, which can cause trembling or shaking. Tense muscles may also trigger a constriction in the throat, leading to a higher-pitched voice.

In the "fight or flight" state, you may feel severely agitated, alert, or argumentative. Or you may feel like leaving wherever you are. A "fight or flight" response that is more intense than usual can become a panic attack. It can also induce an asthma attack in someone with the condition.

What happens in 'freeze' mode?

The 'freeze' response's physiological process differs from fight or flight. Scientists describe it as a state of "attentive immobility." While you're "frozen," you remain extremely alert but cannot take physical action against the perceived threat.

If you experience the 'freeze' response, you may develop the following:

- Physical immobility
- Muscle tension
- A rapid decline in heart rate

While freezing seems like a counterintuitive response to danger, it has its purpose. First, it prepares you for action. Scientists have observed that it allows animals to scan the environment to decide their next step. When you freeze, your brain uses that time to contemplate the best way to respond to the danger.

Also, freezing enables you to perceive your surroundings better. In a 2015 study, researchers monitored people's reactions to shock and its effect on their ability to process visual information. They found that participants who froze in response to shock better understood poorly defined images and were able to process threat-relevant information more quickly.

In some situations, the 'freeze' response can help you hide. Sometimes, hiding and staying very still keeps you safe from an attack or causes the attacker to lose interest in harming you. In animals, tonic immobility is used as a last resort when "fight or flight" fails since many predators don't eat something dead.

Finally, freezing can cause dissociation, thus reducing the impact of an event. Dissociation occurs when an individual experiences trauma. It makes a person feel detached or numb in the face of a threat, which makes a severely distressing event feel less real. This could be why the freeze response happens more frequently in individuals with a history of trauma.

There is psychological fear when the fight-flight-freeze response triggers physiological reactions without an apparent cause. That fear is conditioned, meaning you've associated an event or thing with negative experiences. This psychological response is activated the first time you're exposed to the situation, after which it develops over time.

We refer to that as a perceived threat – something you consider potentially dangerous. Perceived threats vary from individual to individual. With a phobia, your brain thinks you're in danger because it considers the situation that triggers your phobia to be life-threatening. As a result, your body activates the fight-flight-freeze response to keep you safe.

However, the response can be overactive. Thus, a non-threatening situation can trigger the associated physical reaction.

That is how panic attacks happen – resulting from the activated fight-flight-freeze response.

An overactive stress response is typically more common in individuals who have experienced the following:

Trauma

Some people develop an exaggerated stress response after going through a traumatic event. It involves a repeated pattern of physical reactions linked to the actual event. So, you're more likely to experience panic attacks if you have a history of PTSD, assault, childhood trauma, accidents, natural disasters, or stressful life events.

In this case, your brain activates fight-flight-freeze in response to related triggers to prepare you for future traumatic events. Unfortunately, that can lead to an overactive response, causing panic attacks.

For example, if you've been in a car accident, the sound of a car may remind you of the traumatic event. You might have a panic response from simply hearing a car honking.

Anxiety

As I've established, anxiety is a natural response that helps you respond appropriately to a perceived threat. But if you have an anxiety disorder, you're likely to experience anxiety attacks triggered by non-threatening stressors. For example, you could develop an exaggerated stress response to simple activities, such as sitting in traffic or speaking at a business meeting.

Fortunately, you can learn to cope with an overactive stress response and control your panic attacks. But first, let's discuss why it is essential for you to learn how to control panic attacks.

THE IMPORTANCE OF LEARNING HOW TO CONTROL PANIC ATTACKS

Remember the autonomic nervous system? It has a subsystem known as the sympathetic nervous system: your body's default alarm system. The sympathetic nervous system (SNS) is a harmonized network of nerves, hormones, and brain structures. An imbalanced SNS can cause serious complications.

You learned earlier that the ANS is the body's involuntary response center. Without conscious decisions, the ANS controls vital bodily functions, including heart rate, digestion, blood pressure, body temperature, pupil dilation, etc. This is how we can make quick internal adjustments and external reactions without consciously thinking about it.

However, the sympathetic nervous system is specifically responsible for the stress response. When the SNS activates the involuntary response to a stressful or dangerous situation, it floods the body with hormones that boost alertness, heart rate, etc.

It triggers the physiological reactions of the fight-flight-freeze response, and this happens so quickly that we don't even realize it's happened. For example, you may jump from the path of an oncoming car before fully registering that it is racing toward you.

The sympathetic nervous system activates the stress response but doesn't deactivate it once the perceived threat is eliminated. This is done by the parasympathetic nervous system – another subsystem of the autonomic nervous system.

The parasympathetic nervous system activates the 'rest and digest' to calm the body down after a stressful situation. As a result, heart rate, blood pressure, hormone production, etc., revert to normal levels as the body enters a state of equilibrium, also called homeostasis.

Chronic stress occurs when the body spends too much time in fight-flight-freeze mode and not enough time in 'rest and digest mode. The parasympathetic nervous system activates after a meal or during a pleasurable activity, and the physical effects include:

- Reduced heart rate and respiration
- Drop in blood pressure
- Increase in intestinal activity
- Blood flow to the digestive tract increases
- Cortisol and adrenaline decrease
- Neurotransmitters that regulate muscle contractions increase

Normal body function is achievable only if the sympathetic and parasympathetic nervous systems work harmoniously to maintain the standard baseline.

The SNS controls the body's stress response by interacting with the hypothalamus-pituitary-adrenal (HPA) axis. Stress triggers the secretion of hormones like cortisol, epinephrine, and norepinephrine to increase blood pressure and blood sugar.

As I said, after a stressful event, the parasympathetic nervous system kicks in to decrease the production of the hormones mentioned before and lower blood pressure by releasing neuro-transmitters, including acetylcholine.

It would be an oversimplification to say that the SNS and PNS are antagonistic. Both systems exist to maintain homeostasis throughout the body. To do this, they can work together, against each other, or independently. The key is to maintain balance.

Think of the SNS and the PNS as existing on either side of a scale: each work to counteract the effect of the other. If balanced, the body enters homeostasis and functions as usual. However, this balance can be disrupted by several factors, including disease.

Some physical and mental conditions can make the sympathetic nervous system overactive. This makes it impossible for the parasympathetic nervous system to activate 'rest and digest.' This imbalance underlies mental health problems such as chronic stress, anxiety, depression, and panic attacks.

The SNS' stress response is incredibly useful in short bursts, especially with the boost of mental focus. However, if prolonged, it wreaks havoc on your physical and mental health. Besides keeping you in a constant state of stress, the continuous production of stress hormones like cortisol and epinephrine can increase blood pressure, damage blood vessels, and lead to unhealthy fat accumulation.

Symptoms of an overactive stress response include:

- Anxiety
- Panic attacks
- Insomnia
- Breathlessness
- Poor digestion
- High blood pressure
- High cholesterol
- Palpitations
- Inability to self-soothe or relax

So, while the SNS' stress response serves a purpose, you don't want it overactive or "on" all the time.

Are you stuck in a "fight or flight?"

It is referred to as a sustained sympathetic tone when you're stuck in the "fight or flight" mode. And it can lead to:

- **Fatigue or exhaustion** – You are in a constant state of tiredness. Even though you're eating healthy and taking care of yourself, you still feel like you have no strength or stamina.

- **Poor immune response** – Attention shifts somewhere else in your body, leaving your immune response unsupported and dysfunctional.
- **Slow metabolism** – The digestive system slows down because the blood supply is constantly redirected to your muscles. This makes your resting metabolism suffer.
- **Lack of focus** – When you're stressed and overwhelmed, you tend to forget things.

Being stuck in "fight or flight" can also make you generally unwell. You may become snappy and irritable with the people in your life. You may also experience migraines, dizziness, sleep issues, anxiety, and panic due to being stuck in the "fight or flight" state.

The solution is learning to induce the 'rest and digest response' whenever you feel stressed. This can help you maintain the balance between the sympathetic and parasympathetic nervous systems and reduce stress response activity.

CALMING THE BODY BACK TO A REST AND DIGEST STATE

Panic attacks happen with very little warning, so you should have readily available coping strategies to stop a panic episode as soon as it happens. To do this, you must explore different ways to deactivate the sympathetic nervous system's response and instead seduce the parasympathetic nervous system to take over.

- **Breathing exercise**

It's normal for physical sensations, such as chest tightness and rapid breathing, to become intense and overwhelming during a panic attack. However, a breathing exercise can help you feel calm and relaxed despite the unpleasant physical symptoms.

By directing attention to your breath, you can focus on that instead of fixating on what's happening to you physically. Breathing exercises can also help with hyperventilation and palpitations common in intense anxiety or panic attacks.

Breathe slowly and deeply, focusing on each breath. Gather your breath from your abdomen, filling your lungs slowly as you count to 4 when you inhale or exhale. You can also try the 4-7-8 technique, where you inhale for 4 seconds, hold for 7 seconds, and exhale slowly for 8 seconds.

Note: Breathing exercises can amplify some people's panic attack symptoms. In such a case, you can try the following strategy.

- **Retreat to a peaceful spot away from stimuli**

Stimuli can overwhelm the senses and intensify a panic attack. You can stop a panic attack by finding a calmer and more peaceful spot. For example, if you are in a busy room, leave and find a spot with zero distractions. An alternative is to move to rest against a nearby wall.

Retreating to a calm and quiet place creates mental space, making it easier to practice breathing exercises or try another coping strategy.

- **Focus on one stimulus to drown out others**

Focusing on a physical object in your immediate surroundings can help you feel grounded when you're overwhelmed with distressing physical symptoms. The idea is to drown out other stimuli by focusing on a single stimulus.

Choose a specific item in your environment and focus on it. As you look at the object, you may start to think about its texture, wonder how it was made or who made it, and how it came to be in the room. This can help reduce panic attack symptoms.

If you suffer from recurrent panic attacks, you can carry a familiar object around to help you stay grounded. This could be a tiny toy, a crystal or smooth stone, a seashell, etc.

- **5-4-3-2-1**

Panic attacks can make you dissociate due to the intensity and how it overwhelms your senses. The 5-4-3-2-1 grounding technique helps you reroute your focus away from stressors. You can practice this method by completing the following steps slowly and carefully.

1. Look at 5 different items. Focus on each one for a few minutes.
2. Listen for 4 different sounds. Think about their source and what distinguishes them.
3. Touch 3 separate objects. Think about their texture, temperature, and usage.
4. Sniff 2 different smells. It could be the scent of your soap or brewed coffee.
5. Identify one thing you can taste. You can focus on whatever taste you have in your mouth or taste a piece of candy.

- **Repeat a mantra or an affirmation**

A mantra is a sound, word, or phrase that helps you focus and ground yourself in the present. You can use a mantra to reassure yourself, such as "This too shall pass" or "I am strong, brave, and calm." Or you can try something with a deeper, more spiritual meaning. Repeating a mantra aloud or internally can help you stop a panic attack in its tracks.

Focus on gently repeating the mantra, and your physical responses will start to slow, making it easier to regulate your breathing and relax your body.

Another way to stop a panic attack is to stimulate your vagus nerve – a cranial nerve located on both sides of your voice box. The vagus nerve is the longest cranial nerve and is connected to branches of the parasympathetic nervous system. Therefore, you can induce the PNS' 'rest and digest' response by stimulating the vagus nerve.

You can stimulate the vagus nerve by humming, singing, or chewing gum. This lets the brain know that your body isn't under attack and there's no real or perceived threat. Other ways to stimulate the vagus nerve include massage and cold exposure.

Affirmations to repeat during a panic attack

An affirmation is a positive statement about yourself. Positive affirmations are positive self-talk, meaning you can use them to counter negative thoughts and self-beliefs. You can use self-affirmations to ease stress and anxiety and promote positive life changes. Repeating affirmations can help you stop a panic attack as soon as possible.

Below is a list of affirmations you can repeat during a panic attack. But you can also create unique affirmations by drawing on the things that speak to you. Regardless, the goal is to use affirmations as a healthy tool to manage anxiety attacks.

- "I am in control."
- "This too shall pass."
- "I believe in my strength."
- "I inhale peace and exhale fear."
- "This feeling will pass."
- "I am strong and capable."
- "I am enough."
- "I am safe and protected."
- "I let go and free myself."
- "I will move past this moment."

If you're suffering from an obsessive or addictive behavior, you need a more tailored, hands-on approach to CBT. We will look at the methods you can use in the next chapter.

Chapter Six Highlights

- Panic attack symptoms vary from individual to individual. Still, the common symptoms are intense anxiety, dizziness, shortness of breath, numbness, sweating, and a racing heart. A panic attack episode might feel like you're dying or having a heart attack.
- Panic attacks aren't dangerous or harmful in themselves. However, they can be a symptom of other severe psychological conditions or health problems. Therefore, you should get a proper diagnosis from a medical expert to determine the specific cause of your attacks.
- You can experience panic attacks with no apparent trigger. An episode can happen suddenly anywhere, any time – driving, during a meeting, or even while sleeping. It's possible to experience one or two panic attack episodes without ever experiencing any after that. It is called a panic disorder if you suffer from recurring panic episodes.
- Avoidance isn't the best tactic for dealing with panic attacks. Don't be tempted to avoid event triggers or social situations. Avoidance only exacerbates your fear. Instead, the best policy is to face your fears head-on using the recommended CBT approach, such as Exposure and Response Prevention therapy.

- Certain CBT techniques can help you treat panic attacks successfully. For example, you can combine stress management methods with other CBT techniques to reduce the frequency and intensity of panic attack episodes. They will also help you cope better when an episode starts to happen.

OVERCOMING OBSESSIVE AND ADDICTIVE BEHAVIORS

One of the scariest things anyone can experience in life is feeling out of control. Unfortunately, this is something that individuals with obsessive behaviors and addiction struggle with daily. Obsessive behavior can look different in people – compulsive gambling, spending, sexual behavior, and behavioral rituals are only a few examples.

Individuals with obsessive-compulsive disorder (OCD) experience never-ending distress due to their obsessions. Yet, they feel compelled to perform any behavior or ritual that provides them temporary relief.

The thing about these types of mental health problems is that you not only struggle with anxiety, depression, and negativity. You also live with guilt, shame, and poor self-worth.

Cognitive behavioral therapy can help you take back control of your life. You don't have to let OCD, substance abuse, chemical dependence, shopping addiction, or any other kind of addiction and other compulsive behaviors rule your life. With cognitive behavioral therapy techniques, you can address problematic thoughts and feelings to overcome obsessive behavior or addiction.

CBT is used widely in treating all types of addictions and obsessive disorders. It teaches you to find connections between your thoughts, feelings, and behaviors to increase awareness of how these three things impact your recovery process.

Alongside addiction, CBT is an effective treatment for co-occurring disorders like:

- Obsessive-compulsive disorder
- Eating disorders
- Bipolar disorders

CBT shows that many harmful thoughts and feelings behind addiction and obsessive behavior are neither rational nor logical. They sometimes stem from negative past experiences or environmental and biological factors.

When an individual struggling with addiction or obsessive behavior understands why they think or feel a certain way and how their thoughts and feelings lead to compulsions or substance use, it becomes easier to overcome their mental health issues.

If you struggle with addiction or OCD, CBT can help you to identify your "automatic negative thoughts." As I've explained, these thoughts originate from impulse and are based on misconceptions and feelings of fear and self-doubt. It's common for people to try to self-medicate intrusive thoughts with substance abuse or behavioral rituals.

Not all obsessive-compulsive behaviors are the same. So, let's first discuss how CBT can address different types of compulsive behavior.

CBT AND OBSESSIVE-COMPULSIVE DISORDER

Obsessive-compulsive disorder involves a pattern of intrusive thoughts, ideas, images, urges, and fears (obsessions) that leads one to perform specific repetitive behaviors (compulsions). Compulsions can be physical rituals, such as hand cleaning or checking on something, or mental rituals, like counting and other activities, which compel you to do something repetitively to eliminate the distressing, unwanted thoughts in your head.

We all have varying degrees of unwanted thoughts and repetitive behaviors, but this doesn't mean we have OCD. For those with OCD, these thoughts are persistently intrusive – they don't go away until you give in and complete the associated compulsion.

Not performing the behavioral ritual causes great distress, usually linked to an intense fear of negative consequences, if one does not complete the behavior. In addition, obsessions and compulsions interfere with the daily functioning of those with OCD and can cause a significant decline in their social interactions.

You may try to fight the obsessions by ignoring the thoughts or ideas inside your head, but that only significantly amplifies your fears and distress. Ultimately, you feel like you have no choice but to perform the compulsive act that will ease your distress.

They only keep coming back despite attempts at ignoring or suppressing the bothersome thoughts or urges. And that leads you to engage in more ritualistic acts – keeping you in a vicious cycle of obsessions and compulsions.

As someone with OCD, you might suspect your thoughts are unrealistic and false. But even if you know they are not realistic or true, you may find it incredibly hard to disengage from the obsessive thoughts or stop the behavioral rituals altogether.

Think of the different forms of OCD as subtypes of obsessive thoughts. Though OCD and compulsive behaviors generally have similar symptoms, they present differently in people. Here are examples of common OCD subtypes:

- **Contamination obsessions:** Fear of contracting germs or diseases and getting sick.
- **Harm obsessions:** Fear of harming self or potentially harming others.
- **Symmetry obsessions:** being fixated on the organization of items.
- **Body-focused compulsions:** Compulsively picking, biting, or pulling at hair, skin, or nails.
- **Relationship obsessions:** Focusing on the "rightness" or uncertainty of intimate relationships.

Anxiety is at the root of obsessive and compulsive behavior. But CBT can help you understand that while the obsession-related anxiety is real, not giving in to the intrusive thoughts won't affect you – even if it feels that way.

CBT strategies for treating OCD act based on the fact that obsessions and compulsions develop and intensify due to deeply ingrained, dysfunctional thought patterns that push an affected person to react to their thoughts and feelings in dysfunctional ways.

CBT aims to teach you to form a new relationship with your thoughts to stop them from maintaining your anxiety. More importantly, it also aims to help you develop a more effective and healthier approach to responding to your obsessions and compulsions. You can also use CBT to identify and challenge the cognitive processes that intensify your OCD symptoms and their associated meanings.

Leaving compulsive behavior unattended can have significant emotional, physical, relational, financial, and legal consequences. Therefore, the sooner you start your recovery process, the greater your chances of success.

There are many highly effective CBT techniques for treating obsessive behaviors, but we will focus on Exposure and Response Prevention. This strategy breaks the bond between automatic negative thoughts and ritualistic compulsive actions. They also train you to stop ritualizing when you feel overwhelmingly anxious.

You can start noticing improvements within weeks of practicing either of these treatment therapies. OCD treatment is typically short-term, but it has lasting benefits. Of course, this depends on how severe your symptoms are.

Exposure and Response Prevention (ERP)

Many therapists argue that this is the most helpful CBT technique for treating OCD. This is because ERP involves exposing yourself to distress-inducing intrusive thoughts without engaging in the compulsive ritual.

The aim is to prevent yourself from getting the temporary relief associated with performing the compulsion, forcing you to face the anxiety until it fades. Eventually, with consistent practice, you become desensitized to obsessive thoughts.

With ERP, the exposure to situations that trigger intrusive thoughts must be gradual and controlled. The symptoms usually become mild to the point where you learn to ignore them; sometimes, they disappear entirely. Over time, you will learn to respond differently to the trigger, causing a significant decline in the intensity of obsessions and frequency of compulsive behaviors.

Below are the steps in practicing exposure and response prevention by yourself.

1. First, write down a detailed description of your triggers, obsessions, and compulsions. Now, rank them

from the most difficult to the least bothersome. After this, begin with the easiest obsession and the symptoms.

2. Put yourself in situations that trigger your obsessions (exposure). During this phase, avoid performing the behavioral ritual for 15-30 minutes (response prevention). Then, with every session, avoid performing the compulsion for longer periods. Soon, you will notice that when you don't perform the ritual, your anxiety increases rapidly, peaks, and then goes downward.

In situations where it is impossible to expose yourself to the actual situation that triggers obsessive thoughts and compulsion, you can use visualization or recordings to practice imagined exposure and effectively increase your anxiety levels for the CBT exercises.

Once the associated anxiety with the least bothersome symptoms decreases significantly or completely fades away, you can take on more challenges until they become manageable. Effective ERP exercises result in "habituation," meaning you learn that nothing bad happens when you don't perform rituals.

For example, suppose you have contamination OCD, i.e., an obsessive fear of contracting germs or disease. In that case, you may start by getting yourself to touch a dusty desk – which you believe may be contaminated – and then wait for at least 20 minutes to wash your hands. Subsequently, you can wait for longer and longer periods before you clean your hands.

Over time, the gradual, repeated exposure and delayed response will condition you to respond differently to the fear of germs, which, in turn, will cause a decrease in the frequency of the obsession.

OVERCOMING ADDICTION WITH CBT

Cognitive behavioral therapy can be life-saving if you struggle with chemical dependence, substance abuse, addiction, or dependence. By teaching you to identify and address negative thought patterns and feelings, CBT can help you overcome addiction.

When an individual with addiction understands the underlying reason behind their feelings or behavior and how it contributes to substance use, it becomes much easier for them to overcome addiction.

I explained early in the book that negative thought patterns are the primary cause of anxiety disorders and depression. It's no coincidence that these conditions typically co-occur with addiction. The presence of negative thinking patterns can make you more likely to abuse alcohol and drugs or develop other kinds of addiction.

As I said, addiction sometimes develops because people try to self-medicate the unpleasant or distressing thoughts and feelings in their heads with drugs or alcohol. CBT can help you defeat addiction by:

- Providing valuable self-help techniques and tools to improve your mood.
- Helping to identify, challenge, and dismiss the inaccurate beliefs and insecurities that contribute to addiction.
- Teaching how to communicate effectively.

CBT also helps you cope with addiction triggers in three key ways:

- Recognize – identify triggers that lead to engaging in addiction (drinking, drug use, shopping)
- Avoid – remove yourself from trigger situations when appropriate and possible.
- Cope – practice CBT exercises to address and neutralize dysfunctional emotions and thoughts contributing to addiction.

CBT for addiction treatment requires you to identify any co-occurring psychological disorders and analyze how addiction negatively impacts your physical, social, emotional, and spiritual development. Understanding the impact is central to getting back on track with recovery.

My favorite thing about CBT for overcoming addiction is that you can work with a therapist to create a personalized treatment plan. You can replace ineffective coping mechanisms with healthy and safe skills.

CBT Addiction Exercises

You can employ specific CBT exercises to overcome addiction such:

- **Recording thought**

This exercise is to help you examine automatic negative thoughts and find objective evidence to challenge, support, or disprove the thoughts. You must record and cross-examine evidence for and against your negative thoughts and assumptions.

Example: "My partner thinks I'm unlovable, and drinking makes me feel better about myself" can be challenged and replaced with "*I can learn how I am unlovable and become a better person. I don't need to drink to feel good about myself.*"

- **Behavioral exercise**

This exercise compares dysfunctional thoughts against positive, healthy ones to determine which can effectively alter behavior. For example, self-criticism works for some people, while self-kindness is the best route for others. A behavioral exercise will help you see which approach is best for your recovery process and journey.

Example: "If I criticize myself harshly after drinking heavily, I drink less" versus *"If I practice compassion after drinking heavily, I drink less."*

- **Pleasant activity exercise**

Create a list of healthy and fun activities you can practice daily. There should be enough activities to last a week. Ensure the tasks are easy to complete while evoking positive emotions. The aim is to reduce negative thoughts and, by effect, the need to drink, use drugs, or go on a shopping spree by scheduling pleasurable and enjoyable activities.

Example: When you get the urge to drink or use drugs, use that time to dance to your favorite music.

- **Advantages and Disadvantages**

This is a warm-up exercise to try before starting your CBT recovery journey. Get a journal and write down the advantages and disadvantages of your addictive behavior. For example:

Addictive behavior	Advantages	Disadvantages
Excessive drinking		
Quitting alcohol		
Using drugs		
Quitting drugs		

- **Identify external triggers**

Triggers are those situations that affect your brain and can push you toward an addictive behavior even when you've decided to stop. Therefore, the intention to quit must reflect in your behavior, keeping you away from potential triggers.

So, write down the strongest triggers for you. Then, write down specific triggers that could interfere with your recovery process – at least 20. Your triggers should include people, places, feelings, times, objects, and situations.

- **Thought-stopping technique**

The thought-stopping technique is key to interrupting the *trigger-thought-craving-use* sequence. It helps to disrupt the process. It would help if you stopped the thought as soon as it begins by promptly taking action.

Try this technique in two ways: Visualization and Relaxation. With visualization, imagine a switch in your mind and picture yourself moving the switch from ON to OFF to stop your unhelpful thoughts. Replace the thoughts with something healthier and more positive.

Relaxation involves practicing a breathing exercise. Take a deep breath from the belly and slowly exhale. Do this at least three times. Repeat this whenever your thoughts are triggered.

Note: Cravings last up to 15 minutes, so practice any of these exercises for that long.

- **Identifying internal triggers**

Your internal triggers set off the brain to think about engaging in addictive behavior. Below is a list of feelings and emotions that might trigger thoughts about engaging in addictive behavior. Place a checkmark next to the ones that apply to you.

- Angry
- Frustrated
- Afraid
- Bored
- Jealous
- Nervous
- Insecure
- Criticized
- Sad
- Embarrassed
- Pained
- Irritated
- Hungry
- Worried
- Overwhelmed
- Exhausted
- Lonely
- Excited
- Guilty
- Sleepy
- Envious
- Anxious

Write down other emotional states that trigger you to engage in an addiction. Describe situations where a specific change in mood triggered cravings for an addiction. For example, you argued with someone, got angry, and felt the urge to use it.

Overcoming addiction requires working with a support network. So, don't be afraid to seek people out and join groups for recovering addicts.

SELF-HARM AND EATING DISORDERS: HOW TO CHANGE THOUGHTS AND BEHAVIOR

Self-harm is the deliberate act of hurting oneself by causing pain or injury. It includes behaviors such as cutting, biting, burning, or scratching at one's skin, hitting oneself, pulling out hair, or repeatedly getting in dangerous situations. It can also involve substance abuse, including deliberately overdosing on medications.

People who engage in self-harm do so in response to intense emotional pain, overwhelming feelings of distress, and painful memories. Many people have described self-harm as a way for them to:

- Express thoughts and feelings that are difficult to put into words.
- Make invisible thoughts and feelings visible to all.
- Turn emotional pain into physical pain.
- Create a feeling of being in control.
- Reduce the intensity of overwhelming thoughts or feelings.

- Detach from traumatic memories.
- Punish themselves for traumatic experiences.
- Stop feeling detached, dissociated, and numb to emotional pain.
- Express suicidal thoughts and feelings without committing suicide.

Individuals who self-harm don't necessarily want to die but may have suicidal ideations. For some, the physical pain caused by injuring themselves offers temporary relief from the overwhelming emotional pain. In this way, they use self-harm as a coping strategy to continue to live.

Even though self-harm provides short-term release, it doesn't remove the source of your distress. Instead, it can bring up some strong emotions and amplify underlying feelings. You may self-harm with no intention of taking your own life, but there is still a risk of accidental death.

Suppose self-harm doesn't offer the brief respite you seek. In that case, you may feel the need to injure yourself more severely or may start to believe that your emotional pain will never end. This can make suicidal ideations stronger.

Self-harm often co-occurs with eating disorders. Both are maladaptive coping strategies for mental distress. They are also dysfunctional in communicating a need for help or support.

For example, suppose you attempted to communicate your needs and were not listened to until you engaged in self-injurious behavior. In that case, it can reinforce the beliefs that it is the only way to get the support you need.

That belief is harmful and ineffective, but it makes sense to the individual self-harming. So, you might continue to engage in that behavior, fearing that you won't receive care or support otherwise.

Many argue that eating disorders are self-harm behaviors. However, eating disorders such as bulimia nervosa, anorexia nervosa, or binge eating typically occur with other psychiatric conditions and disorders.

The motivations behind these disorders are similar to self-harming behaviors. So, it is common for people struggling with an eating disorder to engage in self-harming behaviors, such as cutting simultaneously.

Low self-esteem is one of the biggest underlying causes of self-harm and eating disorders. Self-esteem is defined as "a realistic, appreciative opinion of oneself." In other words, it is accurate, positive, and self-adulatory.

Self-esteem is usually stable, but it may fluctuate depending on thinking patterns influenced by your looks, physical health, relationships, etc.

Individuals with low self-esteem have unrealistic and negative opinions of themselves. They believe they are unworthy of love and respect and below other people. Research has shown that low self-esteem contributes to the following:

- Anxiety and depression
- Stress
- Psychosomatic illness (headache, fatigue, and insomnia)

- Alcohol and drug abuse
- Dependency
- Social challenges
- Unhealthy dieting
- Eating disorders

Self-esteem is directly linked to happiness, optimal mental health, and overall life satisfaction. Individuals with high self-esteem are less troubled by internal problems and mental health issues than those with low self-esteem. Combating self-esteem with cognitive behavioral therapy can help you stop engaging in self-harming behaviors.

CBT for Low Self-Esteem – 5 Key Tools

These five tools can help you build your self-esteem and self-confidence:

Valuing yourself

Low self-esteem may begin in childhood, but it can fluctuate or fall due to traumatic events or life challenges. Think about what you were doing when your self-esteem was higher than it is now. Did you stop doing those things? If so, consider starting them again. Here are some ways to practice valuing yourself:

1. Do things that you genuinely enjoy. This should be anything healthy, such as writing, reading, cooking, gardening, traveling, painting, walking in nature, etc.
2. Recognize your positive traits and strengths.

3. Affirm yourself to improve your sense of personal identity.
4. Challenge limiting beliefs.

Accepting yourself

Self-acceptance means valuing yourself even when you aren't how you think you should be. Know that making mistakes or having flaws doesn't make you worthless.

1. Don't judge yourself for failings or weaknesses.
2. Replace prescriptive statements with preferences. For example, don't say, "I mustn't make another mistake," say "I will try my best not to make another mistake."
3. Embrace your looks.
4. Acknowledge your faults and accept them by reminding yourself that everyone has faults.
5. Challenge your beliefs.

Looking after yourself (self-care)

Taking good care of your body and mind can help you feel your best mentally. Don't ignore your physical or emotional needs or cater to them with a quick fix.

1. Exercise regularly – up to five times a week.
2. Get an appropriate amount of sleep daily.
3. Adopt healthier eating habits. You can switch to a Mediterranean diet.

Understanding yourself

1. Identify underlying personal causes of low self-esteem.
2. Create a more rounded image of yourself, your aspirations, and your values.
3. Confront your fear of what people might think about you.
4. Start a self-esteem journal. Write down personal notes of reflection and express your true feelings and thoughts.

Empowering yourself

Empowering yourself means adopting assertive communication. Be assertive when you express your thoughts, feelings, and needs. Allow others to express themselves constructively.

1. Describe any situation or behavior that is upsetting you clearly and specifically.
2. Try your best to explain how the situation makes you feel.
3. Ask the other person to make reasonable changes that you believe would help.
4. Listen to their perspective and negotiate a solution that works for both parties.

Building your self-esteem takes consistent, intentional effort. Create a plan to implement these steps in your life in the long term.

WHY SELF-CARE IS CRUCIAL

We often overlook self-care, thanks to the number of stressors and responsibilities in life. Despite what you may think, self-care isn't something you practice just for stress, anxiety, depression, OCD, or other mental health issues. You don't have to be struggling with mental health problems to take care of your mind and body.

Self-care doesn't have to be elaborate. It can be as simple as eating healthy, getting enough sleep, exercising, and engaging in fun physical activities. Everyone should take a more active role in protecting their physical and mental well-being – even more so when stressed.

Here are my top ten activities for physical and mental self-care.

- Read a book or magazine for at least an hour. Reading is an excellent way to escape life's many challenges and practice self-care.
- Go outside and walk in nature. Any activity at all is better than none.
- Listen to your favorite artists or any soothing music.
- Get out of bed, shower, and dress your best for no particular reason.
- Declutter your home or workspace.
- Drink water first thing when you wake up, instead of coffee or tea.
- Get some naps regularly.
- Do some yoga.
- Use positive self-affirmations.

- Unplug from social media and technology

Think of more activities you can enjoy and engage in more frequently than you currently do.

Having a great support network makes overcoming addictions and obsessive behavior easier. Asking for help doesn't make you weak or needy. And if you try these techniques on your own without any apparent success, that doesn't make you a failure. These are complex mental health issues, and needing extra help is expected.

Chronic pain requires making a special effort to care for yourself. Thankfully, there are CBT techniques to help you manage pain levels. In the final chapter, I discuss the cause of pain and how CBT can help you change your relationship with pain.

Chapter Seven Highlights

- Obsessive behaviors and addiction are a byproduct of negative thought patterns. Challenge negative thoughts and self-beliefs by writing them in a journal and cross-examining them with objective evidence. Even a 15-minute journaling session every day will make a significant difference.
- Exposure is the fastest way to weaken anxiety's hold over you. Take as little as 30 minutes weekly to expose yourself to situations that trigger your compulsion, and practice ignoring the anxiety until it fades away.

- Mindfulness plays a key role in OCD and addiction treatment. Stay in tune with your emotional state at all times.
- Healthy self-esteem is essential for optimal mental and emotional health. So workout, visit a spa, watch a romantic comedy, and participate in pleasurable activities to nourish your self-esteem with regular self-care.

8

MANAGING CHRONIC PAIN WITH CBT

Pain is a physical sensation and an emotional experience that is often the result of tissue damage. It alerts the body to react to and prevent further damage. While there is no doubt that pain is real, the brain has a way of amplifying chronic pain and making it seem worse than it is. However, how you view pain, and your relationship with it, can be improved when you adjust your thoughts. In this chapter, we will be looking at CBT techniques for successful pain management.

We all experience pain differently. If I were to ask you to describe pain, your description would vary from mine. That is because there are different ways to feel pain. Unfortunately, this variation in the experience of pain can, in many cases, make it difficult to diagnose, define, or treat it.

Pain ranges from tingling to burning, prickling, stinging, aching, etc. And it can be sharp or full. Additionally, pain is either acute (temporary and brief) or chronic (long-lasting and problematic for your health).

You feel pain when a signal is sent to the brain via nerve fibers for interpretation. More specifically, a group of nerves called "nociceptors" are the body's pain alarm. These nerves detect tissue damage and immediately send words about the damage to the brain, traveling along the spinal cord.

For example, a message is immediately conveyed via a reflex arc in your spine when you unknowingly touch a hot surface. That triggers your muscles to contract, causing you to pull away from the hot surface. Ultimately, the goal is to limit further damage.

The reflex reaction to touching the hot surface occurs before the pain signal reaches the brain. But when it arrives, you feel the unpleasant sensation we all know as pain. Your brain's interpretation of the signal and the efficient operation of the communication channel via which the message is conveyed dictates how you experience pain.

Usually, the brain also releases feel-good neurotransmitters, like dopamine, to counter the unpleasant sensation of pain.

I mentioned that there are two types of pain: Acute and Chronic. Acute pain triggers the fight-or-flight response to alert you to localized tissue damage or an injury. We all experience acute pain every now and then; it is intense and brief. You can get rid of acute pain by treating the underlying injury.

On the other hand, chronic pain is much more intense than acute pain and has no cure. It can be continuous or intermittent, mild or severe. For example, arthritis causes persistent pain, whereas migraine episodes happen intermittently. Intermittent pain happens repeatedly but typically stops between flares.

A key difference between acute and chronic pain is that the latter doesn't trigger the fight-or-flight reaction. At first, it does, but eventually, your sympathetic nervous system adapts to the pain stimulus, causing it to halt the activation of this response system.

Chronic pain is what I want to focus on, so let's delve into the common causes.

COMMON CAUSES OF CHRONIC PAIN

Depending on the cause, the pain has a normal healing time. But once pain lasts over three months or beyond the normal healing time, it becomes chronic. Chronic pain is complex, and it is usually experienced on most days – whether mildly or severely.

Typical pain becomes less severe as the source of injury heals. However, with chronic pain, the body continues to transmit pain signals to the brain. Often, this happens even after the injury behind the pain heals.

Chronic pain may last several weeks, months, or even years. It limits mobility and reduces strength, endurance, and flexibility. It can make it much harder to complete your daily tasks and activities. From experience, it can occur in any body part, but the feeling often differs across the affected areas.

Some common types of chronic pain you should be familiar with are:

- Migraine
- Post-trauma pain
- Post-surgical pain
- Cancer pain
- Lower back pain
- Arthritis
- Neurogenic pain (caused by nerve damage)
- Psychogenic pain (isn't caused by injury, disease, tissue, or nerve damage)

The American Academy of Pain Medicine reports that over 1.5 billion people globally suffer from chronic pain. In addition, it is the number one cause of long-term disability in the U.S., with about 100 million United States citizens affected.

Chronic pain doesn't just happen. Varying factors can cause it. Sometimes, the primary cause may be an initial injury, such as a pulled muscle or a back sprain. Chronic pain is said to develop after nerve damage occurs from the initial injury. That makes the pain more intense and long-lasting. You cannot eliminate chronic pain simply by treating the original underlying injury.

However, there are many cases where chronic pain doesn't have any underlying injury. The specific causes in these cases aren't well understood yet. Often, certain health conditions accompanying aging may cause chronic pain in how they affect the joints and bones.

Some kinds of chronic pain can have multiple causes. For example, lower back pain may be caused by one or more of the factors below:

- Long-term poor posture
- Traumatic injury
- Obesity – which puts strain on the back and knees
- Wearing high heels all the time
- Poor sleeping habit
- Aging of the spinal cord
- Improper lifting of weights or heavy objects
- A congenital physical condition

Chronic pain is sometimes caused by disease. The following diseases and medical conditions may result in the development of long-term pain.

- **Chronic fatigue syndrome:** a condition characterized by prolonged tiredness typically accompanied by pain.
- **Fibromyalgia:** intense, widespread pain across the bones and muscles.
- **Endometriosis is** a disorder where the uterine lining grows outside the uterus, causing severe pain.
- **Inflammatory bowel syndrome:** a set of conditions characterized by chronic inflammation in the digestive tract.
- **Interstitial cystitis:** a disorder marked by pressure and pain in the bladder.

Rheumatoid arthritis, osteoarthritis, cancer, AIDS, multiple sclerosis, gallbladder disease, and stomach ulcers are some other diseases that can cause chronic pain.

Despite all the causes we've identified, the source of chronic pain can be complex and mysterious. Although it may begin with an illness, injury, or any underlying conditions highlighted above, persistent pain can take a psychological turn after the physical cause has healed.

That alone makes it incredibly hard to pinpoint a specific course of treatment and why you are advised to try various curative techniques for chronic pain.

BRAIN MECHANISMS AND PAIN

Without a doubt, chronic pain is every bit as real as it feels, but the cause isn't always what we think it is. For example, when there is tissue damage in the lower back, the brain receives signals.

Chronic pain charges the front area of the brain cortex to run at full throttle. This wears down the neurons, changing synaptic connections in the brain. This continuous neuron firing can cause the brain to develop a dysfunction that feels like lower back pain.

That pain is present, but the source is the brain, not the back. This demonstrates that brain dysfunction is not directly linked with pain sensation in chronic pain patients.

As a result, people with chronic pain rarely only suffer from the physical sensations of burning pain. They also struggle with anxiety, depression, and sleeplessness. Some may even have trouble making the simplest decisions.

Research has established that chronic pain can trigger these pain-related symptoms. In other words, due to the brain mechanisms of chronic pain, there is a real connection between pain, anxiety, and depression.

Everyone has to deal with pain at some point in their lives. Still, for individuals with anxiety or depression, pain is particularly intense and difficult to define or treat. As an example, if you suffer from depression, you're also likely to experience extreme, long-lasting pain compared to other people.

This overlap of pain, anxiety, and depression is particularly highlighted in chronic pain disorders, such as irritable bowel syndrome, fibromyalgia, migraine, nerve pain, and lower back pain. Some psychiatric disorders also contribute to the intensity of pain and an increased risk of disability.

In the past, researchers believed that the relationship between anxiety, depression, and pain was purely a product of psychological factors rather than biological ones. Chronic pain can be depressing, and major depressive disorder likewise causes physical pain sensations.

However, with more advanced research and an increased understanding of how the nervous system interacts with other body systems, it has been established that pain has biological mechanisms similar to anxiety and depression.

Shared anatomy is a major cause of this interconnectedness. The somatosensory cortex, which is the area of the brain responsible for interpreting sensations such as touch, interacts with the hypothalamus, the amygdala, and the anterior cingulate gyrus (parts of the brain in charge of regulating emotions and the stress response) to create the physical and psychological experience of pain. These regions also contribute to the experience of anxiety and depression.

Additionally, serotonin and norepinephrine (both neurotransmitters) contribute to alerting pain signals in the brain and nervous system. They both contribute to anxiety and depression as well.

Chronic pain can be challenging to manage or treat, even more so when it overlaps with anxiety or depression. Sometimes, a clinician may focus on pain, masking the awareness of the presence of a psychiatric condition. But even when both conditions are accurately diagnosed, chronic pain is still difficult to treat.

Living with chronic pain is one of the hardest things to do. It can make it hard to work, care for yourself, and do the things you like. More often than not, chronic pain leads to anxiety or depression. It can also negatively impact your mood and sleep.

Medications aren't the only way to effectively manage or treat chronic pain. If you are on medication for chronic pain, it's best to take a psychological approach to treatment. Individuals with chronic pain who take an active approach to managing their pain daily do better than those who try passive solutions such as medication or surgery.

Cognitive behavioral therapy is one of the best treatment approaches for when pain occurs alone or with anxiety or depression.

HOW CAN CBT HELP THE SYMPTOMS OF CHRONIC PAIN

"It's all in your head."

This is something you've probably heard a few times as someone who suffers from chronic pain – especially when the pain has no apparent cause. But you know the discomfort is real, and you can feel it all too well in your body. So when you're lying in bed, aching and hurting, pain becomes your whole world. Fortunately, that's where cognitive behavioral therapy as an approach to pain management comes in.

As you know, CBT advocates that we create our own experiences, including pain. CBT tells you that pain perception is in the brain, meaning you can affect physical pain by challenging the thoughts and behaviors underlying it. By changing your negative thoughts and attitude toward pain, you can change your awareness of pain and learn better ways to cope, even if the pain intensity never changes.

If you live with chronic pain, what can CBT do for you?

Cognitive behavioral therapy can help you relieve pain in a few ways. First, it changes how you view your pain. With certain CBT techniques, you can change the thoughts, emotions, and behavior related to what you're experiencing and view the discomfort in a much more positive context. You learn that pain doesn't have to interfere with your quality of life, allowing you to function better.

You can also use CBT to change how the brain physically responds to pain. As you know, that is what makes the pain worse. Pain triggers stress, impacting pain control chemicals such as serotonin and norepinephrine.

You can reduce the arousal that affects these brain chemicals using CBT pain management techniques. That, in effect, improves the brain's default pain relief response, making it more powerful than ever.

Combining CBT with other pain management strategies to treat chronic pain would help treat your symptoms. This could be medications, massage, physical therapy, or surgery. Compared to these other remedies, CBT has fewer side effects and risks.

Cognitive behavioral therapy for pain relief encourages you to adopt a problem-solving attitude. One of the worst things about chronic pain is that it induces a sense of helplessness – "I can't do anything about my pain." But if you take action, no matter how little, you will find that it gives you more control and the ability to impact the situation the way you choose.

Perhaps the best thing is that you can do everything necessary yourself. Practicing CBT techniques on your own to control your pain is why CBT is so popular; in fact, self-help CBT sessions are just as effective for treating chronic pain as one-on-one sessions with licensed CBT therapists.

Before you begin pain management with CBT, you should talk with your doctor first. You need a professional to assess your level of pain, as well as the history and current pain management remedies. Your doctor may refer you to a cognitive behavioral therapist to conduct a general psychological assessment to identify underlying issues that may worsen the pain.

Whether you see a professional first or not, you can still start a CBT pain management program. You only need individual sessions for at least 45 minutes and up to two hours weekly. However, you might need between 8 and 24 sessions to achieve your pain control goal.

Before you begin, here's how you can get the most out of the process.

- First, you have to believe it will work. Some people take a cautious approach to CBT because they think, "How will it work?" If you don't believe it'll work, you won't participate in the process as you should or do well.
- You have to engage with the techniques actively. As with most things, you get what you put into the process. The more work you put into sessions and assignments, the better your pain management outcome will be.
- Practice all recommended skills. Engage with new ways of thinking and acting in response to pain, even when you aren't in pain. You should keep a log of your pain and the specific skills that work in your fight against it. The more you practice, the easier it will be to draw on your skills when needed.

- Keeping an open mind is essential. You have to accept that an alternative way of viewing things may be more helpful for you. CBT may not work for pain relief if you have difficulty taking a different approach

The Chronic Pain Cycle

Many factors contribute to pain and fatigue, on top of whatever condition is underlying the pain. Due to the fatigue caused by persistent, chronic pain, it's easy to fall into a pattern of inactivity and rest that is, unfortunately, not the best way to deal with pain. Therefore, breaking this seemingly harmless cycle is important by stopping before the pain or fatigue forces you to stop.

An example is resting too much for too long. The more you rest, the more symptoms will develop. In addition, prolonged rest after an injury or illness can make it harder to become active once again, thus increasing fatigue. Also, it negatively affects the heart, lungs, muscles, and nervous system.

Doing too much too soon after an injury or illness because you have some energy can also contribute to pain and fatigue. It can make you feel more tired and put you in even more pain, forcing you into prolonged rest.

Fixating on pain and fatigue is another way to complicate chronic pain. Worrying about your pain makes it more prominent in your thoughts. That can affect your emotions, resulting in fatigue and even more pain. If you worry that your symptoms mean the pain is worsening, especially after physical activity, you might worry that you're harming yourself by becoming active again.

These can make you feel low, frustrated, anxious, helpless, and even depressed. In turn, this can make you feel more tired and in pain. These are all psychological factors that interact with each other, so it's like having multiple double-ended arrows pointed at you while stuck in a circle.

PACING YOURSELF

As someone who suffers from chronic pain and fatigue, you know how difficult it can be to complete tasks when you're having a flare-up, i.e., an episode of severe pain. As a result, you may feel the urge to push yourself too hard or avoid tasks altogether. Unfortunately, this creates a "boom or bust" pattern of activity.

"Boom" is used for days when you're bustling with energy and overactive, whereas "Bust" is when you're tired and underactive.

Pacing yourself, which means taking a break before the pain forces you to, is a technique to limit the interference of pain flares in your daily life. It is specifically for people who cannot effectively manage their pain and fatigue. It helps you manage the "boom or bust" pattern to find a balance.

The framework for pacing yourself includes the following:

- Recognizing unhelpful behavioral patterns
- Finding baselines

- Learning to exercise self-compassion
- Being flexible
- Gradually increase your progress in different activities

It's important to embrace flexibility rather than rigidity when thinking about the things you need to get done.

Some key components of pacing yourself include:

- Breaking down your tasks into smaller, more manageable ones.
- Be kind to yourself.
- Saying 'no'
- Creating a structure or routine.
- Using every lunch or rest break

It's possible to experience "boom and bust" if you do too much in a day, even if you feel energized and okay. For example, if you're suffering from chronic pain due to fibromyalgia, you may want to clean the house and do some stuff here and there because you don't feel as much pain and have some energy. But you may have to pay for that for the rest of the week.

Learning to pace yourself can be difficult. You may feel like it takes longer to complete some tasks or activities, even though it isn't the case. For example, it will take less effort to plan to do some gardening over two days compared to exerting yourself to complete it one day and dealing with increased pain and fatigue throughout the following week.

It would be best if you devised a pacing strategy that works well for you when working independently. Here are the steps to pace yourself effectively:

- **Calculate your baselines**

Your baseline is how long it takes to perform a task without worsening your symptoms. When you have an activity, set a timer for your baseline. For example, if standing for 25 minutes flares up your pain and makes you tired, your standing baseline should be 15 minutes.

Note: Time isn't always the measure of pacing. For activities such as exercises, you can use repetitions as a measure. Set your baseline according to a "bust" when you can still do an activity, no matter how little.

- **Structure your day**

There is a traffic light system to help you structure your day and practice better pacing. Use this to create a table of your daily activities for every day of the week and mark each activity with the right color. For example, red = demanding; amber = moderate; and green = relaxing. It will help you structure and improve your day.

Below is an example of what your table should look like.

	Mon	Tues	Weds	Thurs	Fri	Sat	Sun
7-8 am	Breakfast	Breakfast	Breakfast	Breakfast	Breakfast	Sleep	Sleep
8-9 am	Get ready	Get ready	Get ready	Get ready	Get ready	Sleep	Sleep
9-10 am	Work	Work	Work	Work	Outdoors	Sleep	Sleep
10-11 am	Work	Work	Work	Work	Shopping	Breakfast	Breakfast

You can fill the table in to include activities that you do every day.

- **Plan your week**

Think of ways to classify the long periods of red activity by mixing in some green or amber activity. For example, if certain tasks must be completed at specific times, highlight them with appropriate colors. Also, break tasks into smaller ones according to priority.

Once you've established and stabilized a routine, you can start pacing up to increase daily activity. Again, choose a realistic baseline buildup rate and allow your body to adapt before climbing. Most importantly, make the increases gradual, steady, and routine.

QUESTIONING THOUGHTS REGARDING PAIN

I know what you're thinking – that I want you to question if your pain is real. This is inaccurate. Questioning thoughts regarding pain isn't about challenging the realness of your pain. Rather, it's about challenging your negative views of pain. Negative thoughts contribute to worsening pain and fatigue symptoms more than you know.

Living with chronic pain often means struggling with overwhelming negative thoughts and feelings — pain catastrophizing. The mere sound of "catastrophizing" can make this concept seem judgmental, but it's just negative thinking.

Pain catastrophizing is when you have persistent negative thoughts and feelings related to chronic pain, which interfere with daily functioning. Negative thinking patterns related to chronic pain arise from the 3 "I"s of pain – infinite, insurmountable, and incurable. All refer to our perception of pain.

You have to understand that the experience of pain is more layered than how we physically perceive it. Negative thinking related to pain affects self-efficacy and the ability to function normally in social situations.

Negative thinking may be impacting your quality of life in these three ways:

- Magnification – magnifying your pain and the possibility of it getting worse.
- Rumination – constantly thinking about your pain to the point where it distracts you from other things.

- Helplessness – losing hope in your ability to overcome your pain.

Some negative thoughts associated with chronic pain include:

- *"My pain will never end. I'm stuck with it for the rest of my life."*
- *"I can't keep my pain out of my mind."*
- *"It hurts so bad. I don't think it will ever stop."*
- *"Something serious is bound to happen to me."*

Positive Self-Talk is a great CBT technique to challenge negative thoughts related to pain. The idea is to slow the waterfall of negative thoughts before they send you over the falls. You can use positive self-talk to replace the narrative building about yourself inside your head.

We've covered positive self-talk (affirmations) extensively. Nevertheless, here are three positive affirmations regarding pain to get started.

- *"I am learning to change my pain."*
- *"I might still have some level of pain, but I am making great progress, and I'm proud of how far I have come."*
- *"My pain may not be gone, but I am becoming more resilient and dealing with it better."*

Another technique to challenge pain-related thoughts is "Moving with your mind." It is effective for anyone struggling with lower back pain, rheumatoid arthritis, fibromyalgia, etc.

As you pace and slowly rebuild your strength, it's normal for your mind to get anxious. Anxiety is meant to protect you from potential danger.

So, your mind resorts to constantly showing you the worst-case scenario or highlighting potential *doom and gloom* situations.

Try this exercise:

- Notice any negative thought that arises with the activity you're trying to do.
- Label the negative thought.
- Do the activity anyway.

It may look like this:

- *"I shouldn't walk because what if I fall and hurt my knees some more? Walking isn't good for me."*
- *"No! This is a negative story created to stop me."*

Start walking and see if the thought subsides.

You may be surprised at how quickly you can change your thoughts or make them subside. These techniques can make negative thoughts go away or dissolute into unrelated thoughts. You can improve your self-confidence and decrease pain-related anxiety and depression. CBT offers a simple way to overcome pain and live your life to the fullest.

BODY SCANNING: GUIDED MEDITATION FOR PAIN RELIEF

Do this body scanning exercise for 45 minutes every day.

- Lie down comfortably on a flat surface. You may use your bed or a meditation mat.
- Shut your eyes and focus on your breath.
- Inhale and exhale deeply. As you breathe in and out, notice the rise and fall of your belly.
- Focus on your left foot. Pay attention to how you feel and if there's any pain in that part of your body. Continue to breathe in and out gently.
- Keep the attention on your foot. Even as your thoughts come and go, keep focusing on the foot.
- Notice any pain and what you're feeling at the moment. Observe the pain; don't judge or try to alleviate it.
- Slowly pull your attention away from your left foot and bring it to your left ankle. This is scanning.
- Continue scanning and work up, repeating the steps above.

Regular meditation can positively impact all aspects of your physical and mental well-being. It can help you reduce stress, improve focus, and cope better with chronic pain.

Chapter Eight Highlights

- CBT for chronic pain focuses on changing thought and behavioral patterns to address the problematic thoughts-feelings-behaviors cycle contributing to pain. CBT techniques may not eliminate pain entirely, but they can help you change your thoughts and behaviors to increase tolerance and decrease pain intensity.
- Pain often presents with other psychological problems such as anxiety, depression, borderline personality disorder, etc. CBT can treat all possible underlying mental health problems while treating chronic pain.
- Chronic pain often leads to fatigue, creating a cycle where being in pain makes you tired, and being tired puts you in further discomfort. Pacing is a CBT pain management method that can help you break free of this cycle.
- Cognitive reframing can change your perception of pain, thus positively influencing how you respond to it.

CONCLUSION

Wow! It's been such an exciting journey with you, and I am glad you made it to the end. I believe you've now gained invaluable skills you can use to live a peaceful and fulfilling life. But before I go, let me leave you with a few words.

Like me, I want everyone suffering from the effect of distorted thoughts to benefit from CBT skills and techniques. When you use the skills discussed in this book, you can now deal with the issues you're presently facing due to unhelpful thought patterns.

So far, you've learned what CBT entails and how to help your-self with it. You've discovered where thoughts come from and the connection between your thoughts, emotions, and actions. By examining cognitive distortions, you can easily identify and become aware of them when it happens.

We discussed learning how to rewire your brain and overcoming negative thoughts. When you know this, it will be easier to change your emotions by addressing your cognition and behavior.

You've learned how to use CBT to address OCD, anxiety, chronic pain, and panic attacks due to negative thoughts. When you know more about your triggers and emotional regulation, you can take control of anxiety and depression.

As you navigate life, don't give up on the hard work you've dedicated to this journey. Even if you find yourself slipping, re-strategize and keep on moving. I encourage you to always approach what you've learned positively. Allowing negativity means you're setting the stage rolling for failure, and that isn't what we want. So, approach any issue you may face with an open mind. Put in the effort, and you'll see that the result will be worth it.

As I end this journey, I'd appreciate it if you could take a few seconds to help someone by dropping a review and mentioning how this book has been helpful.

See you on the positive side of life!

KEEPING THE GAME ALIVE

Whoa! You did it! You've zoomed through "What The Heck Is CBT?" by R.J. Miller and now you're like a mini-expert on all things CBT. Pretty cool, right? But guess what? Your adventure doesn't end here. It's time to pass the torch and help others find their way too.

Now that you've got all these awesome skills and tips, it's super important to share your thoughts about the book with others. By leaving your honest review on Amazon, you'll be like a guiding star for other kids, parents, and friends who are searching for the same answers you were.

Your review is more than just a few words – it's a helping hand, a high-five, a "you got this" to someone out there who really needs it. You're showing them where they can find the help and happiness they're looking for.

Thank you so, so much for being part of this journey. The world of CBT and understanding our feelings stays bright and alive because awesome readers like you pass on what they've learned. And guess what? You're helping me, R.J. Miller, to spread this knowledge even further!

Ready to make a difference? Just leave a review by scanning this QR code:

It's a small step for you, but a giant leap for kindness!Thanks a million for your help! Together, we're keeping the game of understanding our minds and emotions alive and kicking. You rock!

- Your pal, R.J. Miller

REFERENCES

Ackerman, C.E. (n.d). *CBT Techniques: 25 Cognitive Behavioral Therapy Worksheets.* Retrieved from https://positivepsychology.com/cbt-cognitive-behavioral-therapy-techniques-worksheets/#cbt-tools

Ackerman, C.E. (n.d). *CBT's Cognitive Restructuring (CR) For Tackling Cognitive Distortions.* Retrieved from https://positivepsychology.com/cbt-cognitive-restructuring-cognitive-distortions/

Ackerman, C.E. (n.d). *What Is Neuroplasticity? A Psychologist Explains [+14 Tools].* Retrieved from https://positivepsychology.com/neuroplasticity/

Action News. (July, 2021). *Best Life: Practice these tips to stay calm during a panic attack.* Retrieved from https://www.actionnews5.com/2021/07/16/best-life-practice-these-tips-stay-calm-during-panic-attack/

American Psychological Association (n.d.) *Different approaches to psychotherapy.* Retrieved from https://www.apa.org/topics/psychotherapy/approaches

American Psychological Association (n.d.) *What Is Cognitive Behavioral Therapy?* Retrieved from https://www.apa.org/ptsd-guideline/patients-and-families/cognitive-behavioral

Anxiety Canada. (n.d.). Tool 4: *Resisting the Quick Fix.* Retrieved from Tool 4: Resisting the Quick Fix - Anxiety Canada

Barrell, A. (April, 2020). *Stress vs. anxiety: How to tell the difference.* Retrieved from https://www.medicalnewstoday.com/articles/stress-vs-anxiety

Begdache, L. (March, 2019). *Ask a Scientist: Neurons help explain how our brains think.* Retrieved from https://www.pressconnects.com/story/news/local/2019/03/18/ask-scientist-how-do-thoughts-work-our-brain/3153303002/

Better Health. (n.d). *Panic attack.* Retrieved from https://www.betterhealth.vic.gov.au/health/conditionsandtreatments/panic-attack

Bjarnadottir, A. (June, 2019). *Mindful Eating 101 — A Beginner's Guide.* Retrieved from https://www.healthline.com/nutrition/mindful-eating-guide

Bravely She Blogs. (November, 2019). *How To Challenge Negative Automatic Thoughts When You Are Depressed.* Retrieved from https://www.bravelyshe blogs.com/how-to-deal-with-automatic-negative-thoughts-ants-when-

382 | REFERENCES

you-are-depressed/
#Always_remember_depression_does_not_define_you_Y
ou_are_stronger_than_you_think_you_are_and_every_step_you_
take_in_this_journey_reflects_your_true_strength

Bowers, S. (June, 2011). *Managing Chronic Pain: A Cognitive-Behavioral Therapy Approach.* Retrieved from https://www.webmd.com/pain-management/features/cognitive-behavioral

Butler, S. (n.d). *Are You Stuck in Fight or Flight?* Retrieved from https://www.thejoint.com/florida/orlando/town-park-27010/202407-are-you-stuck-in-fight-flight

Calzadilla, S. (March, 2022). *41 Journal Prompts for Depression.* Retrieved from https://www.choosingtherapy.com/journal-prompts-for-depression/

Carpenter, J. K., Andrews, L. A., Witcraft, S. M., Powers, M. B., Smits, J., & Hofmann, S. G. (2018). *Cognitive Behavioral Therapy For Anxiety And Related Disorders: A Meta-Analysis Of Randomized Placebo-Controlled Trials.* Retrieved from https://doi.org/10.1002/da.22728

CBT Los Angeles (n.d). *Does CBT Work?* Retrieved from https://cogbtherapy.com/how-effective-is-cbt-compared-to-other-treatments

Cherry, K. ((August, 2022). *What Is Cognitive Behavioral Therapy (CBT)?* Retrieved from https://www.verywellmind.com/what-is-cognitive-behavior-therapy-2795747

Clack-Jones, T. (June, 2014). *Stress less with mindful walking.* Retrieved from https://www.canr.msu.edu/news/stress_less_with_mindful_walking

Cleveland Clinic. (n.d). *Diaphragmatic Breathing.* Retrieved from https://my.clevelandclinic.org/health/articles/9445-diaphragmatic-breathing

Cognitive Behavioral Therapy Los Angeles. (n.d). *Does CBT Work?* Retrieved from https://cogbtherapy.com/how-effective-is-cbt-compared-to-other-treatments

Cooper, M. (n.d). *7 Ways to Face Down Your Fear of Failure and Come Out Stronger on the Other Side.* Retrieved from 7 Ways to Get Over Your Fear of Failure | The Muse

Cronkleton, E. (April, 2019). *10 Breathing Techniques for Stress Relief and More.* Retrieved from https://www.healthline.com/health/breathing-exercise

Davies, M. N., Verdi, S., Burri, A., Trzaskowski, M., Lee, M., Hettema, J. M., Jansen, R., Boomsma, D. I., & Spector, T. D. (2015). *Generalised Anxiety Disorder--A Twin Study of Genetic Architecture, Genome-Wide Association and*

Differential Gene Expression. Retrieved from https://doi.org/10.1371/journal.pone.0134865

Department Of Health Republic Of The Philippines. (n.d). *Patient's Workbook For Cognitive Behavioral Therapy Sessions.* Retrieved from https://www.jica.go.jp/project/philippines/013/materials/ku57pq00003ud3mz-att/material_02a.pdf

Domschke, K., & Maron, E. (2013). *Genetic factors in anxiety disorders.* Retrieved from https://doi.org/10.1159/000351932

Lanese, N. & Dutfield, S. (February, 2022). *Fight or flight: The sympathetic nervous system.* Retrieved from https://www.livescience.com/65446-sympathetic-nervous-system.html

Ellis, M. (June, 2020). *How to Cope With Crippling Anxiety and Knowing When to Seek Treatment.* Retrieved from How to Cope With Crippling Anxiety and Knowing When to Seek Treatment – Bridges to Recovery

Fenn, K & Byrne, M. (September, 2013). *The Key Principles Of Cognitive Behavioural Therapy.* Retrieved from https://journals.sagepub.com/doi/10.1177/1755738012471029

Felman, A. (February, 2022). *What is pain, and how do you treat it?* Retrieved from https://www.medicalnewstoday.com/articles/145750

Fitzgerald, S. (2017). *The CBT Workbook: Change Your Life With Cognitive Behavioral Therapy.* John Murray Learning , Camelite House.

Forhims.com. (February, 2021). *Anxiety Triggers: How to Identify & Overcome Them.* Retrieved from https://www.forhims.com/blog/common-anxiety-triggers

Gillihan, S. (2006) *Retrain Your Brain: Cognitive Behavioral Therapy In 7 Weeks.* Althea Press.

Good Therapy. (n.d). *Self-Criticism.* Retrieved from Therapy for Self Criticism, Therapist for Self Criticism (goodtherapy.org)

Groff & Associates. (n.d). *5 Easy Steps to Changing Your Thinking Using Cognitive Behavioral Therapy (CBT).* Retrieved from https://groffandassociates.com/2017/10/12/5-easy-steps-to-changing-your-thinking-using-cognitive-behavioral-therapy-cbt/

Ground Work Counseling. (n.d). *Anxiety and Criticism* – How CBT Can Help You Overcome Your Anxiety. Retrieved from Anxiety and Criticism – How CBT Can Help You Overcome Your Anxiety | GroundWork Counseling

Harvard Health Publishing School. (January, 2022). *What causes depression?*

Retrieved from https://www.health.harvard.edu/mind-and-mood/what-causes-depression

Heads Space. (n.d). *Meditation for stress.* Retrieved from https://www.headspace.com/meditation/stress

Heads Up Guys. (n.d). 18 *Male Athletes And Celebrities Who've Talked About The Value Of Therapy.* Retrieved from https://headsupguys.org/18-male-athletes-celebrities-whove-talked-value-therapy/

Health Direct. (n.d). *Chronic Pain.* Retrieved from https://www.healthdirect.gov.au/chronic-pain

Ineffable Living. (September, 2022). *Top 18 Self Esteem Exercises (+FREE CBT For Self-Esteem Worksheets PDF).* Retrieved from https://ineffableliving.com/raising-low-self-esteem/#3-cbt-for-low-self-esteem-%E2%80%93-5-key-ingredients-

Jovanovic, T. (n.d). *What Is Anxiety?* Retrieved from https://www.anxiety.org/what-is-anxiety

Kaczkurkin, A. N., & Foa, E. B. (2015). *Cognitive-behavioral therapy for anxiety disorders: an update on the empirical evidence. Dialogues in clinical neuroscience.* Retrieved from https://doi.org/10.31887/DCNS.2015.17.3/akaczkurkin

Kasper S. (2006). *Anxiety disorders: under-diagnosed and insufficiently treated.* International journal of psychiatry in clinical practice, 10 Suppl 1, 3–9. Retrieved from https://doi.org/10.1080/13651500600552297

Keelan, P. (n.d). *A common misconception about cognitive behavioural therapy: It's just about positive thinking.* Retrieved from https://drpatrickkeelan.com/psychology/a-common-misconception-about-cognitive-behavioural-therapy-its-just-about-positive-thinking/

Lee, W. E. et al. (2006). *The Protective Role Of Trait Anxiety: A Longitudinal Cohort Study.* Retrieved from https://www.cambridge.org/core/journals/psychological-medicine/article/abs/protective-role-of-trait-anxiety-a-longitudinal-cohort-study/919A2F6F0C52E512A5F67E3AFE7B7A0F

Let's Talk CBT. (February, 2020). *CBT for Self-Harm.* Retrieved from https://letstalkaboutcbt.libsyn.com/cbt-for-self-harm

Lim, C. (n.d). *This Is Why You Should Be Proud of Making Mistakes.* Retrieved from This Is Why You Should Be Proud Of Making Mistakes (lifehack.org)

Lyle, L. (n.d). *When You Can't Think Away Your Anxious Thoughts, Do This Instead.* Retrieved from When You Can't Think Away Your Anxious Thoughts, Do This Instead (happify.com)

Mayo Clinic (n.d). *Stress symptoms: Effects on your body and behavior.* Retrieved from https://www.mayoclinic.org/healthy-lifestyle/stress-management/in-depth/stress-symptoms/art-20050987

Micah, Abraham. (October, 2020). *How to Perform Exposure Therapy for Anxiety at Home*. Retrieved from https://www.calmclinic.com/anxiety/treatment/exposure-therapy

Mindful.Org. (n.d). *How to Manage Stress with Mindfulness and Meditation*. Retrieved from https://www.mindful.org/how-to-manage-stress-with-mindfulness-and-meditation/#mindfulness

Mind My Peelings. (n.d). *How Cognitive Distortions Creates an Irrational Perception of Reality*. Retrieved from https://www.mindmypeelings.com/blog/cognitive-distortions

Mind Your Mind. (February, 2020). *7 Eating Disorder Recovery Strategies*. Retrieved from https://mindyourmind.ca/blog/7-eating-disorder-recovery-strategies

Mistry, M. (n.d). *7 Signs Your Mistakes Have Made You Stronger Even Though You Don't Feel So*. Retrieved from 7 Signs Your Mistakes Have Made You Stronger Even Though You Don't Feel So - Lifehack

Nawaz, S. (January, 2020). *How Anxiety Traps Us, and How We Can Break Free*. Retrieved from How Anxiety Traps Us, and How We Can Break Free (hbr.org)

NHS Inform. (n.d). *How to deal with panic attacks*. Retrieved from https://www.nhsinform.scot/healthy-living/mental-wellbeing/anxiety-and-panic/how-to-deal-with-panic-attacks

Northwestern University. (February, 2008). *Chronic Pain Harms The Brain*. ScienceDaily. Retrieved December 1, 2022 from www.sciencedaily.com/releases/2008/02/080205171755.htm

Oxford CB UK. (November, 2018). *16 Things To Do For Self-Care*. Retrieved from https://www.oxfordcbt.co.uk/self-care/

Pietrangelo, A. (December, 2019). *9 CBT Techniques for Better Mental Health*. Retrieved from CBT Techniques: Tools for Cognitive Behavioral Therapy (healthline.com)

Pogosyan, M (February, 2021). *Positive Psychology in Therapy: What is Positive CBT?* Retrieved from https://www.psychologytoday.com/intl/blog/between-cultures/202102/positive-psychology-in-therapy-what-is-positive-cbt

Priory Group. (n.d). *How are CBT and mindfulness used to treat OCD?* Retrieved from https://www.priorygroup.com/blog/how-are-cbt-and-mindfulness-used-to-treat-ocd

Psychology Today (n.d) *Cognitive Behavioral Therapy.* Retrieved from https://www.psychologytoday.com/us/basics/cognitive-behavioral-therapy#the-origins-of-cbt

Cassabianca, S. & Shatzman, C. (April, 2022). *46 Positive Affirmations for Anxiety Relief.* Retrieved from https://psychcentral.com/anxiety/affirmations-for-anxiety

NHS. (n.d). *Practical Pacing and Fatigue Management.* Retrieved from https://www.ehlers-danlos.com/wp-content/uploads/Parry-Practical-Pacing-and-Fatigue-Management-S.pdf

Quintero, S. (n.d). *Toxic Positivity: The Dark Side of Positive Vibes.* Retrieved from https://thepsychologygroup.com/toxic-positivity/

RBS Rehab. (n.d). *Cognitive Behavioral Therapy Exercises for Addiction.* Retrieved from https://rbsrehab.com/cognitive-behavioral-therapy-exercises/

Roncero, A. (June, 2021). *Automatic negative thoughts: how to identify and fix them.* Retrieved from https://www.betterup.com/blog/automatic-thoughts

Saxena, S. (Dcember, 2021). *Avoidance Behavior: Examples, Impacts, & How to Overcome.* Retrieved from How to Spot & Overcome Avoidance Behavior (choosingtherapy.com)

Shah, N. (n.d). *Relationship between thoughts, emotions and behaviours – Complete guide.* Retrieved from https://www.visitmhp.com/mental-health/relationship-between-thoughts-emotions-behaviours/

Smith, J. (September, 2020). *How can you stop a panic attack?* Retrieved from https://www.medicalnewstoday.com/articles/321510

Stoppler, M.C. (January, 2022). *Progressive Muscle Relaxation for Stress and Insomnia.* Retrieved from https://www.webmd.com/sleep-disorders/muscle-relaxation-for-stress-insomnia

Tartakovsky, M. (August, 2015). *5 Ways to Expand All-or-Nothing Thinking.* Retrieved from https://psychcentral.com/blog/5-ways-to-expand-all-or-nothing-thinking#1

Teachman, B. (May, 2020). *Why Anxiety Should Not Be Feared.* Retrieved from Why Anxiety Should Not Be Feared | Anxiety and Depression Association of America, ADAA

The OCD and Anxiety Center. (March, 2021). *Rumination.* Retrieved from https://theocdandanxietycenter.com/rumination/

Tyrell, M. (n.d) *15 Core CBT Techniques You Can Use Right Now.* Retrieved from https://www.unk.com/blog/15-core-cbt-techniques-you-can-use-right-now/

Youthful Dynamics. (n.d). It's Exhausting. 16 Quotes Illustrating Life with Anxiety. Retrieved from https://www.youthdynamics.org/its-exhausting-16-quotes-illustrating-life-with-anxiety/